Richmond upon Thames Libraries

Renew online at www.richmond.gov.uk/libraries

LONDON BOROUGH OF
RICHMOND UPON THAMES

D1419970

90710 000 455 545

BACK IN THE FRAME

JOOLS WALKER
aka Lady Vélo

BACK IN THE FRAME

JOOLS WALKER
aka Lady Vélo

CYCLING, BELONGING AND FINDING JOY ON A BIKE

sphere

SPHERE

First published in Great Britain in 2019 by Sphere
This paperback edition published by Sphere in 2020

1 3 5 7 9 10 8 6 4 2

A CIP catalogue record for this book
is available from the British Library.

ISBN 978-0-7515-7077-9

Typeset in Sabon by M Rules
Printed and bound in Great Britain by
Clays Ltd, Elcograf S.p.A.

Papers used by Sphere are from well-managed forests
and other responsible sources.

Sphere
An imprint of
Little, Brown Book Group
Carmelite House
50 Victoria Embankment
London EC4Y 0DZ

An Hachette UK Company
www.hachette.co.uk

www.littlebrown.co.uk

For my mother, Gemma.

Thanks for always believing in me.
I love you.

Contents

Introduction:
This was not the plan

One of the things you'll discover while reading *Back in the Frame* is that I'm very honest about my relationship with cycling. I don't shy away from talking about the lows alongside the highs when it comes to the bike life – and if you follow me on social media, you'll know that's how I've rolled for the last ten years … so I wanted to share a new part of my cycling story with you.

This was something that happened while I was in the final stages of writing this book, and I'm talking *very final* so no chance to get it in the first edition. So I'm quite chuffed that I can now share the story in this brand spanking new introduction, because life doesn't always go according to plan, and this part of the story feels more appropriate than ever to my cycling journey.

November / December, 2018

I'm a December baby, and also a massive festive freak. My love for the season is so strong that my birthday on the 10th serves as a 15-day countdown to The Big Day. Everything in my house is Christmassed-up to the max: the tree is overly blinged-out with the most OTT baubles I can find each year, my 'Banging Christmas Hits' playlist on Spotify is on heavy rotation, and when there's a marathon of cheesy Hallmark Holiday movies on the TV, you'll find me on the sofa, dressed in my most festive PJ's, glued to the screen.

Christmas 2018, though, was a year when my absolute favourite month turned into a physically and mentally exhausting challenge. In November, Mamma Velo went into hospital for major surgery. As long as everything went according to our plan Mamma V would be back home two days after the op. Except, she had a bad reaction to the anaesthesia, so remained in hospital under close observation for an extra week.

I made the almost 3.5 hour round trip to visit her every day. I considered cycling to the hospital, but I knew that I didn't have it in me physically or mentally to ride 16 miles there and back everyday. Forcing myself to ride would have done me no favours and at least on the Tube, I could zone-out for a bit. Going everyday was exhausting, but I had to do it, so that we could all get some peace of mind. We're incredibly close, so I couldn't bear the idea of her being miles away from home, in pain and alone. Was Mamma V being well looked after by the amazing Nurses and Doctors at Central Middlesex Hospital? Yes. Does the Carer in me know how to switch off? No. Every visit would start with a hug, me asking 101 questions about how she was doing, and her asking the same amount of questions about things at home and how the cats were coping without her. (Terribly. Peggy and Gin were missing their grandmother immensely). Then would come the same question from Mamma V, something along the lines of:

'*Julie, why are you here again today? Don't you have a big deadline to meet? You didn't have to come!*'

To which I'd answer:

'*Yeah, but it's fine ... I've brought my laptop so I can do a bit of writing while I'm here*'.

Luckily, Mamma V had been put in a side room so I had somewhere relatively quiet to work when I came to see her. A hospital doesn't sound like the *best* place to write a book and it maybe seems a little insensitive that I'd pitch-up next to her sick bed and to zone into my laptop screen, but it worked. I couldn't concentrate at home and I was hours away if she needed me. Being by her bedside, I could keep her company *and* get my head down and smash out a few more words.

Mamma V was declared fit enough to go home on 5th December. But my joy was soon swamped by feelings of utter panic when the discharge nurse started schooling me on everything I'd need to do for Mamma V when she was discharged. It dawned on me that, except for the once-a-week home visit from the District Nurse, she would be totally under my care.

There was a tonne of new medication she'd need to take, accompanied by a 4-page list of current medication she *absolutely must not take* while on these. Then there were the daily injections I'd have to give her. Alongside that was a bag containing saline solution pods, swabs and sterile dressings for me to change her wound, just in case there were any issues that the District Nurse wasn't able to come over and deal with. Mamma V would be completely dependent on me; and Ian, my boyfriend, was only able to visit at weekends.

One thing that fell away in all of this? Cycling. Of course it did. I was tired. There was far too much going on at home for me to leave it all and go ride. Spending my days writing about cycling was the same as being on a bike ... right? All the excuses returned – I'd lost the joy of cycling again. My old nemesis Anhedonia (you'll meet her properly the book) had come back to keep me company.

I found the time and energy to put the decorations up, but though everything looked Christmassy all around me, I didn't feel very Christmassy at all. My birthday went by in a blur. In truth, I spent it in A&E, as something was wrong with Mamma V's wound and I certainly couldn't fix it.

When Ian was back in London for his weekend-off-work visits and I didn't have my head buried in finishing the book we'd have conversations about Christmas. I guess he was trying to get me in the festive mood, but I just didn't have the headspace for it

'The last thing I want to be given this Christmas is anything related to cycling!', I blurted out while having a tea break on the sofa. He shot me a look over his mug of tea.

'Really?' he asked.

'Yep. It's really not the one this year.'

I truly felt that way. Mamma Vélo was ill, I thought I was doing a terrible job as her carer and almost every book deadline my editor gave me throughout December was a hurdle that I didn't have the strength to jump over. I was convinced that any words I did manage to write about cycling were absolute trash. Actually *getting* on a bike? No way.

Things did become a lot more festive when The Big Day arrived. My big sister Michele and her two boys came to stay for a few days and from the moment they all arrived on Christmas Eve, the house felt full of life again. It certainly cheered Mamma V up having two grandkids staying. We were thankful for the happy distraction *and* I was excited about seeing the boys faces when it came to opening presents on Christmas morning.

At 11am on Christmas morning, after the boys had ripped into their presents, Ian nudged me and said, 'Go on.' He gestured to the massive box next to the Christmas tree, 'That one's yours'. With Michele and the boys staying over, I'd assumed the present was something she'd shoved by the tree overnight while her little ones were sleeping. I started to unwrap the mystery box. As soon saw the logo on the cardboard underneath, I lost all power of speech – I could only squeal; Ian had surprised me with a Brompton bicycle! It got even better when I looked inside the box. It was metallic purple – my favourite colour.

'I'm worried now,' Mamma V said to Ian. 'That vein in the middle of her forehead is bulging!' It's true, I have to admit, but this wasn't from stress but absolute excitement.

Staring at this beautiful bike, which I still couldn't believe was mine, my jaw locked into a gaping smile that didn't move all day. All I wanted to do was get outside and ride it – never mind the fact I was still in my festive Disney pyjamas! I was that kid who got their dream toy on Christmas morning and had to take it out to play, immediately. And so I did. I shoved my bare feet into a pair of trainers, carried my new bike out to the garden path, unfolded it and hurried Ian to get the Brompton he'd got that September. It was absolutely freezing outside but we didn't even stop to put coats on – in our excitement we didn't care.

Both in our PJs, we cycled around the housing estate. We were that 'his and hers Brompton couple'. We stopped and chatted with some of our neighbours who laughed at the spectacle of two grown-ass adults bezzing around the estate. It had been so long since I'd felt that kind of fun and excitement, and, oh my, the feeling of being back on a bike – I was loving it.

Anything that could possibly bring me joy – including being

on a bike – had been pushed out of my mind by the exhaustion and stress of the preceding month. But those moments on that Christmas morning were another cycling touchstone for me, one I can always turn to in tough times.

At the time of this new edition being published, I'll have had Paisley (you'll find out that I love naming my bikes) for two years. I now laugh about almost putting the kibosh on her existence whenever Ian reminds me of my flippant comment in the run-up to the festive season.

I'm so glad he didn't listen to me.

In the last two years, Mamma V has turned a corner with her health since the op, and Paisley has given me a new lease of life. Being on two wheels (any of them!) doesn't feel like pressure anymore ... it's pleasure, just like it used to be. I can turn to cycling when I need to clear my mind, instead of running as fast as I can in the opposite direction. The joyrides me and Paisley have been on, including cycling to publishing meetings, or cycling to parts of the UK for the *Back in the Frame* book tour have been huge milestones. And mean I can spread the joy that I wanted to capture in this book! Whenever I can, I grab Ian or friends and we cycle to the local shops via the longest route possible to stretch out the fun. We do whole days out, riding from cafe to cafe to seek out the best coffee, sandwiches and cakes in the city (#PedallingForPastry is becoming a thing).

Something about cycling had become really complicated – and that's the last thing that it should be. That pure joy of just jumping on a bike and riding as far as you can go – even if it's to the end of the street and back – that's the magic. December 2018 had me convinced I was going to jack this whole bike-thing in. I was out. But Ian's surprise present gave me a new lease of life, and a whole new chapter in my cycling journey opened up.

And cycling can do the same for you.

Life doesn't always go according to plan, and you know what? It tends to work out better than you think it does when events take you down an unexpected path. Follow it.

Changing Lanes

I didn't study Classical Greek History at university, but I am about to apply (or utterly butcher, depending on your opinion) some of Aristotle's philosophical musings to the whole riding a bike thing. You'll probably have come across some variation of Aristotle's famous quote, 'The whole is greater than the sum of its parts.' That quote is about how much better things are *together* than as separate pieces. A bit like a bicycle, really. All those different components – frame, wheels, pedals, saddle – some sleek, some shiny and some incredibly sexy (hello, vintage Campagnolo Super Record Groupset). They are absolutely beautiful in their own right, but once you put those individual parts together and end up with a whole bicycle, it's a different kind of beauty. Because it's not *just* a bicycle you get at the end of it. You get a glorious vehicle for new ideas, adventures and discovery, both physical and mental.

Just as the bicycle is greater than the sum of its parts, the whole narrative of cycling isn't the binary act of getting on a saddle and riding. It's not just for so-called 'hipsters' or 'enviable East Londoners on their fixed-gear bikes' as the then Mayor of London Boris Johnson put it in 2013. Nor is it just the 'Beautiful Godzillas', a term coined by the excellent BikeSnob: a particular kind of female urban cyclist who rides around on a Dutch-style bike as though the rest of the world were created simply to yield to her. That was something I was described as being in *many* more angry words by a rather angry man on an Internet bike forum once upon a time. Cycling isn't only for affluent city types, riding to work on their fold-up Brompton bikes, or people jumping on cycle hire bikes to quickly get from one side of town to the other. It's not just the hard-as-nails mountain bikers, or the BMX riders, going off road on rough terrain and doing tricks and flips that would make your eyes water if you came off at the wrong point. Cycling is not just middle-class white men and women in Lycra. Nor is it the images of competitive racing that we see on-screen: Spring Classics, the Tour de France, the Tour of Britain, track-cycling competitions and all other prestigious professional events around the world in between. Ignore the marketing. Ignore the hype. Because although they form part of it, cycling isn't those stereotypes. It's so much more. In the best possible way, becoming part of the industry forced me to look beyond my own wicker basket, and re-examine what I thought I knew about cycling. There are so many parts of the narrative that exist, all intersecting with one another and making up the strong and diverse tapestry that is cycling as a whole. In recognizing the boundaries and unspoken rules that make up the 'norm' in cycling, I can now see ways to tear down the existing structure, spoke by spoke.

First up, this journey is about surrounding yourself with people in the industry who inspire you, and for this book I spoke to some of the valued friends I've made along the way. They've each taught me something different about how to challenge the status quo and move forward in the industry. Their invaluable advice is something I wanted to include and pay tribute to, as this has been a team effort as well as an individual one.

To delve into stats for a moment, a 2017 analysis carried out by Transport For London (TfL) found that 70 per cent of frequent cyclists (those who cycled at least once a week) are men, along with 59 per cent of infrequent cyclists (those who cycle at least once a year). In contrast to these numbers, women make 27 per cent of current cycle trips, and all BAME (Black, Asian and Minority Ethnic) groups account for only 15 per cent of current cycle trips. If these statistics reflect upon a situation that I am still conscious of *now*, I can only imagine how the landscape looked seven years earlier when I started cycling again. My immediate peers, from those that I worked with on a day-to-day basis to various cycling business associates never set out to make me feel like I didn't belong. They were my colleagues, fellow 'cycling nuts' and most importantly friends, but it was hard not to sometimes feel like a bit of an outsider within that world. As a black woman, I felt like I was the complete opposite: both in what I was seeing in the industry and also outside of it as a recreational rider. So, that led me to wonder what it must feel like if you're in the industry as another type of 'something else' that doesn't fit the *de rigueur* of that world ... say, a black female competitive-racing cyclist? Or a female frame builder? What about female endurance cyclists or older women in cycling – how are they represented? Although they might all be on different journeys, all these demographics cross paths. Cycling, and all of the different stories within it, is not homogenous. We don't all share the exact same life experiences, and mine is just one part of a brilliant whole.

Our House

Like many families, my mum has all our old family-photo albums stashed away in a safe spot in the house – for us, it's the downstairs storage cupboard. We don't have a loft, and Mum assures me that the darkness and low temperature of the cupboard preserves the photos for longer. When I started looking back over my cycling journey, I found hundreds of pictures taken by Mum – who, with her little 110-film cameras, is probably responsible for 90 per cent of the contents of the albums. In them, I found some of the childhood moments I was after, and those images helped to jog those *really* early memories.

There were a handful of snaps of me out and about on my beloved Raleigh Burner – but I wasn't looking for those ones in particular. I was looking for validation of the vague, pedal-powered memories rattling around my head, ones that came long before the days of cruising around on red Snakebelly BMX tyres. I carried on searching through Mum's vast archives and pulled out the 'big one' – a burgundy leatherette four-ring binder album, with a rectangle outline embossed in gold on the front. The look of it always reminds me of the big red book Michael Aspel presented to celebrities on *This Is Your Life*. Our version is kind of like that book – it's filled to the brim with pictures from the 80s: from me in my maroon corduroy pram, right through to the class photos from my years at Keir Hardie Infants School. So much of my childhood is held between the pages of that album – grainy 4 x 5s of bank holiday family outings to Dreamland Margate and Southend Pleasure Beach, birthday parties, christenings and other gatherings with relatives now long-gone but frozen in time ... and more Jheri Curl hairdos than you could pull a metal pik comb through. Honestly, we all had one at some stage, apart from my dad, who remained steadfast in his commitment to his natural 'fro. And then I found them: the batch of photos that confirmed where my love of being on wheels came from. The three-year-old me, on an impossibly small, green tricycle.

It's incredible that just looking at those photos evokes the sounds, textures and even the smell on the days on which they were taken. How on earth can you possibly remember the emotions and experiences you had on certain days when you were in the earliest stages of being a single-digit human? It's kind of bonkers how some of the stuff from when you were a child can stick in your brain. Those slightly yellowed self-adhesive pages took me back to that time, but also track a path so strongly to my life now. That green tricycle sparked off so much joy and happiness every time I got on it. Deep down, I still feel the echoes of that anticipation of adventure every time I get on one of my bikes. And I wonder if Mum's pictures inspired me to record my cycling life and more – she always seemed to have a camera to hand and catalogued everything in those albums, a true Instragrammer before its time.

I was born and raised in East London. The district of Canning Town, London Borough of Newham to be exact. Long before it became one of the trendiest places in the capital to live, synonymous with hipsters, edgy art galleries, and third-wave coffee shops, the East End had a bit of a rough reputation. That was certainly the case for the corner of it I grew up in. It still does to be honest. Although major regeneration works started there over thirty years ago, and Canning Town is now neighbour to the affluent developments that have sprung up across the Docklands, Newham is still ranked as one of the most deprived areas in the UK. It wasn't exactly a picnic growing up around there but there really is no place like it. The diverse mix of ethnicities and nationalities who settled in Newham – from West Indian families like my own, along with African, Pakistani, Jewish and Bangladeshis to name but a few – make up a vibrant community. We fostered friendships that went way beyond our immediate neighbours. Mum's weekly shopping trips were a major way in which those community links and friendships were forged. We'd always bump into someone she knew, and we became pretty familiar with the market stall traders we visited. Under the canopy of music blaring out from the reggae and bhangra stalls, there would be throngs of Saturday morning shoppers – some armed with those lethal two-wheeled trolleys that take the skin off your shins if you walk into one – weaving their way between the stalls like a slalom course. Market traders would be bellowing over one another, selling everything from cheap and cheerful clothing and shoes to fruit and veg and meat and fish ('like you'd get back home', according to my parents). All of these fragrant and exotic smells converged to create that distinct marketplace whiff. I loved, and still take pride in saying, 'I'm a Newham girl' whenever people ask where I'm from. My answer still raises the odd eyebrow and sometimes even reactions like, 'Really – you come from around *there*?' Pffft.

Home was, and still is, a three-bedroom, ground-floor maisonette on a post-war social housing estate. The Freemasons Estate was built during the 1960s and 1970s – the era of radical concrete and high rises – and was a vast mix of residential buildings in various blocky shapes and sizes. When I was little, I thought our neighbourhood looked a bit like a concrete beach. There were nine dark grey and sooty white tower blocks, twenty-three stories high, that dominated the local skyline like tall waves. The parks and smaller orange-brick buildings, like ours, made up the sandy, seaweed-laced shores below. There were five of us inside our maisonette: Mum, Dad, my brother Anthony, my sister Michele and me. That council estate in East London is still where I proudly call home, but with a few noticeable changes, both outside and in. Tall buildings still dominate the local skyline, but now they are an array of expensive multi-coloured apartments, with rooftop gardens, indoor gyms and penthouses offering panoramic views of the Millennium Dome, Canary Wharf and the City of London, not that cluster of 1960s high-rises. That change has taken some of the old community with them. Ferrier Point remains, but that last post-war monolith of Canning Town is now clad in blue and white panels, softening its Brutalist concrete so it blends in with the newer developments. It's a whole new world up there, as well as down at our level. Regeneration works gave our tangerine-hued blocks a Barratt Homes-style facelift for a toned-down modern aesthetic. Pastel-coloured pebbledash terraces, with uniform double-glazed windows, and identical neat front porches. I still miss all our bare orange brickwork.

On the inside, our house is no longer filled with the exuberant, rowdy energy given off by three children and two adults living together. It's a lot calmer these days with just me, Mum and two cats as its occupants – although saying that, a stint babysitting my two young nephews can see a return to high-spirited behaviour within those four walls and take Mum straight back to the days of dishing out That Look: the one all mums have in their repertoire. Universal in its application to any telling-off situation, That Look translates into, *'Chyle ... tell me wah di hell you jumping cross my settee for?'* without Mum having to utter a single word. In an instant my nephews will stop bouncing on the sofas like manic acrobats, and even I – the grown-ass adult that I am – will still freeze on the spot if caught in the crossfire. Seeing the next generation of children in the family home takes me straight back to what it was like there when I was that young. Plenty may have changed since then (back in the day, it'd be arguments over whose go it was next to complete 'Mr Pop' – now it's over whose turn it is to play football in the front room on a virtual reality headset), but I can still picture everything about a typical day in our house in the 80s, from the look and sounds of the place through to the wonderful chaos of all five of us being home at the same time.

And there really was nothing quite like the decor I was surrounded by when I was little. Coarse woodchip (or 'Rice Krispie' as I used to call it) wallpaper painted mustard was the big theme across almost all the walls in our house. I think my dad, the self-designated DIY guy, must have had a thing for citrus colour schemes, as he was responsible for those walls and the surprise orange paint job he did to all of the once-white bedroom doors. Mum wasn't best impressed when she came home from work and discovered the fruits of Dad's artistic labour. Judging by her reaction, it's probably fair to say she was seeing nothing but a mist of Pantone 2035 that day. One thing that did run through every 'comfy' room of the house was our colourful carpet. It was a busy floral affair with a spiral pattern that would make me dizzy when I looked down at it from my tricycle. It gave a special kind of motion-sickness edge to every fast whizz I took around the house, which I guess in a weird way, added to the experience.

Those rides would always start from the same spot: the far end of the downstairs passageway, by the front door. It was a bit like getting ready for a Grand Prix. I'd get my tricycle from under the stairs, pedal over and park on the 'Welcome' door-mat, my grid position for the race. I'd then do a little warm-up lap at slow speeds – ensuring that the conditions were safe (that I wasn't going to crash into any of the grown-ups walking about the house) and that there was no debris on the tracks (any of my or Michele's toys left lying around). A Grand Prix is always a hive of activity with revving engines, team engineers and mechanics, accompanied by the noise from the crowd. I had an equivalent buzz going on around me, especially when all five of us were at home. During my warm-up lap, I'd listen to that household commotion. The first thing that would catch my ear (and you couldn't miss it anyway) was the muffled basslines vibrating through the walls. If he wasn't out with his mates, my older brother Anthony would be upstairs in his bedroom listening to music, flipping through crates of vinyl or stacks of CDs, deciding which of his albums to stick on his Hi-Fi next. Anthony's room was like an audio library, almost rivalling the collection Mum and Dad had amassed over the years. It was a random but pretty decent musical mixed bag in our house though: if you were in the mood for a bit of Marvin Gaye and Tammi Terrell, Johnny Cash, Nina Simone, John Holt or Earth, Wind & Fire, it was straight to Mum and Dad's collection. If you fancied some Afrika Bambaataa, Kraftwerk, Run-D.M.C, Prince or Talking Heads, my brother was your DJ. Commotion coming from the kitchen would be the next thing to grab your attention. Riding further down the passageway, I'd come to a halt at the kitchen doorway, turning right to wheel myself into the room and have a peek at what was going on. When it sounded that busy in there, the kitchen would usually be filled with the following things:

1) The sweet sounds of pan music.

2) The incredible smell of cooking.

3) Plenty of company and conversations.

In there I would find Mum in her usual spot, stood at the corner worktop adjacent to the window and the kitchen sink (to this day it's her space for prepping food in), and my big sister Michele, sat at the table doing some homework or playing with a board game she'd spread across the whole surface. She could have been doing that upstairs with much more space to herself, but there was something fun about hanging out with Mum in the kitchen, chatting, laughing and joking. The thing with kitchens is that they are *never* just a space for cooking for a family – they've always been more than that. No matter how small a space – and no matter what the occasion – that's where everyone ends up congregating. It was the same at Nanny Lucy's place. She was my maternal grandmother, and whenever we went over to her place in Archway, the kitchen would be where we'd spend 99 per cent of our time. That's where you were always likely to find her – either putting on rounds of egg, chips and beans for us when we'd pile over on a Saturday afternoon or sat at the table, listening to the radio and doing one of her jumbo crossword-puzzle books. When Nanny Lucy came over to see us, you could bet money on her commandeering our kitchen and all of us gravitating towards that room for hours on end. The kitchen was the beating heart of Nanny Lucy's home, and Mum naturally made our kitchen the same thing too. You'd know Mum was going to spend a serious amount of time in there when the Ferguson 3-Band Radio/Cassette player that lived on her dressing table was in the kitchen with her. She'd put it on top of the washing machine and stick on one of her Soca Monarch, calypso or old carnival mixtapes, with the likes of Crazy, Baron, The Mighty Sparrow and David Rudder coming out of the little speakers. With all those steelpans, horns and melodies, it's hard not to dance to tunes like 'Doh Rock It So'. Michele would be there making some moves around the kitchen with Mum too. The music aided Mum's cooking sessions, whether it was finishing off the family meal for that evening or doing major dinner prep for the next night. This was especially important if she was going to be cooking one of her Dutch Pot brown stew-downs: she'd be coating chunks of beef or a chopped-up boiling fowl in her homemade 'Trinidad Green Seasoning', tossing them around in her beloved white Luminarc glass bowl, and leaving them to marinate overnight in the fridge. The smell of the seasoning alone was enough to make your mouth water, never mind the thought of the plate of food you'd get to devour the following night.

Pedalling down to the other end of the passageway, I'd come to the last corner of the house: the front room. Dad (if he wasn't working the night shift) would be sat in his usual place, the armchair. Unlike most 'Dad Chairs' it matched the rest of the furniture – Mum would probably never have had it otherwise. 'His' chair was the single-seater of our orange, white and brown-striped three-piece suite, a colour scheme that, looking back, was *really* similar to the moquette fabric you'd see on London buses and the Tube in those days. Mum always jokingly referred to that seat as 'Leo's Throne'. Dad didn't mind if anyone else sat in that chair – there were no actual objections from him if you were discovered in it – but it was an unspoken rule that it was his spot. It was his chair to sit and read the papers in with a cup of Nutmeg tea in his *Muppet Show* 'Animal' mug; his chair for watching the Test Cricket; his chair for eating his dinner in or having a post-dinner Hofmeister Lager in his favourite dimpled glass pint tankard with a packet of salted peanuts, probably watching something like *Tales of the Unexpected*. It was the seat you'd find me in when I wasn't on my tricycle – either bundled up asleep in Dad's arms after failing to stay up and watch TV or curled up in it with some toys while he was at work.

After this inspection of the track conditions, I'd pedal my way back to grid position. Picture the scene: three-year-old me, in a two-piece green and red jersey tracksuit and my favourite mouse-shaped fluffy slippers, poised on the starting line. Bum on the edge of the seat, hands on the bars and feet on the pedals.

Three ... Two ... One ... GO!

Setting off down 'Hallway Straight' and clearing it without incident, it's straight into the front room. The enormous brown wooden sideboard would be to the left of me (careful not to clip that). Take a right at 'Leo's Throne' (turn one) and then keep heading straight to swing a left at 'Don't You Dare Lean On That!' roundabout (turn two), aka Mum's round coffee table made of tempered glass atop a black-and-white moulded plastic base on wheels. Knock that or any of her ceramic figurines and framed pictures on top of it, and you'd *know* about it later. Once I'd cleared the roundabout without incident came an even more important rule: 100 per cent *under all circumstances* avoid the Ferguson Colourstar-TX TV in the corner of the room. I'm pretty sure if it fell on you, the weight alone of the wooden casing and chrome-wheeled stand would kill you – toddler or adult – and no hero-points are to be gained for sudden death. Now the home-straight of the course was in sight, but first I had to tackle 'The

Big Peoples Corner' (turn three): the drinks cabinet. This was tricky and required serious technical skill, which is why you *always* took it on last – riding behind it you've got to avoid its white electrical cord trailing on the floor (you could plug it in to light it up), then, on emerging, be careful not to clip it with the back-left wheel of the tricycle. On top of the cabinet would be the plastic-pineapple ice bucket, along with Schweppes soda syphons and a cut-glass decanter with three tiny matching glasses on an ornate silver-plated tray. The top glass shelf was filled with Mum and Dad's fancy coloured drinks glasses (which were *always* for 'The Big People Dem' when they came over to ours for parties), all carefully arranged by collection, shape and size. The shelf below that: booze. Bottles of Cherry B, Babycham, Mum's Angostura Bitters (which, of course, came direct from Trinidad), luminous yellow Advocaat and various bottles of Overproof Rum that Dad had collected over the years, which – as I learned later in life – would blow the top of your head off just from sniffing them. And then the bottom shelf: MORE DECORATIVE GLASSES. The cabinet was a cycling minefield, but having cleared that without incident, I'm now on the home straight, alongside tall, lush palm trees (in reality, the Rubber Plant, Cheese Plant and Weeping Fig, which all sat on another smaller side table), back along the big wooden cabinet which was now on my right, and over the finish line (the front room door frame) while taking my right hand off the handlebar and attempting to hit the spider plant suspended from the ceiling in a puka-shell hanging basket by way of celebration. The crowd (more framed family photos hanging on the brown cork-tiled wall) would be going wild, celebrating my epic win and cheering me on during my victory lap. And in amongst all those cheers, one chant would ring out above the rest of them:

'Julie! Calm down on that thing, please! You're going to run over and hurt someone's feet soon!'

Which would mark the end of my race. Fair play, I suppose. It's not like I wasn't allowed to ride around the house on my tricycle, but acting like Danny Torrance in *The Shining* – minus the luxury space of the empty Overlook Hotel – probably didn't really bode well.

Mum and Dad gave me that tricycle for Christmas in 1985, and I loved it. I was never off the thing, probably to the bone-crushing annoyance of my older brother and sister in the battle of their exposed toes or shins versus my three wheels. I'm really sorry about that, guys. To say I was besotted with that trike and how it moved and looked would be an understatement. It was the most magical 'toy' I'd ever been given, and an absolute wonder to look at: a steel frame in metallic green, with red stickers dotted on either sides of the front fork and the body. I think they were supposed to be 'go faster' stripes. There was a step between the two rear wheels to make it easier to hop on to it, big black handlebars that were wide enough for me to wedge my favourite teddy bear in between, and a curved black faux-leather seat, like you'd get on a hog-style motorcycle.

Even back then, separating me from the saddle was a mission for anyone. Unless I was eating, sleeping, or glued to the TV watching *T-Bag* or *Emu's World* (children's TV really was the best in the 80s), you were guaranteed to find me on that tricycle geared up to go, probably with a slightly naughty twinkle in my eye. The happiness that came with being on that tricycle was amazing, and as a child with a vivid imagination (when your sister is eight years older and your brother has sixteen years on you, they're not exactly playmates in your own age range, so my own imagination was key), I could be anywhere I wanted to be while riding it.

When an activity is so magical that it takes you beyond what you're physically doing, it sticks with you for a long time. There was always a sense of freedom that came with being on that tricycle and it's pretty fair to say that it never went away.

Inevitably as I got older, nature and physics meant that I got way too big for that beautiful green machine and eventually I had to let it go. However, what I didn't let go of was my desire to be on a bike. Like I said before about early memories and how wild it is that they can stick with you – in those years I was riding that tricycle, the tracks were being laid for a life on wheels becoming my 'thing'.

That feeling was further cemented by another early memory that's seared into my brain: watching my sister riding her bike and the IDGAF attitude she carried with aplomb towards what some people thought and vocalised about her riding it. When Michele was about to turn eight, she picked out the present of her dreams from the Littlewoods Catalogue: a 1982 Raleigh Team BMX Ultra Burner. Flipping past the pages of girls' bikes, Michele came to the boys' section. As she recalls, it had many, *many* more pages than the preceding one, with young lads on bikes popping moves in the air, almost jumping out of the book. She made it pretty clear to Mum that the Burner was *the one*. Her choice for a bike went against the grain of the type little girls were expected to want. It wasn't pink, it didn't have hearts and flowers on it, there were no rainbow-coloured handlebar streamers and it wasn't a step-through frame (traditionally, bicycles with a step-through frame were known as 'Ladies', 'Women's', or 'Girls', mainly for their advantage to riders wearing skirts or dresses).

That Burner was a stunner: it was a diamond frame (which has a high top tube or cross-bar) painted in 'flame red', with the classic Raleigh Bikes Heron Crest head badge in gold, red and black on the head tube. The front fork was shiny polished chrome, which matched the alloy pedals. The components on it in bright yellow looked wicked: those sharp contrasting pops from the thermoplastic 'aero-style' saddle, rubber handlebar grips and the Team BMX pad-set attached to the cross-bar (the pads were there to cushion your bits if you came off the saddle at a bad angle and landed on the bar) really set the thing on fire. Not to mention the chrome V-brace handlebars and head tube. It all looked so good. Michele's Burner had thick, rubber Snakebelly tyres that were bright red instead of standard black, and the wheels were built with 12-gauge spokes on hubs that looked like they were made of pure silver.

Despite it being the most awesome-looking bike, all these decades later Michele can still recall some of the reactions she'd encounter while riding it: 'I had rubbish said to me like I should be on something less boyish, or not be riding it because I didn't do proper BMX riding.'

Bicycle Motocross (or BMX as it's more widely referred to) is a type of off-road bike racing that originated in the USA in the early 1970s, when my sister was born. By the early 1980s, when Michele was older, it had started to gain traction and eventually exploded in the UK. She was one of the thousands of kids (including young girls) across the country that wanted a BMX bike, though the marketing for the sport was heavily geared towards boys and men. She still remembers – long after getting her bike – the promo magazines and posters for BMX she'd see in the old local bike shop (LBS) on Barking Road, whenever she went in there for parts or accessories, and the kind of messages that campaign was putting out.

'It was usually images of the Raleigh Burner Team riders, all kitted out or just ordinary kids riding circuits together. They were always the same: young white boys, doing tricks on their bikes. When I was out riding, boys I didn't even know would shout out stupid things like, "Oi! Ain't that your brother's bike?" trying to be funny. Most of the boys at my primary school were riding BMX's at one point, or bikes like it ... maybe being one of the few girls or being maybe the only black girl in school to have one was too odd for some people to get their heads around.'

Witnessing my sister's BMX bike-riding defiance in the face of a few idiots and some pretty blinkered advertising (a problem which still lurks within the industry today) was creating a legacy for me in the future. Michele also managed to create another cycling legacy that I've carried with me into my adult life. Being eight years older than me and a teenager in the 90s, she was automatically a Cool Big Sister. I've got to put this straight out there: she's one of my best friends now, but growing up that was *not* the case with Michele and me. As kids we could have a laugh together, but there would be fights and squabbles that would get a bit out of hand. A great example of how ridiculous our arguments could be: when Anthony left home, me and Michele rowed so much over who would get his bedroom – the second biggest bedroom in the house – that Mum moved us *both* out of the box room we shared and into his room to settle it.

Michele was the bane of my life when she was winding me up (to be fair, I was probably exactly the same for her) but she would raise hell with anyone who tried to mess with me. Part-time enemy, full-time role model, I always thought my big sister was the coolest person, even if I was sometimes aloof in showing it. Although we had an age gap that seemed massive back then, we had shared interests:

a) Our taste in music. Obviously I could never go out raving with her (especially when she did stuff like getting into Camden Palace for an all-nighter with her friends), but I could listen to music with Michele at home. The radio in our bedroom was always tuned into Kiss 100 FM – and if I touched that dial, she'd kill me. That was no bad thing, as I loved what they used to play. Back then, it was DJs like Lisa I'Anson, Coldcut and Tony Humphries bringing you sounds like 808 State, Frankie Knuckles, Alison Limerick and really early stuff from The Prodigy. Kiss provided the backing tracks to being upstairs with Michele, on the occasions I was 'allowed' to hang out with her and her cool friends when they came over, who also thought I was pretty cool for liking that music too. Well, I like to tell myself that.

b) Our taste in style and bikes – I guess what I call 'cycle style' now. Michele always looked cool when she was on her Burner. She inherited Mum's sense of flamboyant style as well as rocking looks influenced by the icons of the 90s. Absolute queens like Salt-N-Pepa, Monie Love, and Neneh Cherry were the shit (and they still are) with their fly-girl style. It wasn't just the first ladies of hip-hop that had an impact on her: kings like Run-D.M.C, Eric B & Rakim and The Beastie Boys also had a huge influence on Michele's style too (her look was often aided by occasionally 'borrowing' items like oversized old-skool Adidas track-tops and Kangol bucket hats from Anthony's room). The fact she had that entire thing going on while riding around on a BMX was a source of both little sister envy and inspiration for me.

I'd admire that Burner all the time, looking at it stored away under the stairs, or watching her set off for a ride with Sarah and Sophia, her two best friends from primary school. The three of them would ride over to the Mayflower Family Centre and Kids Club or if they were feeling adventurous, further out of Canning Town, towards Beckton or Stratford. I have memories of times when Sophia would turn up at ours on her roller skates instead of her bike and hold on to the back seat of Michele's Burner while she'd pedal off, pulling her along. They never took their riding seriously, and seeing how happy the three of them were always had me wishing I was out cycling with them. I was a bit too young for that, and I still didn't have my own 'big' bike. That only made me more determined that one day, when I was a 'big' like them, I'd be out on my own bike having my own cycling fun too.

The three of them absolutely loved riding, but the epidemic that's all too familiar for teenage girls and cycling struck: by the time they were around fourteen, Michele, Sophia and Sarah stopped riding their bikes. They all went on to the same secondary school in our Borough, and still hung out together, but cycling became less and less of a 'thing' they did as a group, and ultimately, as individuals. When I was about six years old, I'd started to notice that when Michele, Sarah and Sophia went out, it was now often without any bikes. Michele was on the Burner less and less and it would stay under the stairs for longer periods of time. Eventually, it was relegated to the downstairs storage cupboard by our parents, tucked away like a relic of her childhood.

When the three of them stopped cycling, it wasn't just down to not being into it any more. Conversations with my sister revealed there were many factors involved: 'When young girls stop riding, there is a different story for each one who shuffles off the saddle and puts their bike away, possibly for good. I'm sure all three of us had personal reasons – different from each other – when we stopped, but probably influenced each other's decision at the same time.'

Secondary school played quite a large part in them no longer cycling around together. It was, in Michele's words, 'A whole new world that took over. We made new friends, and more of the girls we started hanging around with at school were into different things and activities that didn't include cycling.' The fact that cycling wasn't an activity included in Physical Education also could have had an effect: 'It was all about netball, swimming, and hockey: cycling wasn't an option.'

It was a shame my sister stopped riding with her friends. Of course it was. There isn't really anything to celebrate in yet another young woman getting off the saddle. But what it *did* mean was that her legacy was fully passed on to me. When I outgrew my tricycle, it ended up being dismantled by Dad and put in one of the big metal bins in the estate chute room. It was sad to see it go, but it had a good innings – I'd cycled that three-wheeled wonder into the ground. When it was thrown out, I was too old for another tricycle, but too young to get on my sister's bike – and she was sometimes still riding it then. The notion of Mum and Dad buying me a brand-new 'proper' bike was out of the question. Aside from the fact that storage space was an issue (it's still *so weird* thinking that five of us used to live in our house), we weren't exactly swimming in money.

We were a working-class family: comfortable enough with the wages Mum and Dad were bringing in, but not to a point where every time one of us wanted something mega-huge like a brand-new bike, it would appear just like that. My parents are immigrants of the Windrush Generation; they worked all the hours possible and saved where they could. Dad was a machine tool-setter – a job he held from age nineteen when he arrived in England from Jamaica – at the Ford car plant in Dagenham. It was definitely a job for life as it was the only one he ever had; he remained there happily right up until he retired. Work-wise I'd never known anything other than Dad being at the plant on earlies, night shifts, or doing overtime when it came his way. He'd arrive home with a distinct whiff of motor oil and grease coming from his Afro, and his dark blue overalls and steel-toe-cap boots stuffed in his battered duffel bag. He was proud of what he did and what he made with his hands, and even when he wasn't at the factory, he would spend his free time with his head under the bonnet of a car. Dad LOVED tinkering with motors, or anything else that that had working parts and *might* have needed fixing – like the time he took apart our Grundig VS200 VHS Player on a Sunday afternoon just to put it back together again. It was fun watching him do stuff like that, though – looking at the inner workings of a machine, and what made them move. I guess that side of things came back to me later in life, with bikes.

Mum's line of work involved factory floors too, but completely different ones to Dad's. Long before I arrived on the scene, Mum had an array of jobs. She came over to England from Trinidad in 1964, when she was just sixteen. Mum joined Nanny Lucy, who was already over here. Nanny Lucy had come over to England first, in order to build a life for her children. When she was ready, she then sent for them to join her in North London. Nanny Lucy had a job working at a zip and fastener factory that used to be just off Old Street (which by coincidence is where I now spend a lot of time on my bike). She managed to secure Mum a job on the factory floor with her not long after her arrival. I can only imagine what the atmosphere must have been like with those two side by side on the production line.

Growing up around them, there was never a dull moment, so that factory floor must have been pure sass when they were on it together. Later, Mum spent a year working at Mattesons, weighing and packing processed hams, before going on to what always sounded like the coolest job ever: a machine operator at Lesney Matchbox Toys Factory in Hackney Wick. There, she used to put the windows into die-cast fire engines and cars. Anthony and Michele reaped the benefits of that particular job, and to this day I wish some of those cars had filtered their way down to my toy box. But it was my mum's job as a swatch maker for Progressive, a textiles company, that was undoubtedly a massive influence on my love of fashion and the cycle-style side of what I do.

Progressive designed knitted and woven fabrics, which would be sold to fashion houses in London and Europe. Mum's role was to plan the design of textile sample books, make them and send them off to potential buyers. Occasionally, if childcare couldn't be sorted, Mum would have to take me to work with her. I'd always cross my fingers for a babysitter to fall through, as going in with her was so much more fun! Mum's work place was a wonderland to visit. A warehouse building in Upper Clapton, it was owned by a large Jewish family who had been in the East End textile industry for years. The owner ran it with his three brothers and his two sons worked for the company as well. It was a real family affair – every single person in that three-storey warehouse building was my 'Uncle' or my 'Auntie' and they really seemed to enjoy it when Mum brought me in with her. They were happy to have a mini-me around, darting between the offices, fascinated by the hundreds of rolls of beautiful fabrics stacked up and waiting to be cut and shaped. I would drape some of the larger offcuts over my shoulders, styling them like expensive designer scarves, while pretending to be as cool and knowledgeable as Caryn Franklin from *The Clothes*

Show on BBC One. I loved asking Mum hundreds of questions about what she did, how the textiles were made and about the clothes they would one day become. Nowadays, I can't walk into a clothes shop or pull garments out of my wardrobe to wear on my bike without wanting to know exactly what their back story is.

Bingar's Burner

I waited patiently to get big enough to ride that Burner. In all those years that passed, my desire to own it never died. There was something so sad about seeing that bike just living in the cupboard, doing nothing. And after all those years Michele spent riding and the joy she got out of being on it, I couldn't help but be convinced my sister felt that way too. The dust gathering on the handlebars was an epitaph: 'Here stands stationary, the BMX Burner of Michele. Many memories made. Gone but never forgotten.' That Burner could be back out in the world, igniting the fire inside of another young girl desperate to get out on two wheels. But it would have been rude to have just assumed ownership of it – after all, it was still Michele's bike. Finally, one day when I was seven, ten magical words were all it took from Michele to make my dreams come true.

'You should have it if you still want it, Julie'.

You *bet* I still wanted it. I *always* wanted it. From that day onwards, the most coveted Raleigh Burner in London, perhaps the world, was officially mine.

Two things needed to be done before I could really get to grips with what was now my Burner. Number one, give it a bit of a spruce-up so that it was back in perfect working order. Even though it had been sitting pretty in the cupboard, it would still need some TLC. And number two, learn how to actually ride it. As desperate as I had been to be out there cycling with my sister and my own friends, I was quite apprehensive about the whole thing. Learning how to balance, pedal and steer on a bike that looked gigantic, had two wheels instead of three and was much higher off the ground?! That was all a bit much once it became reality.

I had done myself zero favours a few years earlier with an ill-advised attempt to emulate Michele, hoisting myself up on to the Burner and trying to ride it through our house. I learned fast it was *nothing* like the days of bombing up and down the passageway on my tricycle. Having legs too short to reach the pedals and no sense of balance really doesn't make for the best bike-riding combination. That incident had knocked my confidence a bit, but didn't put me off wanting to learn how to ride a big bike when the time was right. The question then was, who was going to teach me?

I guess my sister could have done it, but she was busy with homework every evening or hanging out with her friends on the weekends – and I'm not sure how much fun it would have been for her trying to teach a slightly nervous seven-year-old how to ride a bike. Or how that would have helped or hindered our fraught relationship! Dad worked crazy shift patterns so wasn't always around after school, and he would be sleeping in the day if he was on nights. Mum wasn't sure about teaching me to ride at all. 'Yuh crazy? I've not been on a bike since I was a chyle in Trinidad!'

Luckily, my adored big brother Anthony was up for the challenge. I was beyond thrilled! He had taught Michele how to ride, and he was going to be back at it again with another little sister on the very same bike. In my opinion – and no matter what age you are when you do it – learning how to ride a bike should be a fun experience because: a) the memory will stick with you for ever, b) there will be times when it's as scary as hell and you don't want that to be the lasting legacy of something that is so much fun, and c) being able to laugh through the hard parts, false starts and potential tumbles is *so very necessary*.

Despite our sixteen-year age gap, Anthony was my best friend when I was a little girl, in contrast to my tumultuous relationship with my sister. Mum always believed the bond my brother and I had was forged the day she came home with me from Forest Gate Maternity Hospital in an ambulance, three days after I was born. Anthony was the first person to come straight out of the house to greet us, at which point he took me from Mum and brought me indoors. When I was a toddler, I'd follow him everywhere around the house and he'd even pop me in my pram and take me over to his mates if he was heading out and Mum needed a break from a crying baby. I used to go in Anthony's room to sit and listen to the music he played. I owe most of my old-skool musical knowledge and love for bands like Talking Heads to him. When Mum or Dad couldn't pick us up from school, Anthony would be the one to collect Michele and me. Those were some of the best days: he'd take us out for a bag of chips and babysit us, playing music loudly in the front room until our parents were back from work. When he left home and moved into his own place, me and my sister (in between rowing over his room) were gutted. He'd only moved half an hour away to East Ham, but it might as well have been the other side of the world. So him coming back home to teach me how to ride a bike? That was a huge treat.

But before I could actually get out there and learn how to ride the thing, we had to make sure it was roadworthy. To the untrained eye, it looked like nothing was wrong with the Burner. Michele had kept it in pretty good condition, getting it serviced on a regular basis at our local bike shop and keeping it stored indoors. Though it hadn't been left in the garden to be battered by the elements, it had been a while since the BMX had seen the light of day.

Anthony took on the role of fixing the Burner up, squeezed into his weekly return home. Every Sunday afternoon, he'd come back for the big Sunday dinner cooked by Mum – because, no matter how old you get, or how grown-up it is having your own place, *nothing* beats Mum's Trinidadian cookout on a Sunday afternoon. The house would come to life: everyone in and out of the kitchen, getting under each other's (well, mainly Mum's) feet, music drifting out of the front room (Sunday was definitely a *1000 Volts Of Holt* vinyl kind of day), multiple conversations and laughter bellowing over the records, and then the silence that would fall when a plate of delicious food was put in front of each of us to eat. After the wonderful chaos of Sunday lunch at ours, Anthony would get to work on basic maintenance on the bike. He'd wheel it out to the garden and prop it up on the pathway. Then he'd set to work: cleaning and oiling the chain; checking the brakes were still in working order and adjusting them; checking the frame, tyres and wheels for signs of serious wear. He may not have been massively into cycling at that time but he still knew a thing or two about how bikes worked. Watching him tinker away on the Burner was always really cool, partly because he was restoring it back to its best for me and partly because it was amazing to see how all the machinery worked.

Now, I say 'we' needed to make sure it was roadworthy, but other than bringing my brother mugs of coffee and handing him the occasional tool, I didn't get that involved in that side of things. Looking back now, not diving in is something I regret. It took me years to become confident in asking technical questions about my bikes. If I'd been introduced to it from the start of my cycling journey, would that have made me more technically minded? I'll never be 100 per cent sure, but it's a thought that rattles around my brain to this day. I'd certainly suggest seizing the moment to ask as many questions as you want and getting stuck in with both hands! No question is a silly question when it comes to learning something new.

After a few weeks of visits, cookouts, coffees and tinkering, everything was all set on my Burner. Anthony had cleaned and restored it to its former glory and – even though I'd witnessed Michele riding on the same bike hundreds of times – when he presented it to me on that final Sunday it looked like a brand-new machine. Even Michele was impressed. There were a few minor changes to it which came as a lovely surprise: Anthony had attached some amber and clear reflectors to the spokes, along with a brand-new set of Ever Ready bike lights he'd bought and put on the front and the back of the frame. They looked awesome, encased in yellow plastic that matched the yellow saddle, handlebar grips and padding of the Burner perfectly. Even back then, anyone who knew me clocked that I have to co-ordinate my cycle style down to the last detail. By today's standards, those bike lights would probably be considered *lamps*: they must have been about four inches in height and three inches in width and depth. Each of them took two massive Ever Ready batteries (Lord knows how many lumens the lights gave off but they were bright enough to leave floaters in your eyes) and was attached to the frame with metal brackets you had to screw together to clamp on to it. None of the easy-install, quick-release versions we've got now. They were obzocky and heavy . . . but absolutely perfect.

The other change was a pair of stabilisers. During those weeks while 'we' were working in the garden, I'd plucked up the courage to tell Anthony just how scary I thought it might be learning how to cycle. That disastrous first experience I'd had on the Burner still stuck in my head and the idea of face-planting on concrete instead of our psychedelic carpet sent shivers down my spine. I'd expressed my fears but didn't actually ask Anthony for stabilisers as I so wanted to be like the big kids I saw riding around the estate. I had visions of myself whizzing around just like them, or even better, just like Michele and her friends used to. But Anthony had been listening, which meant everything to me. My fears didn't mean that I was a baby or that I was weak – and he understood that a little bit of help would go a long way.

Now that the Burner was spruced up and ready to go, everything had all got pretty real. The time had come for Anthony to teach me how to ride. We didn't head out on that Sunday – Anthony had finished the Burner quite late that afternoon and said it might be better to have a full day of riding, so I was happy to wait until next week when he would be back. The idea of taking the bike out after school one day and giving it a go on my own crossed my mind, but thinking about what had happened the last time I attempted to go solo I decided it probably wasn't a good idea.

In the end, I didn't have to wait until next Sunday though. The following Tuesday, walking home from school I spotted Anthony's car (an impossible-to-miss bright red Ford Escort convertible) parked on our road. He'd finished work early, so decided to come over and surprise me with an afternoon lesson! I remember how exciting it was when he wheeled my Burner out of the house; he had a great big smile on his face, knowing how happy this was making me.

The plan Anthony suggested was to ride up and down my

road, staying on the pavement so I could get a feel of the bike without being panicked by any passing cars. I was so transfixed by how beautiful the red and yellow Burner looked, glistening brightly in the late afternoon sun, I don't think I'd have noticed anything else around me. Part of me hoped some of my classmates and friends who lived on my estate would walk past and see me with my gorgeous machine. I got on the bike, positioning myself comfortably on the saddle, feet on the pedals and proudly holding on to the handlebars. I hadn't set off yet but I was buzzing so much, I felt like I could take on the world on two wheels.

'There's nothing to worry about, Julie,' said Anthony, as he bent down and adjusted the position of the pedals and my feet. He brought the left pedal up to the top of its rotation, telling me to push down on it as hard as I could and giving the advice that, 'All you have to do is pedal in a straight line.'

I pushed off with my left leg just like he told me, somehow managing to wobble with the supports on either side of me. The wheels started turning and just like that, my Burner was going. I was away and it felt incredible.

After that first time, I'd count down to every Sunday when Anthony would return, and look forward to the full routine he had planned: we'd practise on one of the quiet side streets just around the corner from home, never going too far away so I could find my feet and get used to the feeling of being on the bike. Then we'd go around the estate and a little further out: down to the corner shop at the bottom of my road, loop up and around to the parade of shops opposite my primary school, do some of the roads around there and loop back home via Canning Town Recreation Ground. I knew the area like the back of my hand, but seeing it from the perspective of the saddle was eye opening. I'd be riding alongside my brother on the pavement, listening to him schooling me about riding on the roads. It all felt so different, and going about the neighbourhood on four wheels made me even more excited to get out there with my friends and ride around on two with them. With every practice session, I was getting more and more used to the feel of riding a bike. Anthony didn't pressure me to go beyond a pace that I wasn't comfortable with and encouraged me every pedal of the way.

Starting off on stabilisers was a huge boost for me, though not every child starts off with them, or indeed needs them. Some learn straight away on two wheels with an adult gently holding on to the handlebars, guiding them along; others (like my nephews did when they were about eighteen months old) start off on balance bikes. A balance bike is a training bike with no pedals or cranks, which you push along with your feet. It helps kids learn the crucial skills of balance and steering, so that eventually, instead of pushing along, they start gliding by lifting their legs and utilising the momentum of the bike. The point here is this: there is no right or wrong way to get into cycling, whatever age you are, and there is certainly nothing wrong with asking for a little help. Going at your own pace is totally okay.

It was after quite a few of these practice rides that the big day came. Both Anthony and I felt it was time to say ta-ta to the stabilisers and give it a go on two wheels. I wanted to feel the thrill of freewheeling without them, and my confidence had grown to such a point that I was absolutely desperate to give it a go.

I've fuzzy memories of that significant Sunday, but parts of it stick out in my mind. While Anthony was unscrewing the stabilisers in the garden, Mum was out there chatting with him. I asked Mum recently what they were talking about. She recalled, 'I can't remember exactly what I said to him, but I know I told your brother to make sure he was careful with you.' I could understand her worry. She'd probably had a similar conversation with Anthony when he taught Michele how to ride a bike. This would be the first time I'd be out riding without the safety cushion of the stabilisers and the beginning of a whole new set of outdoor adventures for her youngest girl.

I remember growing impatient to get out of the door, desperate for Mum and Anthony to stop talking so I could go and ride. But patience is a virtue, and when they *finally* stopped and it was time to go, I was too nervous to cycle out the gate! So we wheeled my Burner over to Canning Town Recreation Ground. It was *the* park to go and play in with your family or your friends. Sprawling over nineteen green acres with long, flat, tarmac paths that snaked around the climbing frames, merry-go-rounds, swings and slides, it was the perfect place for me to get started. The park had plenty of space to practise navigating corners and stay safe while learning.

We wheeled the Burner over to the start of one of the long, wide paths that led all the way to the other side of the grounds. I knew I wasn't going to ride the entire length of it, but I was sure as hell willing to give it a go. Holding on to the handlebars and staring down the path, a mix of nerves and excitement swirled through my mind. It was so bizarre – this was a park that I probably could have navigated with my eyes closed, yet suddenly it felt like a strange alien planet that I'd just landed on.

'Am I gonna fall off?'

'Probably, Bingar,' he replied, reassuring me with my childhood nickname. 'But if you do we'll just try again, innit.'

I got on the Burner. Feet on the pedals. Anthony stood behind me and held my waist to help me get balanced. Then he started to gently push me and the bike along the path. With him holding on to my waist, I was in control of the bike and steering while my feet were moving with every rotation of the pedals. It was happening! I was wobbly and it felt really weird, but it was happening! We got to the end of the path, turned around and repeated the route a few more times. With each try, Anthony would let go of me for a few seconds at a time, allowing me to find my balance on my own. My hands were tightly gripped on to the handlebars, and I was getting used to the sensation of the front of the bike reacting when my arms or body veered a little from the straight and narrow. There was only one moment when I managed to slip through his grip and fall to the side with the bike, but it was in slow motion and I was far too excited to let a little setback like that stop me. At least it wasn't like what had happened to me that first time on the Burner.

On what felt like the thousandth attempt, something felt different. I was concentrating on what was ahead of me and chattering at Anthony, but he wasn't answering back. I realised I couldn't feel his grip on my purple puffer jacket. He wasn't holding on to me any more and I was riding my bike all by myself! I could hear Anthony laughing and clapping in the background as I carried on down the path, albeit with a few more wobbles. Eventually without panicking (and remembering what Anthony had taught me weeks before about how to gently apply the brakes so I didn't go flying over the handlebars), I stopped the bike, steadied myself, turned around and cycled back towards him. We were both over the moon. Slowly cycling that Burner back home with my big brother walking beside me was one of the best feelings in the world.

Not long after this major breakthrough, I was faced with a situation similar to the one my sister found herself in when she first got that Burner: my bike was *nothing* like those of all my peers. When I was at primary school, it was all about having a fancy bike like Stephanie (one of my best mates who lived on my housing estate) had: a Falcon Mont Blanc Girls Bike. Stephanie's bike was the absolute business. It says a lot that almost thirty years later I still remember it: 12-inch gloss-white frame with bright purple accents and colour-coordinated brake cables; 20-inch wheels; a padded black-leather saddle, *and* it had Shimano gears and was a 6-speed. Back then – even though Steph was confidently bragging about it and I was confidently pretending to understand – neither of us *really* knew what that gearing jargon was about (think of gears as the same thing as speeds: a Falcon like Steph's with six gears is a 6-speed bike). With that many at her fingertips, versus my single-speed Burner, it was easier for Steph to power her way up the Canning Town Flyover without her lungs and legs exploding (you're going uphill and it's too difficult = shift down to a lower numbered gear) or accelerate across the flat ground of the Park (your legs are spinning the pedals way too fast = shift up to a higher numbered gear).

It's not like any of us lot really had to worry about not having enough gears – we were kids riding around the flat streets of Newham, not cycling up and down the Pyrenees. Maybe my bike wasn't as impressive as some and it wasn't brand-new, but that single-speed, flame red and yellow beauty was brand-new to me, and nothing (not even my best mate's bragging) would shake it from its spot as the bike of my dreams. Having it and knowing how to ride it meant I could finally cycle around with Stephanie and all my other friends instead of just watching them riding around from my bedroom window. It didn't really matter what your two wheels looked like – just having them was the main thing.

Being on a bike took on a whole new meaning and significance in my life. Before I'd be playing out with my friends on foot, but playing on two wheels gave us a whole other level of freedom. Adventures were out there to be had and I was determined that my Burner and I were going to have them, just like my sister did before me. After school and at the weekend, I spent as much time as possible out riding with friends – some from my class, and some new ones from my estate. I didn't know them pre-Burner, but being out on a bike, we'd clock other kids out riding, and we'd naturally latch on to each other and ride in groups. Our bikes had the power to bring us all together.

It was such a wonderful scene: a crew of Canning Town's most colourful misfits, all hailing from different backgrounds and all on mismatched bikes, full of energy and joy. I'm pretty sure we all fancied ourselves as the BMX boys of *E.T.* Our favourite time for riding our bikes was always the summer holidays – they were the best! Six glorious weeks of long, bright (and if we were lucky) hot days, with no school to interrupt our time. The only thing holding us back were the curfews from our parents, which we certainly broke on more than one occasion (those bike lights my brother got me sure came in handy when I lost track of time). We'd ride around the other estates in our area – especially fun when all the demolition and regeneration works were going on with their 'forbidden playground' vibes. All of the parks in our area were our dirt tracks and cycling circuits to explore. Anywhere we could get to by bike and ride around freely was an adventure playground. Newham may not have exactly been 'green-space' rich, but it was still an amazing place to explore. The bond and unity that we had through our love of cycling and the freedom it gave us is one of the things that kept us safe in an area that had a bit of a rough reputation, and where kids on bikes might have been considered to be trouble. We looked out for one another.

I was convinced those days were going to last for ever. When you're that young, why would you imagine otherwise? We all imagined we would always go on those adventures, picking up even more cycling waifs and strays each time we headed out; decimating the ice-lolly freezers in our local sweet shop, then riding over to the park to make ourselves sick with frozen e-numbers, lying on the grass, our bikes piled up next to us. We'd made pacts – proper ones with grubby spit handshakes and everything – swearing on our lives that we would always ride together.

But we had been fooling ourselves into thinking that childhood days like those could last for ever, and sometimes circumstances change beyond your control. I'd never even imagined any of us lot would move away from Canning Town. I'd never moved house in my life, and in the way I knew our house was our forever home, I had assumed that was the same for my friends too. This is where we lived, and this is where we'd be with each other for ever. But stuff like parents getting new jobs outside of London or deciding to move out of the area for a fresh start meant that some of my friends were suddenly upping sticks and leaving. Gradually our once-tight cycle crew started to drift. Hearing Stephanie saying stuff like, 'Dad says we'll still come back and visit' and then never seeing her again was heart-breaking.

One less person in our gang. One less friend to ride with and see at school. And then of course not everyone stays interested in the same thing – tastes and activities change. One summer, cycling with your friends is the *only thing* you want to do. The following summer it's all about going away for football training camps, or trips away with the local play scheme. Pop Top was the summer scheme that me, Claire and Vicki – two of the other girls from our gang – all got places in. The days at Pop Top were filled with different kinds of adventures: coach trips to beach towns like Walton-on-the-Naze, big days out to Alton Towers and five-day camping stints in Debden. It was so much fun. Every year you'd want to go back and spend your summers doing stuff like that, which cut down the time for cycling. Later came secondary school, and not all of us went on to the same one. The others who were still left in our little gang went to either Cumberland or Eastlea – two of the community schools in our area. I joined Sarah Bonnell, the all-girls school my sister attended. It was still in my borough, but half an hour away from Canning Town. The drifting of our cycling crew was complete. We no longer rode together, and new bonds at our new schools replaced those that were lost. The same thing I'd witnessed with my sister and cycling years before was now happening to my friends and me.

I still continued to cycle into my teens and occasionally rode my bike to secondary school, but it became an increasingly sporadic and lonely occurrence. Solo rides on my Burner turned cycling into a very different experience. Somehow, cycling around as a young woman on your own is an open invitation for strangers to shout unsolicited reviews of your anatomy at you. If I was feeling brave enough (because most of the time it was intimidating and bloody scary – and I'd need to make sure I could cycle off fast enough after), I'd stand up for myself and shout something back. 'Can't you take a compliment, love?' or 'I was only being nice, you little bitch,' were the kinds of retorts I'd get back.

Just the thought of facing that kind of harassment, knowing I'm probably going to get jeered at if I ride down a particular road or that someone will say something creepy to me about my school uniform, was enough to make me re-jig my usual cycling routes, or take a change of clothes with me for riding home after school. It was ridiculous to be exposed to that kind of harassment for just riding my bike and that I had to restructure *my* routine because some moron felt it was okay to make me feel unsafe. It's bad enough that catcalling and sexual advances from randoms is something that women deal with *literally every day* while just existing on this planet. So getting it while riding a bike? The vehicle that for some of us is a means of freedom and escape – that sucks on so many levels. Little did I know that those experiences were just a taster of the hurdles to overcome as a woman in cycling. Is it any wonder teenage girls still don't feel comfortable out and about on a bike?

I managed to convince myself that I didn't really need to cycle to get to places anyway. Cycling no longer felt like the 'done thing' to do to get around either, and who doesn't feel the pressure in their teens trying to fit in with what's cool? Steadily my interest in riding a bike waned, and at eighteen I stopped altogether. Both college and then later university were just a bus ride or DLR journey away from home. They'd both have been pretty cool cycle commutes, especially the ride to my uni campus in Greenwich (which I discovered in later years is a gorgeous route in London), but I'd lost my confidence riding in traffic, so didn't even try it once while I was studying.

As time went on, my withdrawal from one of the biggest joy-bringers in my life was complete. The Burner was gone: first, it was put back in the cupboard my sister once relegated it to, and then when space was needed and it was clear I was never going to ride it again, just like my beloved tricycle, the Burner was dismantled and in the estate chute room it went. With hindsight, I really regret that happening; not out of the pangs of nostalgia I hold for that bike now, but because it could have been repurposed and passed on to somebody else to enjoy. There wasn't an immediate family member to pass it on to, so it just got chucked in the bin. I wasn't as socially conscious then, and now, knowing there are organisations like The Bike Project (who take second-hand bikes, fix them up and donate them to refugees and asylum seekers) who can do something life-changing with an old bike, I urge anyone who's thinking of getting rid of theirs to find somewhere like that to donate it to.

I can't deny that I missed cycling – I'd be lying if I did – but at the time there was no real desire to get back on a bike and start again. Life had changed, my interests had changed, and that was a chapter that was over – fun while it lasted, but done and dusted.

Well, that's what I thought.

Girl, Connected

While my love of cycling was becoming dormant, another big part of my life entered on to the scene. The Internet. I've been on the World Wide Web since I was sixteen years old, which means I'll have been online for the better part of *two decades*. Almost everything bike-related I do today revolves around the Internet.

Nearly all the jobs I've had as an adult are related to being online. I've been a PR and social media executive, an online community engagement manager and an online marketing manager. This would have been incomprehensible when I was studying for my GCSEs. I can just imagine how *that* conversation with my careers advisor would have gone down: 'I see myself measuring, monitoring and managing the social media presence of cycling brands, while also spending my day starting conversations, cracking jokes and sharing bike-related memes with thousands of people across the globe I've never met before, all from one computer.'

The careers advisor I spoke to didn't think much of my ambitions to practise law or go into creative writing. 'Perhaps you should consider applying your skill set to something a bit more achievable than that,' was her blunt reaction, 'a career path more suited to your background, maybe?' *My background?* At first I felt shock when she said that ... then the shock turned into a mixture of rage and sadness in the pit of my stomach. She wasn't even trying to disguise what she meant by my 'background', and the fact that she was comfortable enough to be that blatant about it? Strangely, that attitude hurt the most. Her suggestions were nursing or PA and clerical work. Of course there is nothing wrong with either of these professions (my Aunt Josceline came to the UK from Trinidad in the 1960s specifically to study nursing and is amazing at it), but I was being pedalled this old and bogus trope of what black people where professionally capable of in the late nineties. There is something so damaging about making those kinds of assumptions based on 'background' and trying to drill such attitudes into someone at such a young and impressionable stage of their life. I still think about it now – the idea that working-class black girls aren't supposed to have such career aspirations, we're not supposed to go into the creative industries or zones that are primarily dominated by white middle-class men – and it still makes my heart ache. I know that black women have to work twice as hard to get half as far. Having the door to my potential career slammed shut in my face before I'd even finished school made me more determined to make it and to be visible for other young women of colour too who need to see themselves equally represented in every sphere.

Anyway, all of those roles I've held were within the cycling industry, and came from me writing about cycling on my blog. Considering I completed a degree in Politics and Law (big shout-out to my careers advisor if she ever reads this), this career path I'm on certainly wasn't the plan. Need to reach me? Then online is where you'll find me. Check any one of my four new residences: Twitter, Instagram, Facebook or VéloCityGirl. I call them 'new' as I moved into them from my online starter homes: AOL, MSN Messenger and an electronic-music bulletin board (which I still mourn the loss of – erutufon, I will always love you).

Technically, I'm a millennial, though I feel somewhat conflicted about that term. *Time* magazine once declared us lazy, entitled, technology-obsessed narcissists who still live with their parents. Plastering all my cycling antics across social media platforms and keeping VéloCityGirl up to date does admittedly take up a good chunk of my time. And I am still living at home with Mamma Vélo (that's the affectionate moniker she's picked up since I became Lady Vélo), but I'm also her carer, so that's just par for the course. As writer William Hughes put it, millennials are 'generally defined as anybody younger than me who has irritating opinions on politics or avocados', which – especially the latter part – makes me laugh quite a bit. Mamma V is a brilliant example of someone baffled by 'all dat damn fuss ovah a zaboca'. She grew up with a humongous zaboca tree growing in her back garden in Trinidad, which still yields the biggest specimens you'll ever see (when I went on holiday there they were the size of my head). Eating them on a regular basis really wasn't a big deal for her and still isn't to this day.

But here I am, grappling with the truth that I am a millennial. The year I got the Internet was the same year as the dawn of a new generation: iGen or Generation Z, and the year my first niece (Anthony's first daughter – my brother has three now which is still wild to think about) was born. For her generation, the Internet has always just been there. For you fellow bike lovers out there: I got online the same year as the 2016 gold medal-winning UEC European Track Champion Elisa Balsamo was born. Truthfully, though, I've essentially grown up along-side the Internet and it's helped me grow as a person. Much of my life has played out online: from my early blogging days to how I met the boy I cycle with.

I have two people to thank for the digital direction my life ended up taking; Mamma V and Dad for getting me connected to that mysterious world of the Internet aged sixteen: I'm grate-ful to you both from the bottom of my first Netgear cable modem; not just for steering me off the original career path I know you both probably hoped I was going to follow when I was obsessed with watching *Rumpole of the Bailey* and *LA Law* as a child, but for opening my eyes to a whole new world. Even though you both still tell me I'll get square eyes from star-ing at my screen to this day.

Although I can now look back on those years fondly, steer-ing through your teens with all the hormonal baggage that gets dumped on you is a minefield. Through those years, All I wanted was to be was sixteen. I was in such a hurry to grow up, convinced that this magical milestone would banish all my teenage anxiety, pressure and heartbreak. Despite the build-up, I had no idea quite how much 10 December 1998 would go on to shape most of my adult life.

Before I could get to that golden date, I had to make it through 1997. The middle of that year began a series of difficult events, and there was no real-life Garmin to help me navigate my way through it. That June, Mamma V found herself out of a job for the first time in twenty-four years. Progressive were shutting their factory doors for the last time, and every single employee of the company – from Sheffield all the way to Upper Clapton – had been made redundant.

'God is good, you know, Julie,' Mamma V would repeat every time I worked myself into a panic over her situation. Her faith means a lot to her and often sees her through her darkest moments. I'd never known her to not be working, and although she was carrying on like everything was totally fine, the worry of having one less wage coming into the house was always lingering in the air.

While we were all processing the fallout of her losing her job, Mamma V and Dad's relationship was slowly falling to pieces and they were on the brink of breaking up. I've yet to meet a child who's been caught up in the middle of their parents messy break-up and says, 'It wasn't too bad really,' or 'Not that big of a deal,' because it is awful. Their long stints of doling out the silent treatment to each other could be as deafening as their explosive arguments.

To complete the absolutely dreadful summer of 97, Nanny Lucy wasn't well. She was one of those oddities – an old person that *never* got sick. I'd never known her to have so much as a cold – the woman had a constitution of an ox! But that summer, Nanny Lucy was in and out of the Whittington Hospital for check-ups, with Mum always accompanying her. Though I'd figured out it had to be bad, it was weeks before the word was spoken. *Cancer.* Nanny Lucy had been diagnosed with cancer. It was the way that Mamma V said the C word that made me realise the outlook wasn't good.

While all of this was going on riding my bike took a back seat – with all the emotional mess that was going on around me, getting on my bike was one of the last things I felt like doing. That burning desire I had to ride was fading away. Every time I did get on the saddle, it didn't feel as enjoyable as it used to, and that was so confusing – I'd always feel riddled with guilt about why it wasn't fun any more. Surely what I needed the most was the thing which used to make me feel my absolute best, right? In hindsight (and thanks to my depression diagnosis as an adult) I now know that feeling was something called anhedonia; the inability to feel pleasure in normally pleasurable activities. Cycling to school every day eventually turned into every other day ... and then stopped completely. I tried my best to keep my Burner in my life, even if rides had become a lot more sporadic. Heading out on my bike on the weekends seemed like a good compromise. If Mum wanted something fetching from the shops, I'd use that as an excuse to make myself hop on the saddle and go. If I needed head space between panicking about mock exams or not have to listen to my parents arguing, I'd get out for a ride around the local park to clear my head. Those bike rides didn't have to be something major, just *something* to keep the joy of cycling going. Those little spins were coping mechanisms while everything else around me was turning to dust; anything that helped and alleviated some of the sadness – and rider guilt – I was struggling with, was a mini-blessing.

Although 1997 had dealt the cruellest of summers, there were some glimmers of joy to cling on to during the winter. In December, Mamma V got a new job as a supervisor at Marks & Spencer. Things were looking up, and as my parents had somehow managed to stay together and Nanny Lucy was miraculously still with us, we decided to throw my sixteenth (aka my long-awaited 'Big People Dem' party) a year early. As morbid as it sounds, all of us – including Nanny Lucy, who was very matter of fact about the whole thing – knew she wasn't going to be around the following December, so bringing the celebrations forward and gathering the whole family together was a wonderful thing to do. Besides, Nanny Lucy *had* to be there. Being The Matriarch (everyone who knew her, even friends of the family, called her 'Mum') meant she was the one who hosted all our birthday gatherings. She was the head chef with her homemade roti, curry goat & rice, and star baker with her knock-out fruit and dark rum birthday cakes. From her own six grown-up children down to her ten grandchildren, every single celebratory gathering happened at her house. No arguments. Even if that meant Dad driving us all to North London at stupid o'clock on the morning of said celebration to drop us off at hers and spend all day helping organise your own (not so) surprise party: you did it.

10 December 1998.

The day I turned sixteen. I remember lying in bed that morning, thinking about some of the things that I could now legally do now that I'd come of age. Stuff like:

1) Buy a ticket on the National Lottery (to this day I still haven't won more than a tenner).

2) Leave home without parental consent (given I live in London, I'd have needed that Lottery win to do that).

3) Drink alcohol in a restaurant with adult supervision (growing up around parties at Nanny Lucy's meant I consumed the odd sip of booze waaay before turning sixteen).

4) Get married (the teenage fangirl in me is still waiting for Constable Benton Fraser – the Mountie in *Due South* – to sweep me off my feet. But only if he's wearing the brown uniform, not the red one).

I guess turning sixteen had some perks to look forward to, right?

The morning of my birthday started off like a normal weekday in my house: Mum stepping out of the door to head to work while I was still getting ready for school; Dad deciding if he was going to go to bed after coming in from a night shift, or do me a kind favour.

'You want mi give yuh a lift to school?' he offered over his mug of tea. A lift in Dad's Ford Granada Scorpio with its heated seats on a freezing cold and drizzly December morning was pretty tempting, but I was going to get the bus and hop off at the stop near to my best friend's house, knock for her and walk the rest of the way into school together. She wasn't going to be sixteen for a whole three days more, and I was looking forward to telling her how much more 'spiritually and emotionally mature' I felt now. Ha.

I was feeling slightly subdued due to a birthday-related silence from Mum and Dad that morning. There was no mention from either of them about it being my sixteenth birthday, so I spent the whole day at school wondering what was going on. Or wondering what could be going wrong with our family, again. But when I got back home, all my fears of being forgotten or everything turning to crap again were allayed by the stack of presents and cards which greeted me, along with a note, in Dad's flourishy handwriting:

Come upstairs.

I could hear both my parents up there, probably getting ready for the meal that night – even though they'd been silent about my birthday in the morning, I knew we'd be heading out to Beefeater (one of Dad's favourite places) for a celebration meal. They were laughing and joking with each other which was a good sign, but as I walked around to the stairs, a few things were seriously off:

1) I could hear my floorboards creaking.

2) There was another voice I didn't recognise coming from upstairs too.

The fact it was my birthday went clean out my mind – I didn't have anything in my room that shouldn't have been in there, but I couldn't help thinking, 'What the hell have they found, and am I about to get my arse busted for it?' as I stomped upstairs. In my bedroom I found Mamma V, Dad and some bloke in a shop uniform huddled around my desk, a blue glow over their faces. What the hell? Mamma V sensed me in the doorway and clicked her fingers, gesturing to Dad. They both stepped out of the way to reveal a man from Dixons setting up a brand-new desktop computer.

'Ta-da! Happy birthday, Julie!' they chorused, with massive smiles across their faces. 'You didn't think we'd forget your sixteenth, did you?'

I honestly didn't know what to say. This beautiful, shining machine was on my desk for *my* birthday. I think the most I managed to get out of my mouth was 'How?'

The man from Dixons was still tinkering away – he re-booted the computer and the glow of the Windows 98 start-up screen flashed up on the monitor.

'You like it?' my dad exclaimed, barely able to keep the smile off his face. 'The people in Dixons said this would be a good one for you to use for coursework and alla dat.'

Dixon's dude had finished doing his thing. He had a blue and yellow CD case in his hand. 'Okay, so the next thing you'll need to do is pop this install disc in when you're ready for the thirty-day trial, choose your screen names, as you can have more than one on the account, and get connected. Subscribe if you like AOL at the end of it.'

A-O-L.

With both a floppy disk *and* CD ROM drive, a huge (!) 32MB RAM and a 2.1 GB hard drive and AOL waiting to go too, my parents had ushered us into the age of the Internet. At that point, I had no clue about how much this gift would shape my life.

From Barbie to Bikes

In June 2007, almost ten years after getting the Internet at home, I started my first blog, The BlackBarbieExperience.

Before we go any further, I'll explain that name: I'd acquired the nickname 'Black Barbie' in secondary school. At one strange period during my time at Sarah Bonnell, a group of girls who were not my friends would refer to me as a 'bit of a princess – like a living Barbie doll'. I decided many years later to reclaim that moniker and flip it on its head.

'Ten years?' you might be thinking. I'd had the World Wide Web at my fingertips for all that time, but I wasn't ready to leap into the blogosphere straight away. Starting a blog is easy: registering a domain name on a site like WordPress and using one of their web templates takes no time at all. Feeling comfortable enough to share the kind of content I wanted to on it wasn't.

Blogging stemmed from the journals I had kept since my early teens. Everything from the trivial to the traumatic was recorded on the gilt-edged pages of those diaries and kept under lock and key.

Writing down the feelings that were bouncing around my head was a huge help. It always made me feel so much better and gave me a better understanding of myself and the situations I was going through at the time. Highs and lows: like my parents' eventual break-up, grieving for Nanny Lucy, my poor mental health, incredible experiences at university and generally trying to navigate my way through life as a young adult; all went into that safe space. I could express my emotions within my journals, but that's as far as it went. I wasn't great at opening up to people, even those who were closest to me, but over those formative ten years, the more I surfed the Internet, the more I found people who were a bit like me; talking about similar situations and emotional highs and lows: all on their blogs.

That was the beauty of the blogosphere, having such a wide range of bloggers I could discover, follow and connect with! Even though it was via a computer monitor, a keyboard and some wires, I was making personal connections and friendships with people who I felt would understand what I was going through, and that encouraged me to put myself out there with BlackBarbieExperience.

Although BBE was a natural progression from my diary-keeping days, initially I was petrified about the blog. I'd never invited anyone to read my private journals, so posting into the digital ether was scary. Every time I gave out the BBE website address, I felt like I was getting palpitations – I was excited about my blog being out there, but also so anxious, wondering if anyone would actually read it and what they would think if they did.

But the feedback and love I received for BBE was overwhelming in the best possible way. That community and its support inspired me to keep on with my blog and stopped me from feeling so isolated. I blogged because I realised it's okay to be yourself online. I blogged because I didn't want anyone else who might be going through similar situations to feel unsupported or alone. I blogged because I loved it. And I still love blogging to this day.

On BlackBarbieExperience I talked openly about 'fluffy stuff' like fashion and style, the things that had the power to grind me down like my physical health issues (my asthma mainly, which can debilitate me in the harsh winter months) and stuff that could lift my soul higher – like true love and relationships.

The first post I did on BBE was about another defining Internet experience: how I met my boyfriend (of thirteen years at the time I write this), Ian. We were both members of an online message board called erutufon dedicated to electronic music.

I discovered the message board through the album *Head On* by Super_Collider. I was obsessed with that album, listening to it on repeat, probably much to the annoyance of Mamma V. While looking through the sleeve notes, I found the erutufon message board address and was hooked on posting and exchanging messages with other Super_Collider fans on the board, including a user who went by the screen name Grobelaar (spoiler: real name, Ian).

I was getting on like a house on fire with this bloke who I was only talking to via my computer screen. It wasn't just the shared appreciation for the band that kept us in conversation. We had other stuff in common; other slightly unusual music acts we were both into, cult 80s and 90s films, photography, and a bit of cycling. It felt totally normal to both of us – we just clicked – but you have to keep in mind this happened during a time when people thought it was quite strange to chat with 'random strangers off the Internet' and make friends or start relationships through online platforms. Oh, how times have changed!

We continued talking (just as friends) on erutufon, but didn't actually meet each other IRL until six years later in 2005. Again, this didn't seem weird at all; we were two people living in different parts of London at the time (he was north and I was east), who had busy lives. We talked online most days – even when we were at work (he was a senior designer in the computer games industry, and I had just started as a university admissions officer). What did finally bring us together? Ian inviting me to watch *The Hitchhiker's Guide to the Galaxy* at the Holloway Road Odeon, and offering to cook me a Sunday Roast with all the trimmings after the film. There's no better way to my heart than a rosemary roast potato, and Ian is a professional chef now so I doubt many people are going to cook for me better!

Although I was being as honest as possible about life and everything in between on BBE, the one thing that I wasn't talking about on there was the desire I was harbouring to get back into cycling. It was bizarre, I'd never even mentioned bikes and what a huge part of my life they had been when I was a child and in my teens.

The thought of getting back on two wheels was always at the back of my mind – niggling away at me, slowly weaving its way to the front of my mind. When Ian talked about how much he enjoyed his extended ride along the coast to work (after we got together, Ian got a new senior designer role which took him out of London) and how energised he would feel, I really wanted some of that. Ian's commuting bike was a Ridgeback Storm Hybrid – which he nicknamed 'the Beast'.

The term 'hybrid' now covers a pretty wide spectrum of bikes, though at first they were considered to be a combination of two types of bike: a standard road bike and a mountain bike. These hybrid builds bring together the best parts of different styles of bikes and can be suited to your needs – some are ace for commuting with a more relaxed position, other are built so you can load up with bicycle bags for touring rides. Different weights and speeds are available, so you can get a ride that is comfortable over all surfaces and terrains. The Beast was perfect for where Ian was living: the route from his flat in Southsea to the studio in Gunwharf Quays was pretty flat, but if he fancied going off road over the weekend and exploring a bit more of Hampshire's bike trails, he had a machine with the speed of a road bike and the flat handlebars of a mountain bike to be able to do that too. When he decided to leave home a little earlier in the mornings to take a longer ride into work, taking in that gorgeous sea view, I was pleased but a little envious. It would have been a beautiful ride first thing in the morning by the beach – especially on a crisp and bright day – and then riding home with a seafront sunset as company? Yes please. I also wanted to be able to head down to his on a weekend with my own bike so we could go on rides together, and for him to bring his bike up to London so we could head out around town.

But still, I didn't talk about it or all of those feelings I was getting on the blog.

I wasn't worried about scaring readers off with it – everyone who read BBE was used to the multiple themes and my random musings and rants – but something about bikes and BlackBarbie just didn't sit quite right together. I needed to test the water.

It was three years into blogging on BBE before I dropped any hints of my desire to test out being on two wheels again. In a blog post titled 'Not resolutions but goals for 2010' I wrote:

> Getting a bike: Something that I have pondered on for ages and
> *really* want to sort out this year. I know exactly which bike I
> want and will be checking it out for a test ride soon. I'll possibly
> have more to come on that here, soon.

Possibly was the key word. I still had that niggling feeling
BlackBarbieExperience wasn't the place for this, especially as
in my heart I was hoping for encouragement from my readers – affirmation that I was doing the right thing in getting back
into cycling again. Granted, the entry wasn't exactly brimming
over with details, but I did put my intention to ride a bike on
BBE. Only two comments came in on that post about my non-
resolutions. Neither one of them was about me wanting to
get a bike.

After my post quietly died a death, I spent the rest of that
January putting the wheels in motion for Operation Pedal
Push, and decided to do it all away from the blog. It wasn't
that I didn't want to talk about it – I just came to the conclu-
sion that BlackBarbieExperience wasn't the right space after
all. The raw excitement about cycling once again was stirring
inside of my soul like crazy. All I could think about was getting
my hands on the bike of my dreams and learning how to ride
all over again.

Researching and planning what I'd need to do to get the bike
and some of the cycling kit I'd need with it was so much fun.
I was feeling energised and couldn't wait to get my teeth stuck
back into cycling! And if I was feeling like this *before* the bike
had even been bought, imagine the state that I was going to
be in when I got it and was riding once again! It helped that I
already knew exactly what bike I wanted to get: a 'Princess' by
Pashley Cycles. The Princess is a traditional Dutch-style 'sit-up-
and-beg': a steel step-through looped frame. It's designed for an
upright riding position, which Pashley beautifully describes as

'ideal for tranquil jaunts into the countryside and an altogether more peaceful style of cycling'.

OK, so this style of bike was a total departure from my Burner AND Newham isn't the countryside by any stretch but that Princess ticked all the boxes for what I was after in a new bike. It would allow me to commute to work and would be a relaxed way to ease myself back into cycling with after a fallow ten years. I have to be honest, the look of the bike was a huge draw too. Today's Princess is still based on its original 1920s design, which spoke to the vintage-style lover in me.

All this said, there is no denying that some elements of cycling can be eye-wateringly expensive. Affordability is a significant barrier to entry, especially amongst ethnic minority groups, and I know about that all too well. This was a barrier that I'd encountered as both a child via the cost constraints my parents faced and as an adult wanting to get back into cycling.

I was still in full-time employment in 2010 as an admissions officer at the University of East London. My salary was reasonable, but living in London, paying bills and generally trying to survive in this city is an expensive business: my dream bike was something that I simply couldn't afford to buy outright. The cost had held me back from fully investing in my new bike dreams much earlier. I know what you might be thinking: an obvious solution to the cost issue would be a second-hand Pashley – one that was well-maintained and fit for purpose. There is nothing wrong – and a lot right – with getting a second-hand bike, as my relationship with my Burner will tell you. I did spend some time scouring eBay and Gumtree looking for one, and a few Princesses turned up. They were a little bit cheaper than the full RRP (if they're well looked after, they maintain their value too), but I'm going to be honest with you ... I didn't *want* a second-hand one. For the first time ever, I wanted to choose a *bike of my own*. I loved that my sister's beloved Burner got a whole new lease of life with me, but this was my chance to start a whole new cycling story – a story of my own. The desire to have my own 'Day 1' – being with my bike right from the very beginning and starting a whole new adventure with it – meant so much to me. I *had* to make it happen.

Doing my research for Operation Pedal Push, I looked into some other options that could make this dream a reality and perhaps actually keep me in sight of my goal of getting my Pashley Princess that year. Looking at high-street bike shops again, I started investigating the affordable option they were offering: bike finance. Credit and hire purchase was a road that I really didn't want to go down. I'm not saying that I'm *terrible* with money, but the risk of putting myself into debt for something that I wanted to get to make me *happy* was not the solution I was after. And was I even sure that it was going to make me happy? It wasn't the kind of expense I could justify for what could end up being a fleeting whim.

I was feeling slightly deflated when the beauty of the online communities I was hanging around in came through. I let off a little steam in the 'General Discussions' forum of the techno bulletin board I lived on. Moaning about the obstacles I was running into on my search to get my Pashley, a forum member picked up on my woes and asked a question that completely changed my cycling fortunes. 'Haven't you checked with your workplace to see if they do the cycle to work thing? Might be worth giving that a try?'

The 'cycle to work thing'? I had absolutely no idea what they were talking about, but I had a new lead.

The Cycle to Work scheme launched in 1999 and was introduced by the UK Government to promote healthier journeys to work and help reduce environmental pollution. It's a tax exemption initiative and employers of all sizes (including public, private and voluntary sectors) who choose to join the scheme can offer to hire out cycles and cycling equipment to their staff. The 'hire' isn't your workplace lending you one of their own bikes, which was the first thing I thought when I looked it up and was very confused by – no one told me UEL had a secret stash of bikes hidden away on campus?! – so this is the breakdown:

- Your employer (so long as you meet their approval criteria) gives you a financial loan in the form of a voucher for the value of the bike and kit you need.

- You exchange that voucher for the bike and kit you've chosen at a bike shop that is registered with the scheme.

- Technically, you've 'hired' that bike from your employer, and they recover the cost of the equipment from you under a hire agreement.

- You pay for the 'hire' AND make savings by agreeing to give up part of your salary in exchange for a benefit (called a 'Salary Sacrifice' benefit). The sacrifice/hire cost gets taken from your gross salary (before tax) over a set period of time, which means that you also end up paying less Income Tax and National insurance.

Sounds marvellous, doesn't it?

At that time I had already been working at UEL for five years. So that exchange sent me straight to my massive 'Life Admin' plastic storage box in my bedroom, digging through it like a madwoman in the search for my contract and paperwork. In amongst all the bank statements and utility bills I'd chucked across my bedroom floor, I finally found it. 'There has to be *something* in here about the Cycle to Work scheme?' I thought to myself. The contract covered pension schemes, nursery places for staff with young children, reduced membership at their gym facilities ... and assistance with travel in regard to staff parking permits and season ticket loans. That was it. Nothing about bikes. Nothing about cycling schemes. That was a pisser on my parade. My glimmer of hope was that, after five years, the welcome pack was actually totally out of date ...

The next morning I headed into work on a singular mission: to speak to Human Resources and find out if UEL was an employer who had opted into the scheme. My buzz about getting back on a bike really was relentless and my concentration levels at my desk were shot – all I could think about was the joy of taking a bike home with me. I was already imagining how bloody ace it would feel to walk into a bike shop and catwalk out of the place, all togged up in the outfit I had planned for the day with my gorgeous Pashley Princess. As overdramatic as it sounds, it felt like the Cycle to Work scheme was my last hope of my 'Day 1' dream becoming reality. I spent the first half of that Tuesday in investigative mode (if my old boss is reading this: I know it sounds like I didn't do any work while I was there all, but between researching for my Pashley and writing blog posts, I did ...). The staff intranet turned up nothing – all the staff benefits listed on there reflected what I had listed on that print-out at home. Bollocks. It was time to make some calls.

I spent about five minutes being bounced between the switchboard and different members of staff in HR, until finally I got through to someone who knew what Cycle to Work was – and confirmed that UEL was indeed a member of the scheme! At that news I could have leapt out of my chair and danced on my desk. Tom, who I was told looked after the scheme, was out of the office until late afternoon. 'It's fine, it's absolutely one hundred per cent fine,' I said to myself, trying to remain glued to my seat. I fired off an email to him as soon as I hung up, even flagging it as high importance – getting things into place for me to be cycling again was at the very top of my agenda so I stand by it!

The afternoon was spent refreshing my inbox. Every time Outlook pinged I jumped, disappointed when it was one of the usual slew of emails: Staff Training Day notice; Returned decisions on Combined Honours applications; Updated Rota for February Enrolment Centre.

Then, after what felt like an eternity, a reply from Tom – checking my eligibility and laying out exactly how I could get involved with the scheme. In that moment Tom become my favourite person in the whole world and he didn't even know it. A new Jools was in the near future, sat proudly on her Pashley Princess in the London sunshine, pedalling her way to pure happiness. Before I could get to this fabulous future, I had some serious plans to make.

The first thing I did when I got home that evening was email Ian. He would still be in his office until at least 8 p.m., and I really couldn't wait until then to call him and tell him. It was one of those moments when I was reminded that being in a long-distance relationship could be a real kick in the guts. There wasn't going to be a long cosy chat on the sofa about my plans for us to finally start cycling. It would either be a phone call late in the evening, or texts and emails. But the pure delight that I was experiencing wasn't lost in technology – Ian told me later that my euphoria was 'jumping off the screen'. What probably made my emotions digitally bounce from London to Southsea was the thought of us cycling together for the first time in our relationship.

I was straight on to the Cyclescheme website that night to find the retailer closest to me that was part of the scheme. I already knew that there wasn't going to be one in Newham:

back then it was slim pickings on local bike shops or big retailers being in my area. From my plotting of Operation Pedal Push, I was already aware of an independent retailer in South London and happily they came up on the list of approved retailers. London Bridge wasn't *that* far away and in an instant I was planning a visit to check out a Princess up close and personal.

Despite my one-track bike mind, it wasn't until a whole ten days later that I had a chance to visit the retailer. A quiet weekday visit would be ideal, so I booked a Friday off work to begin my new cycling life.

After a *long* ten days, I was a bundle of nerves when Bike Day finally rolled around. You know that feeling you get when you're on your way to a first date or a job interview? It was something kind of like that – a heady mixture of excitement and butterflies-in-your-stomach anxiety … and this wasn't even the day I'd be cycling off on the bike. All I was going into the shop to do was have a proper look and hopefully walk away with a quote. In all my years of cycling when I was younger, I'd never actually been *inside* a bike shop before. I had no reason to: if any problems with my Burner came up, either Anthony or Dad was always on hand to take a look at it. At twenty-eight, this was about to be my first experience of entering such a space.

Although it would be a first, lingering in my head was a preconception of what to expect. Factors like ethnicity, gender and income still strongly affect participation, as referenced in the TFL stats earlier – and this bike shop was a lot posher than the old LBS my sister used to go to on Barking Road – so the thought of this being a rather white space crossed my mind.

'Well, at least I won't have to battle rush hour for much longer,' I thought to build myself up a little as I exited the bustling Tube station and made my way to On Your Bike, a huge shop that sprawled over two floors. The two front windows were dressed with a variety of bikes and cycling accessories:

one had folding and commuter bikes, and the other had road and mountain bikes. My heart beat a little faster as my bike-shop newbie and potential outsider nerves turned into a sense of joyous realisation – my Pashley was somewhere in there. I scanned the shop, looking for a member of their sales team, while trying not to get overwhelmed by the size of the place and everything they had on display. I was also resisting the urge to unleash my inner *Supermarket Sweep* contestant and run around looking for their Pashley section to salivate over. Eventually, I caught the eye of one of the team – a man in his late twenties – who came over to help me.

It didn't take long for him to put me at ease, and for me to blurt out my day's mission: to get myself on to a Pashley Princess. Within seconds we were heading up to the first floor where a stationary peloton of Pashley bikes were gathered together on their display stand, looking absolutely glorious. I'd only ever seen them online, or when someone cycled past, and they certainly didn't disappoint. Their clean and shiny paintwork glistened under the ceiling spotlights, with the chrome-plated raised handlebars catching the reflection of the lights and sparkling like stars. I could see in an instant all those long summer rides with Ian along the seafront.

As I stood gazing at the wonder of the Pashley section (while trying to stroke every single one of them) the assistant sensibly offered some advice. 'I just wanted to check that you are aware the ladies Pashley collection features models other than the Princess?' he said. 'We also carry both the Poppy and the Sonnet Pure, if you wanted to have a look at those as well today and give them a little test in here?'

Despite already *knowing* that the Princess was the one for me, I still needed to make sure that it really was – even if it meant the potential of my set-in-stone cycling dream being shattered.

'As you have them in stock, I'll try the Poppy and the Sonnet, thank you,' I replied, still eyeing up the Princess in Buckingham Black. It'd be rude not to give the others a whirl.

The sales assistant looked me up and down, 'We should have them all in the right frame sizes here for you to try. I'm thinking you're around the five foot nine-ish mark, so the twenty-inch frame could be the size for you?'

Well spotted, and correct. Finding out the right size of frame was something I had done in my planning for Operation Pedal Push. It's pretty straightforward: first measure your inside leg length (from the sole of your foot to the top of your inner thigh) in inches, and check the measurement you get against the measurement of the bike. All good bike manufacturers should have their measurements listed on their website alongside what the appropriate frame size should be. It's also worth noting that some retailers will have sizing charts for specific bikes (like mountain, road and e-bikes).

It was reassuring to be asked about my height and frame size and not just get plonked on a bike, which had been another of my fears about the day. The sales assistant weaved between the bikes, checking the sizes printed on the old-fashioned parcel tags hanging from the back of the antique brown-leather Brooks saddles. When he found the 20-inch frames, he wheeled out the first bike, the Sonnet Pure: similar in build and design to the Princess, but a bit more stripped down. Its frame paintwork was a beautiful two-tone colour scheme: ivory with midnight blue mudguards. Just like the Princess, there was a huge wicker basket at the front attached to the chrome-plated raised bar, with black rubber grips, a big shiny ding-dong bell, and a bicycle pump that fitted to the frame. Even though this wasn't my first choice of Pashley, it was gorgeous! I hadn't been on a bike for years and *never* on a bike as stunning as this. Even though there was a chance that

I might have forgotten how to actually ride a bike and this could end in embarrassing disaster, I *had* to hop on and give it a go! On Your Bike had a faux indoor 'road' on the other side of the showroom, which reminded me of the Yellow Brick Road in the *Wizard of Oz* – pretty fitting as I certainly felt like I wasn't in Kansas any more ...

Oh, it felt good but nervy to be sat on that bike. As I balanced my left food on the pedal, I wobbled a bit, causing the shop assistant to gesture his hands towards me, thinking I was about to fall. 'I'm good!' I yelped to him, steadying myself. 'Remember what Anthony taught you about pushing off,' I told myself as I started the wobbly ride.

Off I went on a few small rotations (and no falls). Hmmm. I thought to myself as I pedalled back towards the stand. It felt like a really nice ride: smooth but almost a little too light, and I wasn't keen on the lack of a rear coat guard (this is a device fitted over the rear wheel of a bicycle which stops long trailing clothing, like a coat or a long skirt, getting caught in the back wheel or in the gap between the rim and the brakes) and the chain case only being a partially enclosed one (I wanted a fully enclosed case to protect the chain and keep it lubricated for a little less maintenance).

Then came the Poppy in Blush Pink. Although it was a stunning colour, it was a bit too much on the pink side for me! As I took this one for a little test ride (also feeling a little trepidation), the position felt different, possibly down to the flat alloy handlebars that had a slight back-sweep to them. Then came the moment I had been waiting for: trying the Princess. I stood almost frozen, clenching my hands together in anticipation, as once again the sales assistant bent over to check the label on the black beauty parked on its stand.

I could hear him sucking air though his teeth as he read the tag. My heart was beating out of my chest – something was wrong. Then he stepped over to the other Pashley Princess, further down the line ... the Regency Green one.

'Is there something wrong with the Buckingham Black?' I asked, already getting nervous about his reply.

'Oh no – there's nothing wrong with it,' he said in a reassuring voice. But I wasn't reassured. 'That one is a seventeen-and-a-half-inch frame,' he continued, 'but the green is a twenty-inch, so you can try this one for size instead.'

In my head it was a 'record scratch, freeze-frame moment' as the magical music of meeting my dream machine was abruptly interrupted.

'Ah. I was hoping to get the frame in black.' I don't even know why I said this out loud – I wasn't buying the bike that day – it could be ordered in, but I was gutted.

'The stock we have on display is what we have available at the moment, I'm afraid, but it's not a problem at all for us to order in the black from the factory if you do decide it's the Princess you want after all.'

Of course it wasn't going to be a problem – I knew I was being irrational but my heart sank a little more when I heard those words.

'Could I still have a look at the black one, please? I'll test the green for size, but it'd be nice to see the details,' I asked, thinking I must seem like a total fusspot.

The sales assistant gave me a knowing smile and wheeled the Buckingham Black bike over to me. Good lord, it was beautiful. I crouched down to look at the details: the lugs (a lugged frame is when the tubing is bonded together at the junctions by other pieces of metal) were cut into very beautiful and intricate shapes. There was a big, broad, antique brown Brooks B66s natural-leather saddle with thick twin-coil springs at the back of it (good for suspension and support while riding) which would mould to the shape of your bum over time, a bit like a trusty pair of slippers. Brooks make supremely comfortable saddles that last the distance. Its wheels were 26-inch polished-alloy rims with stainless-steel spokes, which, just like the chrome handlebars, sparkled under the bright lights. Then the detailing on the mudguards caught my eye: hand-applied gold-line detail, which glistened like treasure, with a reflector on the rear one too. The chaincase was fully enclosed, which protects the bike chain while out riding, but I also made a mental note that I *had* to learn how to remove the casing and maintain the chain once I got the bike. It also had the skirt guard, a big ding-dong bell, and that large wicker basket which I could put to good use while out riding. In short, it was absolutely gorgeous.

After admiring it for what seemed like an eternity, I propped it back on the bike stand, and hopped on the Regency Green one to try it for size. Oh my. Memories of my joy the first time I sat on my Burner came flooding back. This time, I pushed off down that faux road without a single wobble. The Princess felt like a beauty to ride – so smooth and elegant. The weight made it sturdy, giving the sense it was supporting me, and the upright position on the bars felt good. I had just spent the morning being the Goldilocks of bikes and at that point, as I came to the end of that road, I thought, 'Now this one is just right.' It was a done deal – I'd have to wait a little bit longer for the Buckingham Black, but I knew it was going to be so worth it.

With the bike sorted out (and while I was still walking on air from that little ride), cycling extras were the next thing on the agenda. The Cyclescheme voucher would also cover bike accessories, so I went back downstairs to have a look around at some. I knew I'd need to get necessities like some bright bike lights, a good helmet and a decent bike lock, but specific clothing for when I was out riding wasn't on my radar, until it was pointed out by my now trusty sales assistant.

I had never even thought about specific cycling wear while

plotting out Operation Pedal Push. I went to the bike shop deliberately in an outfit that was pretty standard for me: a pair of metallic magenta winkle-pickers, black skinny jeans, a black roll-neck jumper with a loud Tatty Devine statement necklace over it, a vintage leather saddlebag and a purple felt double-breasted dress coat. That was the kind of outfit I'd wear when I was cycling around the city. To test the bike properly I even kept my coat *on* to see how it would feel riding in it. I didn't want to have to sacrifice style when I got back into cycling, and I'd never had any special clothing when I was a kid on a bike, no one I knew did. We all rode around in our usual clothes, be it blindingly bright shell-suits and colourful LA Gears on our feet in the late 80s or All Saints-inspired cargo pants, baggy jeans and Acupuncture Trainers in the late 90s. But I supposed there would be a difference between walking down the street wearing the felt coat in the rain and being able to pop my umbrella out of my bag to keep dry, versus being at the mercy of the elements when out on the Pashley. I'll also admit I wasn't a huge fan of some of the waterproof jackets and trousers I'd seen other cyclists wearing – there was something so utilitarian about them that didn't appeal to me. But if I needed to stay dry it seemed to make sense to pick up some bits while I was kitting myself out.

With a slight sense of reluctance I went to the women's section and came face to face with a rail of Lycra, something that back then I only associated with men cycling really fast on road bikes, and the Tour de France ... neither one of which were on the agenda for me and my Princess. It looked extremely sporty and seemed to come in limited variations: jerseys in black, pink or busy floral designs – none of which were my kind of thing. Then there were the bib shorts, which looked like mankinis at the top, with padded pants at the bottom. I didn't know much about this stuff, but I figured they really weren't for me. Little did I know what firm friends they would become in later years!

I moved over to the jackets, looking at the selection On Your Bike had to offer. I'm someone who lives for loud clothing, but what this wasn't my usual kind of outerwear. I picked up a bright raspberry-pink Altura Women's Nevis Waterproof Cycling Jacket in my size. The other colour option was hi-vis yellow. The utilitarian feel from this jacket was coming on strong. It was waterproof, with specially cut vents in the side to allow air to circulate around your body when you cycle. And it wasn't just bright – it was super hi-vis: reflective detailing was the main adornment: on the front zipper, chest, shoulders, cuffs, arms and the back. I told myself it would be a good back-up to get a waterproof jacket to stash in my basket in case of being caught short on a rainy day. Although it looked like a jacket that I would never usually wear, it would probably make for a good back-up to carry around with me, so on the list it went.

With that sorted, I took my list over to the ever-helpful sales assistant, who was waiting for me at the tills, looking rather conciliatory: there would be a four-week waiting time for the Pashley. I know now that one of the many beautiful things about Pashley bikes is that they are all handmade in the UK, at their factory in Stratford-upon-Avon. That care and attention takes time. I actually quite liked the idea that my Princess was being especially made for me!

The sales assistant started tallying up the items that were on my list, adding them to the CycleScheme quote, which racked up rather quickly to just under £700. Though I steeled myself for it, I was still shocked when I saw the price written down in black and white. In my head, I was tallying up how long it would have taken me to get the money together to have bought everything I needed outright. It brought home to me just how expensive certain elements of cycling can be. But thanks to the CycleScheme, it had all started to come into place.

I logged into my CycleScheme account as soon as I got home to tie up the loose ends. The pop-up at the end of the form telling me my details had successfully been registered might have been telling me I'd won the Lottery. The desire to share my new venture with the world had returned again. Sitting at my desk and jotting down the day's Operation Pedal Push events, I thought again of creating a new blog – a cycling blog. I knew that I wanted to do it. I knew that I *had* to do it. I looked up at my screen – the 'your form has been successfully submitted' browser window was still open on it. I swear there was something almost ethereal about the glow coming from it, coaxing me to just get on with it. The rest of my afternoon was totally free, and there was no more time to be wasted. I sat there playing around on blogger.com, feeling a slight sense of betrayal towards BBE.

'This doesn't need to be all whistles and bells, remember that,' I mumbled to myself as I selected a simple black and white template, and gave the blog a holding-page title: 'Hello Velo'. I'd love to say that it was carefully thought out, but it was the first thing that popped into my mind. I'd made the page private, so no one else could see it, but I knew that it was there, waiting for me to come back to when the time was right.

The following Monday it was back to the office, but I was still floating on air about my bike shop visit. Packed into an overcrowded DLR carriage, even the Monday morning commute couldn't put a downer on my mood. 'Soon enough I won't have to do this any more,' I thought to myself, holding on to the passenger rail, trying not to bash into people next to me as the train swung from side to side. Soon enough I'd be cycling through London streets at this time of the day, locking my bike up in the secure staff bike-parking sheds, and strolling into the office feeling refreshed and ready to take on the world ... or at least another round of UCAS application forms.

At my desk, my concentration kept waning. My mind was wandering back to the two words, 'Hello Velo', and how eager I was to get on with turning the page into a proper blog. It was probably a very telling sign of things to come in the future of how much my blog was on my mind when I should have been focusing on the day job. To further derail my concentration, an email notification pinged up from HR letting me know that the CycleScheme paperwork needed signing.

The notion of working on the pile of UCAS applications on my desk went straight out the window. It was going to be a long month waiting, but that didn't stop my imagination from running away with plans about the bike, the rides that I wanted to go on and a countdown to a whole new lease of life. That said, the waiting game for the Pashley didn't have to be boring – there were other plans and preparations that I could put into place for the arrival of the bike. Almost every evening after work, I rushed home to get back to 'Hello Velo' and poke away at the little bits that would build up the blog.

After some back and forth with HR and sorting a date with the bike shop, we all managed to set a date: Sunday, 7 March 2010 was Pashley day. I published a post on BlackBarbieExperience, inviting my readers to something a little different:

NEW CYCLING BLOG

So, it's happening. I'm picking up my brand new bike this weekend – a Pashley Princess. I've started up a new blog for it too: VéloCityGirl. It's going to be solely dedicated to cycling and cycle style. Lots of photography will be thrown in the mix too. I'll still be blogging about general life stuff and nonsense here, but as getting back on the saddle is quite a big deal for

me, it feels like that needs its own journal. If you're interested
in seeing what happens when a twenty-eight-year-old woman
who hasn't been on a bike in ten years gets back on one again,
please come over to VéloCityGirl and have a look. It's still in
VERY early stages at the moment, and you'll notice that one
blog post is up on there already and a few new features are on
it too (call it a little 'Welcome' gesture!) but more content will
come with every turn of the wheels. And a huge 'thank you' has
to go the brilliant Matt over in Toronto (if you're reading this
Sir) as he helped me come up with the name of the new blog!
Look forward to seeing you on the other side readers . . . J x

It was out there, and Hello Velo was now officially VéloCityGirl
thanks to a quip from Matt, an online friend of mine all the way
in Canada. He'd given me some blog ideas in a conversation:
'hello-velo . . . velo-city . . . velociraptor?'

I knew Matt was joking about velociraptor, but 'velo-city'
jumped out at me immediately. The more I thought about it, the
more it made sense for my new venture. At the same time as I
let all the BBE readers know about the new blog I'd put up my
first ever VéloCityGirl, titled 'The Cycle Revolution'. It's still
there, but to save you searching for it, this is how it read:

THE CYCLE REVOLUTION
So, let's get this started. Even at 20-something, I'm nowhere
near as accomplished as the bloggers I've listed as my
inspiration here. I'm essentially a new girl to the world of
cycling – both as an adult and in this city. The last time I
actually owned a bike was years ago: I'd been given my sister's
BMX, which had been lovingly restored by our older brother. It
may not have been as current as the bikes some of my school
friends had, but I loved it. He taught me how to ride it and
even used to take me to Gloucester Park on a weekend to go

cycling together and build up my confidence on two wheels. As I got older I started to ride less and eventually stopped all together, but the desire to pick it back up was still there. Back then it was 'easy cycling': around the park, down to the shops or with friends after school – carefree and simple. As an adult, the idea of it was taking on a whole new perspective: safety, being aware of cars and traffic . . . trying not to become pavement pizza. In all honestly, the idea of riding around my own beautiful city gave me the fear . . . something that I didn't want at all. Fast forward to now and all I can think about is getting back on a bike – and preferably the one that I've been lusting after for ages. My boyfriend Ian rides and is a keen and experienced cyclist. He's been a major source of encouragement in getting me back on the saddle, and making me realise that I don't have to be a top athlete to own a bike and just enjoy riding again. My weird preconception of cycling being a world dominated by aggressive commuters who have the fastest bikes with 101 gears, Lycra outfits and all the cycling knowledge ever kinda put me off and honestly made me feel that maybe it's not for me. But thanks to blogs like the ones listed on here and The Boy I've realised it's not all like that – and I can do this just for me and the sheer enjoyment of riding . . . and hopefully do it while looking as chic as hell on my wheels!

This weekend it all begins: I'll be heading to On Your Bike with The Boy to collect my new ride that's in their storeroom waiting for me: a black Pashley Princess Classic. This is the bike that I've been lusting after for so long – I can't even tell you what a long time coming this bike really is. It's an absolutely beautiful piece of traditional bicycle craftsmanship. Combining this with my love of photography, fashion and London, I'll be noting all things 'bike and visual' right here. There is no real structure to this blog – it's going to be a diary to keep track

of all things chic and enjoyable about riding. Comments and
followers are of course more than welcome . . . and I'll also be
breaking beyond talking on the blog too. I've set up a Twitter
account under the name 'LadyVelo' (seems only fitting, right?)
The link is on the right of the blog if you care to follow :)

I had no idea what was going to happen once I'd made
VéloCityGirl and that blog post public. Other than the sense
of release of finally being able to talk about taking on cycling
again, I was nervous. Nervous that perhaps it would sink without a trace like that blog post on BBE did. Nervous that I'd just
put myself out there, publicly declaring I was getting back on
the saddle, and would fail or lose interest at the first hurdle I
encountered. Nervous that maybe I'd discover that this wasn't
going to be the space for someone like me. But the excitement
I was feeling? That overpowered all those nerves. This was
something that I wanted so badly. Being honest about cycling
not feeling like a space for someone like me – a black, twenty-
eight-year-old woman who hadn't been on a bike in ten years
and might not be as knowledgeable as others about cycling – in
my very first post could have been a red rag to a bull . . . but I
didn't care. VCG was my space, and getting back on a bike was
my dream. Now the only thing I needed to do was actually go
and get my Princess.

Collection day had finally swung round, and I'd been mark-
ing off the days on my calendar like a kid counting down to
Christmas. Ian was coming with me. The idea was that he'd
ride ahead, and then we'd cycle back home together. I'm not
embarrassed to admit that the thought of doing that ride alone
back home totally freaked me out. The route looked as clear as
water when plotted out on Google Maps, but tackling Central
London alone after such a long absence on the bike was not an
option. Mamma V was also incredibly nervous about me riding

back home, something she *wasn't* hiding as we were getting ready to leave. Her relief that Ian was coming with me put her mind to rest a bit, but it didn't stop her reverting to 'Mother Hen' behaviour before we left the house.

Although I was doing what I think was a stellar job of bouncing off the walls with excitement, the nerves were creeping in. Ian was downstairs, doing the usual checks on his bike before heading out the door. I ducked out of the kitchen and swerved Mum's questions about the route, heading upstairs to get my coat on and give myself a little pep talk in my bedroom mirror.

'You never forget how to ride a bike. I can defo do this.'

I did up the last collar button on my trusty coat and gave myself a nod. It was time for Lady Vélo to go get her steed.

Girl Gets Bike

The journey on the Tube to London Bridge went by in a flash. It was a quiet Sunday so was just me in the carriage, and a teeny-tiny voice of doubt in my head that I was doing my best to ignore. When I got to the bike shop, Ian was stood outside with a massive smile on his face.

'Flash git. I had a feeling you'd be here before me.'

'That's the beauty of the bike, Jools. You'll be feeling like this when you're cycling around town and not on the Tube.'

He had a point. Thinking about how wonderful my cycle to work would be was making me feel a little bit smug, to be honest. Strolling up to the service desk, I explained who I was and produced my paperwork for my bike. Moments later, a sales assistant was wheeling my sparkling brand-new Pashley over to me and I swear everything went into slow motion. The front light had already been attached to the basket for me, the rear light on the seat post. My accessories were peeking out the top of the basket: the D-Lock, that far-too-pink water-proof, and my helmet, all neatly packaged together. I'd been assured that everything such as the brakes and the gears would have been checked (although the assistant checked them again while I was there for peace of mind), and any questions I had would be answered. The bike sure *looked* ready: I was blinded by how gorgeous it was and Ian was pretty impressed too. I hopped on the bike as instructed by the sales person, to see how it felt.

'I know it's is the right size frame for me, but something doesn't feel right about the seat, or the handlebars,' I said hesitantly.

'No worries, we can sort that out.'

The assistant unhooked the cycling multi-tool hanging from the belt-loop of his jeans. I mentally added one to the list of bike things I should invest in. Fiddling with the different allen keys, the assistant found the right one to adjust the saddle. I hopped off the bike and watched while he raised it a bit and tightened it back into place. He then did the same thing for the handlebars: loosening them as quick as a flash, raising them a touch and then tightening them into place.

'Do you want to hop back on and see how that feels now?'

So I did. The sales assistant helping me wasn't being rude nor was he frightening, but I felt apprehensive to say anything more, as if admitting 'this still feels a little bit too low' would have made me look foolish. Instead I said, 'Uhhh, yeah, that's great. Thanks.'

Why did I do that? Why did I allow that to be the end of the conversation on adjusting my bike? I'd allowed myself to become intimidated when I knew something wasn't right, but rationalised the answer to myself in my head: 'They're the person who works in a bike shop and knows what they are doing. Setting it up according to eye must come from all his previous experience.'

So that was it – the end of the conversation. After one last signature to confirm I'd collected the Pashley, I could be on my way. Ian was having a browse of the shop while all of this was going on. Part of me wished I'd called him over to help – part of me wished I could have helped myself. I was still smiling as I was so pleased to have my Princess, but as I wheeled my brand-new pride and joy out of the store, I was kicking myself for not feeling like I could speak up. The circumstances I was in wouldn't allow me to. Those emotions and preconceptions that I had the very first time I went into that bike shop were back in my head again. It was lonely – this didn't feel like a space for me, or not one that I felt I was being represented in, so why would I feel comfortable speaking up? It's hard to speak up if you feel like you don't have much of a voice or you're not hearing voices like your own in certain spaces.

I asked Ian to adjust my saddle and handlebars with his multi-tool when we left the shop. Instead of being on top of the world with bike-powered happiness shining off me like some blinding beacon of light, the experience I'd just had collecting the Princess left me feeling almost invisible, and fearing that perhaps I couldn't handle this. What if cycling wasn't the world for me after all? On top of that, I'd put a huge amount of pressure on myself to nail the grand finale of the day: riding a bike for the first time from one side of London to the other. I really felt like I had something to prove with this ride ... but to who? Was it the other more experienced cyclists I'd be riding alongside on the busy roads of London, trying to prove my cycling worth to? Or was it Ian? My wonderful partner who wasn't going to judge me in the slightest. I don't know where those feelings it had come from, as getting a new bike wasn't supposed to be about that kind of stuff at all.

Let me say it loud and clear: there is nothing wrong with being scared of doing something for the first time! And this was not only the first time getting on a bike in ten years, but the very first time I'd be cycling through Central London. With all the excitement of getting my Pashley and starting VéloCityGirl, I'd blotted out the fact that getting back on the saddle and riding around the city was going to be nerve-wracking. These fears were totally rational – part of the reason I'd stopped cycling when I was eighteen was because I was scared of being out on the road and gradually lost confidence. I'm not going to sugar-coat it (and don't tell Mamma Vélo I said it): roads aren't necessarily that safe for cyclists, and even if I did have a clearly plotted route home, and my boyfriend with me for moral support, some blue paint on concrete wasn't suddenly going to make all of my cycling worries vanish into thin air.

The route was five and a half miles from South London back east, but it might as well have been a hundred considering the state I had slowly worked myself into. It had seemed straightforward enough in theory: the ride should only take about thirty-five minutes, and once I was over Tower Bridge and out of that little pocket of the A100 on the other side of it, the blue lanes of the CS3 would be in sight to guide me to my doorstep. However, five minutes after Ian had adjusted my handlebars and saddle for me, we were still stood on that side street with our bikes, shivering in the March cold.

'Are you all right?' Ian asked, clearly concerned about why I wasn't making any moves to get us home.

Shrugging it off, I answered, 'Ahhh, yeah. I'm cool.'

This was a lie. One which Ian didn't believe for a moment and though he was talking to me, the teeny-tiny voice in my head that I'd put on mute earlier turned up to full volume, drowning out anything he was saying to me. 'Told you this was a mistake,' it said.

I ignored it.

'Getting back on a bike now? That's the last thing you should be doing.'

I ignored it, once again.

Then it returned, delivering the knock-out blow, 'Do you even KNOW how to ride a bike in this city?'

KAPOW! It had really got to me with that one.

Ian was still talking but I snapped out of my haze and forlornly cut over whatever he was saying. 'I don't know what I'm doing, and I don't think I can ride this bike home.'

Sitting on a Pashley and having a practice ride in the shop a few weeks before didn't really count as a return to the saddle. Even though I clearly hadn't forgotten how to physically ride a bike, I was questioning myself and couldn't help but wonder if I had made a big mistake. One of the things that I didn't do while putting Operation Pedal Push into action was look into local cycle skills training or Bikeability lessons. Programmes like these are open to anyone: whether you're a first-time rider or can already ride a bike and are looking to improve your knowledge. Schemes like these are designed with the aim of building up confidence. Bikeability has three levels:

Level 1: In a traffic-free environment, to learn basic bike-handling skills to improve riding confidence.

Level 2: On quiet residential streets close to your home, school or place of work so you can learn how to ride amongst real traffic.

Level 3: On roads with larger volumes of traffic and how to negotiate around traffic junctions.

I didn't even realise these things existed then, just like I hadn't been aware of the Cycle To Work Scheme. I was so out of the cycling loop, the last time I had been guided through any of that stuff was by my brother, when he taught me how to cycle as a kid. This wasn't a ride to the park and these were not those carefree days of my younger years either. I was now an adult, hyper-aware of the dangers of cycling in the city, as well as feeling like I was a bit too old and underprepared for what I'd myself signed up for. At that point, Ian made an offer:

'I could lock my bike up somewhere around here and ride your Pashley back? You hop on the Jubilee Line home instead of waiting in the cold, I'll come back and get my bike after.'

I can't lie, this did sound somewhat appealing. I knew he wasn't trying to take away my thunder and was just trying to help. But if I didn't do this ride now, when would I ever feel brave enough to do it?

His next suggestion played into what I had just been thinking about taking on the ride home: 'We could find somewhere quiet to have a practice ride or something to help you get used to it and maybe try the route home?'

This was the answer. The lesson I learned that day was: if there is an alternative to a situation that you can take that will help you out, but you're worried people are going to think you're a wuss if you do – you're not.

'Let's have a little practice on one of the quiet roads and take it from there,' I said to Ian. It really was now or never.

We wheeled our bikes along the pavement until we found a side street quiet enough to have a few practice runs on. My nerves got the better of me on the very first practice pedal I attempted. I was trying to maintain some kind of dignified grace and ended up wobbling like a cat wearing roller skates on an ice rink. What had happened to that woman riding a Pashley Princess on that yellow brick road a few weeks ago? Ian had to step in and, just like my brother all those years ago, he held on to my back to guide and give me a gentle push. This was the last thing I'd expected of the day but the ace thing about it was that with every off-kilter attempt, I was laughing again, and the jaunt no longer felt like it was turning to disaster.

It was getting colder, so before we headed home Ian ran over to the closest coffee shop to get us hot drinks before we developed frostbite. We leaned against the wall we'd propped our bikes against, slurping tea and holding on to the warm take-away cups like they contained the elixir of life. Tea really does feel like it fixes almost everything.

Tea drunk, off we went on my maiden voyage home. So, it may be that the ride back to East London took a *little* longer than the thirty-five minutes Google Maps said it would, and those five and a half miles had a *few* unscheduled stops along the way. But it made me realise that, though not every experience on two wheels was going to be as rocky as that first, not all of them were going to be textbook perfect either. Aside from showing my bike off to Mamma V when I got back home and answering her questions about the ride, there was something else I couldn't wait to do: update VéloCityGirl about finally having my bike and introducing her properly as below:

There is still so much to learn about the Pashley: exactly how it handles etc. What I can say though: the ride was smooth, and more than enjoyable and has got me so psyched up about cycling. And I can't just refer to her as 'The Pashley' anymore. Yes – I've named my bike and she's called Frankie. Getting back on the saddle (especially this one) may have been the best decision I've made in a long time.

Putting the blog post out in the world confirmed I was really doing this. There was no turning back now. Within three days of it going live, I'd racked up fifteen comments from people all around the world – which for me was a hell of a lot! Some were from friends who had followed me across from

BlackBarbieExperience, and some were screen names that I'd recognised from the online cycling community: ibikelondon, London Cycle Chic and Velo Vogue. I couldn't believe bike bloggers had found VéloCityGirl and were congratulating me on my new journey and offering help and advice if I needed it! Their welcome made me feel a part of the cycling community, and I started to feel like I did belong in that space, and no one had the right to make me feel otherwise.

That Sunday I closed my laptop and carried on with my day on a high. Maybe this was the beginning of the biggest adventure I'd ever go on.

The Joy of Cycling

In the very early days when anyone would ask me questions about how much riding I was doing, how I was finding being back on a bike and what I was getting up to on the Pashley, my stock answer would be something along the lines of, 'Oh, I'm absolutely in love with it! I've not had that much of a chance to get out as often as I'd planned because of [insert totally believable reason here], but it's bloody fantastic!'

Now, that wasn't a complete lie. I was completely in love with cycling, but I wasn't putting the rubber to the road as much as I'd hoped. In truth, in my first week of being a 'cyclist' again, almost zero cycling happened at all, and in the first month, it was still pretty sporadic. It's not that I didn't want to – my cycling spirit was definitely willing. However, there's nothing weak about being cautious in the early stages of a new relationship, right? Because for me, that's exactly what getting back on a bike and being with Frankie felt like – a brand-new relationship. I needed to properly fall in love with cycling again, not just the idea of it.

In my head, I had envisaged myself as an adult who could go out on my bike and come back home at whatever time I fancied without a school-night curfew. Instead, I was surprised at just how little cycling I was actually doing. I wasn't planning on doing the Tour de Newham within the first week of having Frankie, but I'd been envisioning all the things I'd told myself I would be doing as soon as I got her: riding to work every (or at least every other) day, exploring my borough to see how much the old stomping ground had really changed and riding to places like Maltby Street Market every Saturday morning with Ian to feed our flat white and custard doughnut habit.

Nowadays, although my cycling journey hasn't led me to set up home with Frankie and end with, 'Reader, I married my Pashley' (for starters, my relationship with bikes didn't remain monogamous), my connection with cycling has managed to get to the comfortable stability of a well-established couple.

But it took a lot longer to get there than I thought . . .

The Monday after collecting Frankie, I was buzzing from the euphoria of my cycle home the evening before. I was still feeling incredibly proud of the fact that we'd got back to Canning Town in one piece – a ride that I'd convinced myself would be a write-off had actually happened, and it was ace. That said, the next day, even after a long soak, my body felt like someone had gone to work on me. Mild aches pulsed through my torso and every single one of my leg muscles. I'd not felt that kind of exercise after-burn in a very long time, and although I never like to see pain as a mark of a 'proper cycling achievement', it was still making me smile. My aches were a sweet reminder of the ride I had completed and an eye-opening revelation of how much effort it takes to pedal an 18-kilogram bike. There was also the first hint of just how much breaking in that leather saddle would actually require. Why can't I ever remember experiencing that level of saddle-sore when I was younger?! The seat on my Burner was made out of rock-hard moulded plastic, but didn't give me this whole new level of 'OMFF!' – 'Oh my fucking flaps!' – the likes of which I had never had before. Female saddle-sore can feel like an embarrassing subject but we should really talk about it more. Emily Chappell has written an excellent article on 'flap mash' if you want more of this content.

Anyway, the next morning I didn't cycle into work, nor did I ride in for the rest of that week, not due to the aches and pains but simply because I didn't have somewhere to store Frankie during the day. I could have just locked her up on the shared student bike racks on campus, or on the public ones near to the DLR, but – call me precious if you like – I wasn't prepared to take the risk, even with a gold-rated D-Lock. What was a few more journeys on an overcrowded train anyway? If ultimately it meant Frankie had a slot in the secure cycling sheds at work it would be worth it.

'So ... I've seen the pictures of your first ride, but when do I actually get to see you on this *amazing* new bike of yours, Jools?' asked Amanda, one of my workmates one morning. I could sense in her tone that she was asking on behalf of every single person in the office who had listened to me bang on about Frankie and had kindly stopped processing application forms to look at every single picture of my brand-new love as I waved my phone under their noses. I paused before answering Amanda's question. The chorus of keyboards fell silent, eyes peeping over PC screens waiting for my answer. I needed to think carefully about what was going to tumble out of my mouth. The show of interest from the rest of the team made me a little nervous, especially as every single one of them owned a car. I genuinely was the only person on the team that didn't know how to drive. (And still don't. As the daughter of a Ford employee it's almost impressive!)

'As soon as I've got my parking space and key for the sheds, you'll all see me riding in!' I replied. I was grateful to be able to give myself a bit of breathing room with this excuse; there was still a bit of doubt in my head about commuting in on my bike.

'Well, I think you're really brave for doing it, Jools,' replied Amanda. She had the best of intentions, but she'd used the B word.

'Why would you say it's brave? You must have cycled when you were younger. It's just riding a bike, right?' I knew this was an ever-so-slightly loaded question, though I wasn't fishing for confrontation or an argument about cyclists vs motorists. We were all friends, and their opinions genuinely interested me. There was another silence, and I could hear at least one intake of breath through closed teeth coming from someone. Before Amanda could answer, my colleague Sarah chimed in.

'It's different when you're younger though, isn't it? My little ones love riding their bikes around the park, and to school and back, but personally, I know I wouldn't want to ride through London on a bike. It's bad enough driving in from Ockendon every morning down the bloody A13 to get here!'

There were loud groans of agreement. The A13 was the bane of commuting lives and one of our regular office moans. Most of the team lived in various parts of Essex, great when the department had been based there, not so much when it was relocated to the Docklands Campus.

Shooting me a warm and reassuring smile, Amanda jumped back in. 'Anyway, Jools, you don't have far to cycle from your place to here every day, do you? I'm sure it'll be a lovely ride, mate.'

I smiled back at her. Could she tell that I was faking it a bit? Urgh. 'Yeah, I'm really looking forward to it. Right! Anyone for a cuppa? It's my turn for the afternoon.'

Multiple mugs were raised in the air. I gathered them up,

strolled over to the tiny kitchenette area and busied myself getting the brews on. It definitely wasn't my turn to do the office tea round, but I felt the overwhelming urge to excuse myself from the conversation, before anyone got a chance to ask me more questions.

I was being paranoid, but my imagination turned what was just some friendly office chat into an awkward inquisition about why I wasn't out riding my bike regardless of the lack of that key to the cycling shed. In my head, my new relationship would become a water cooler (or a 'gather around the kitchenette urn') moment in the office the next day. And the next day, and the next day, and all the days after that where my bike and me were never seen together on campus.

'So she's not seeing Frankie during the day – fair enough – but they're not going out in the evenings?'

'Jools has shown us just one picture of her and Frankie out together on a ride – nothing more. Are they even really a thing?'

'If you ask me, it's not going anywhere, the poor girl. If it's that bloody good, she'd be spending all her time after work and all her weekends with Frankie.'

Of course this was a ridiculous way to think, but it made me aware that I was shying away from getting to know the routes around me. So while letting the tea brew I decided that it was on. Frankie and I were going out a proper first date.

Saturday morning in Newham had never looked so inviting. Bright rays of sunlight streamed into my bedroom through the glass and the net curtains, beaming random prism patterns across the white walls. I opened my window to take a proper look outside – and to inhale the crisp, fresh air. The breeze felt sharp and refreshing and I couldn't wait to soak that feeling in while out on my bike. There is always something magical about that time of year, when it's no longer grey or finger-numbingly bitter, and you can actually see the changes in the season. March was finally turning and hints of the arrival of spring were on the horizon: early daffodil shoots were peeking through the green spaces in the community recreation park, and the mismatched trees dotted down my road were on the verge of bloom. Perhaps I was over-romanticising just how glorious my neighbourhood was looking but it was the day of my first proper date with Frankie. As the forecast was warm enough to head out in a light jacket and not freeze your arse off, I kept that in mind with the outfit I threw together in my favourite style: colour explosion from head to foot.

Frankie was waiting for me in the downstairs cupboard – the very same cupboard that the Burner used to reside in during its sad relegation. After that conversation with my work colleagues earlier in the week and my already growing paranoia about not riding, I recited my new mantra to myself as I walked down the stairs: 'The same thing will not happen to another bike in this house ever again.' Frankie wasn't even a month old, and already she was gathering dust. Awkwardly, I manoeuvred her heavyset frame and massive basket out of the cupboard and wheeled her outside. Knowing that I wasn't going to be doing this ride alone was reassuring – Ian had come back to London with the Beast for the weekend. While I was still stood in the porch, and somewhat transfixed by the front door, he wheeled up behind me.

'You ready to do this recce then, Jools?' asked Ian, with a smile. He always calls *any* kind of outing we go out on a 'recce'. Even though the main objective was to determine what the best cycle route to my office would be, that wasn't going to be the *whole* point of the day ... because let's face it – how dull a ride does that sound? There was fun to be had by getting out and discovering bits of the borough that I'd never seen via two wheels before. It didn't really matter how long we'd be out for anyway, as there was no timetable for the day. The only thing on the agenda was to figure out where I was heading to, and remembering the route. Who gave a damn if I got lost along the way (which happened more than twice), took way longer than expected (I'd defo need to cut the route short to get to work on time) or cycled down a dead-end (whoops!) that I should have known was there? That was surely half the joy of being out on Frankie ... that and getting to know my bike much better – and what I did and possibly didn't like on a bike.

It seems amazing now, looking back on how fearful I was on those first rides. Getting on a bike these days is second nature – I don't even have to think twice about hopping on for a spin. I still have my moments; believe me, but never like in the very early days with Frankie. See, that's the thing with 'adventures' – as much as they can give you a powerful adrenaline rush of excitement, they're also an unusual experience. Adventures are bold and risky with an uncertain outcome. Bizarre how when I was that kid on my Burner with my friends, adventures were something that I embraced with open arms and a degree of utter abandon – but as an adult embarking on the same thing? I found myself dipping my toe in once familiar waters with trepidation. As I've discovered over the years through my other cycling friends, I wasn't the only one who ever felt that way – after all, it had been a *long* time since I'd popped my bum on a saddle! I did find ways (and still do now when those feelings creep back in) to combat that trepidation – like finding a buddy to go out riding with you. Cycling with a friend – especially one who has a bit more experience and knowledge than you – isn't just a huge confidence boost ... it's a lot of fun too! As a beginner, riding with someone like Ian at the very start came with its technical advantages (like being able to ask questions about my bike, or for tips on cycling through London) but the joy of riding with someone and having a laugh, making memories (and rewarding myself custard doughnuts along the way) was the biggest joy that came from it. Remembering that it's not a competition or a race to become the next Victoria Pendleton when going out for a ride is a good move too. Taking it slow and steady? Why not! Hopping off your bike and wheeling it for a bit if you're feeling a bit intimidated? I've been there, done that, and trust me, I still do.

At last, after what felt like the longest three weeks of waiting, my set of keys to the secure bike sheds at work finally came through. This was it – I was about to start my daily routine of commuting by bike to the office. I could say goodbye to the DLR. No more squeezing into a hot sweat-box of a carriage in the summer, or being left stranded in the cold on the platform, waiting for a delayed service in the winter. I'd have a bit more money in my pocket and get into the office in great mood – thanks to the endorphins from riding and the fresh (well, *fresh-ish* – I was going to be riding on a main road and towards London City Airport) air in my lungs.

I'd spent the weekends doing dry runs of the commute. It's another thing that I totally recommend to anyone thinking about cycling to work. I knew the distance between home and UEL wasn't far, but I was still nervous about how much time it would take me as a newbie to ride that route. I did a few dry runs with Ian and then some on my own, adding some quiet back routes and riding at an easy pace. The feeling of finding my own natural groove when it came to timing was ace! I knew that it was going to be slightly different doing this on an actual weekday when the roads would be busier, but this was a good stepping-stone.

Another thing worth keeping in mind is beginning with an achievable frequency in mind – something I admit to not doing at the very start. As the journey was only a few miles, I was convinced that I would be commuting by bike every single day of the working week! That wasn't always the case for me – things like illness or generally being knackered could get in the way, and I'd beat myself up for not being able to get on my bike. Just remember that you are doing this for yourself and no one else. Don't get caught up in what other cycling commuters are doing on a daily basis – this is *your* journey.

Those weekends of practice runs were about to come to fruition with my first Monday morning commute into the office during normal weekday rush-hour traffic. There was indeed a bit of a difference between Victoria Dock Road on a weekend and a weekday. It's not like I was going to be cycling along the entire A13, but on a bike it felt rather like it.

I left home earlier than usual. I knew the route like the back of my hand, but I wanted to give myself enough time to have as gentle as possible a ride into the office, and allow for anything potentially going wrong. Once I got off my quiet roads and turned on to Victoria Dock, I could feel my heart pounding faster. There were more buses and HGVs passing along that route and a hell of a lot more cars too.

'Just keep on going, Jools – you've got this,' I muttered to myself as I cycled towards the next set of traffic lights. While waiting, I took a gulp of water from the bottle in my basket – my mouth was as dry as a bone, and it's not like I was cycling a speed to work up a thirst. *Green*. Time to go again. I'd taken priority at the front of the traffic in the bike zone at the front, looked around me before I went, and set off down the road. The turning coming up on my left was the one that was going to take me away from the rush-hour noise: it was one of the quiet back routes that I'd factored into my dry runs. It was a peaceful route – past the Leyes Road allotments and through a small park, where on the other side would be the quiet side road I'd take straight into the campus. I looked to my left, took my left hand off the bars to indicate that I was going to be taking that turn. No nervous wobbles – ace. I'd done it so many times on the practice rides, but this one sure as hell felt different – but I cleared it, took the turn and cycled past the allotments and into the park ... and suddenly everything looked glorious! Perhaps I was intoxicated with the joy of not being on the DLR but the whole area looked beautiful as I cycled through it. The idea of doing this as many days as I could was wonderful and put a spring into my pedals.

My biggest worry had been that I was going to do it once and never want to do it again, but when I finally got to the campus, and locked up my bike in the staff sheds, I felt *free*. I strolled into the office to cheers from some of the early birds who were in already. A few of the girls had spotted me through the office window and saw me cycling across the campus. They actually congratulated me on my ride to work. It felt good – it felt really bloody good and I couldn't wait for the working day to be over, so I could take that ride, all over again ... and again ... and again.

It had barely been two months since I started cycling again, which in light of the latest pedal-powered idea I was toying with, really wasn't that long at all. I was still in those newbie stages of being back on a bike: getting reacquainted with my old riding legs, and trying not to bobble around when I took one of my hands off the handlebars and turned my head at the same time to indicate if I was turning left or right. The rock-hard leather saddle on Frankie hadn't even come close to being broken-in or moulding to the shape of my bum, and yet there I was: sat in bed with my laptop perched on my legs, ready to scan through the latest offerings my daily alert email told me were waiting: '19 new "Vintage Raleigh Twenty" items are now available on eBay. Take a look now'.

Yes – I was looking for another bike. It probably sounds like madness – especially as I'd recently moved heaven and earth (and my finances) to get Frankie.

'So, why on earth are you getting *another bike* already, Jools, and why didn't you just get one of these in the first place?' I hear you ask.

Well, Frankie was my 'Day 1' bike, but she'd also set off a chain of events that I wasn't expecting ... the desire to own another bike, namely one that wasn't so 'precious' and that I could leave at Ian's place. Thanks to Frankie, the cycling bug had bitten me much harder than I expected and I wanted to be on two wheels both in London *and* in Southsea, where I was spending a substantial chunk of my life with Ian. There had been some cycling by the seaside on Frankie – I'd taken her down to Portsmouth a few times, but it was a struggle going back and forth between two cities with her. Although Frankie's position as the absolute cycling love of my life was firmly cemented in my heart, it has to be said: a Pashley Princess is *not* the most lightweight of machines. Hulking an 18-kilogram bicycle with the additional weight of luggage on and off a South West Train, playing carriage roulette hoping you'll get a space and *then* getting the bike up and down the stairs of Ian's flat was hard work. Something had to give, and it wasn't going to be me doing less riding, so it was time to sort out an out-of-town bike.

What I needed was a beater bike: a slightly weathered, beaten-up machine that's so past it you don't care much about it getting a bit wrecked and if an opportunist thief did bother to break your lock and steal it, well, you wouldn't give too much of a shit. This beater would be the battered but roadworthy steed for long hot summer rides along the coast – ones that end in fish and chips and one bottle too many of fizzy booze. This beater could get locked up outside all night in the salty sea air while Ian and I walked or got a cab back home from the pub, and still be there waiting to be picked up the following afternoon. As a cycling-lifestyle option, I can't recommend the beauty of a beater bike highly enough.

'Slightly ugly' was supposed to be the plan. But, being the design and style junkie that I am, any beater bike that I got wasn't going to be an ugly affair, and something like a retro Raleigh Twenty from the 1970s was what I had set my heart on. I had to laugh at myself – while still finding my feet after ten years of zero cycling and just fifty-three days into it, I was attempting to buy my second bike. After scrolling through the latest offerings eBay had for me and coming across the usual hurdles (like collection from somewhere that wasn't London), I finally found *the one*. Looking at the photos and reading the description I felt a similar flicker of giddiness to the one I'd got over Frankie. It was a 1973 Twenty in candy-red paint, with chrome detailing. It came with the original rear rack plus the detachable white-leather bag, and a big padded white-leather Brooks Saddle (you know I love a good, comfy Brooks). For a forty-year-old bike, it was in incredible condition and at an incredible price. And the seller was willing to deliver within the M25! My cursor didn't hesitate over the 'Buy It Now' button for long. My inbox pinged:

'Congratulations! You've won this eBay item: Vintage Raleigh Twenty Bike.'

Before I knew it, I was arranging a delivery date over emails with a very nice man in Hertfordshire called Neville, who was also giving me a brief history of the Raleigh. He'd bought it for his now grown-up daughter many, many moons ago, and it had been living in his shed as none of his grandchildren wanted it for themselves. I do like a good back story. and perhaps me taking it off his hands to ride it was repaying the regret I had about chucking out my Burner. It also cemented the fact that I was forming an addiction to all things bike. This wasn't a fad I was going through. It made me think of the Velominati – a tongue-in-cheek organisation and the self-proclaimed 'Keepers of the Cog' – they have ninety-five rules all road cyclists should adhere to while on and off the bike. One of those rules felt particularly apt:

'While the minimum number of bikes one should own is three, the correct number is n+1, where n is the number of bikes currently owned.'

With bikes, there's *always* room for more.

Wish You Were Here

Cycling in Europe was something I wanted to tick off my bike bucket list the moment I started riding again. I'd never cycled outside of the UK before, and I didn't want to go on a cycling break in the traditional sense. Of course those kinds of holidays are ace, but doing the Dolomites or taking on the Catalonian climbs of Girona wasn't what I had in mind. I had never been on a road bike at that point, nor did I possess the cycling legs or guts to do that kind of thing just yet. What I was after was the stuff of dreams I was seeing on one of the first cycling blogs I followed: Copenhagen Cycle Chic. This blog was one of my go-to destinations for cycle-style inspiration as it had everything I love when it comes to being on a bike – getting around your hometown on two wheels like it wasn't a race, and doing it in your everyday (and sometimes super stylish) clothing. The blog's glorious photos of happy people on bikes – women, men, young and old, just getting from A to B with captions like 'Dress for your destination, not your journey' plastered next to them made my cycling heart glow. This was what I wanted so desperately. This is what I was trying to do every single time I went out on my bike and show on VCG. The normalisation of cycling on 'Cycle Chic' blogs (such as Copenhagen Cycle Chic, the originator of the cycle-style moment which spawned sister blogs such as London Cycle Chic and New York Cycle Chic across the globe) was a revolution for me. More of these blogs were popping up across the Internet and growing in popularity, which other than being a refreshing change from the stereotypical 'norms' of cycling websites (filled with sportives, competitive cycling and quite often MAMILS – Middle-Aged Men In Lycra), showed that cycling culture was shifting and being disrupted in a positive and more inclusive way. I wanted to be immersed in the kind of cycling culture where there were more people on bikes than there were cars on the road.

And luckily, though I wanted to save my pennies to get myself to Copenhagen, it wasn't necessary to wait until then to see this cycle culture in action. I was already all booked up for a trip to Berlin with Ian in May 2010. I was excited about going out there for the first time, and losing myself in its diverse art scene, architecture, food and everything else, but the one thing that really blew me away when I was there was the cycle culture. Bleary-eyed and knackered from an early flight, the scene greeted me even from the passenger window of our taxi from the airport. I swear, every other person I spotted was either on a bike or parking one up somewhere. The plan was to rent a couple of bikes from the hotel we were staying at. In my excitement at being there and knowing we had two bikes waiting for us, I was up for dumping our stuff in the hotel and getting out as soon as possible, but adrenaline is a hell of a drug and I realised that going for a cycle the first morning while still feeling knackered probably wouldn't have been a great idea.

After a much-needed breakfast and freshen-up, we headed out for a walk to check out 'home' for the next five days. It didn't take long to encounter more cycle enthusiasts on our walk. Other than being surrounded by seriously chic people on two wheels, we got chatting to a large group at Rosenthaler Straße all of whom had bikes, waiting to set off for a guided tour of the city. Flexing my limited German skills, we got talking to them about how hyped they were about the tour and this got me even more excited about seeing Mitte by bike. The fact that we would be doing it with maps and our own sense of direction made it feel like more of an adventure. This was my first time ever cycling in another country, and I was looking forward to losing myself in unfamiliar surroundings to discover how much I'd enjoy that feeling on a bike.

The following day when we went to pick up our bikes from the hotel lobby, we were given bad news: we'd actually been double-booked and there were none available for us – and there wouldn't be for the rest of the week. After spending the last couple of days walking around the city and plotting cycling routes on our tourist maps, I was heartbroken.

'You could always try Fat Tire Tours,' said the receptionist – I swear he could probably sense the sound of my heart breaking. 'They usually only do organised tours, but you might be able to rent a couple of bikes by the day if they have enough in?'

Fat Tire were the same company that had organised the tour for that big group of people we'd bumped into on our first day. Taking that as a good omen (I'm superstitious like that) as we walked over to their shop, I kept everything crossed they would save our holiday plans. It turns out they're an international touring company who do brilliant guided day trips in cities around the world including San Francisco (one of my cycling bucket-list rides is to cycle over the Golden Gate Bridge), Paris and Barcelona to name but a few. And they're incredibly nice and sympathetic as they let us hire a couple of bikes for the day! Paperwork sorted and fees paid, we set off from under the Berliner Fernsehturm with nothing more than fold-up city guides with dot stickers and red pen lines plotting our routes, a vague idea of some landmarks and museums that might be worth a visit and the name of what we were told was the best currywurst stand in the city.

It was magical – even when I managed to come a cropper and fly off my bike outside the Deutsche Guggenheim (somehow I managed to get my front wheel wedged in between some cobbles, and the rest is ... well, me flat out on the floor, laughing my arse off at my slow-mo crash). The freedom of jumping on a bike and seeing Berlin from the velo-view was excellent. It was also surprising how easy it was to navigate and follow the cycle paths over there. I still considered myself a newbie to cycling, so the idea of riding around the roads of a new city (especially on the other side of the road for the first time) did spook me a little bit. But in comparison to London? I actually felt safer riding in Berlin than I had back at home. At the time, the Cycle Superhighway 3 (CS3) was in its early stages of being extended down to where I live. It was still early days for the infrastructure in my corner of London, and the cycle culture in Berlin felt like a world apart.

In Berlin at the time, cycling accounted for 12 per cent of total street traffic and the city's riders are catered for with wide and smooth cycle lanes on both the roads and sidewalks.

I came back from Berlin promising myself that Copenhagen would happen and the world of cycle travel was my oyster. I was fully converted to sightseeing by bike, be it home, or far, far away.

Winter is usually one of my favourite times of the year. I'm wholly biased due to being a December baby, but I'm one of those people who loves to be cosy. Big coats that act like duvets and thick, roll-neck jumpers that you can snuggle down in when you're out in the freezing cold. Being indoors in the dark evenings – curled up in your spot on the sofa with a mug of something hot or a glass of wine in one hand, and a good book or the remote for the TV in the other.

Having fallen so in love with cycling during the summer of 2010 and feeling like I was inseparable from my bike, I did wonder how I was going to deal with riding in the winter. I used to go out on my Burner all the time in the winter months way back then, but I think when you're a kid who's desperate to play out with your mates, you become immune to the cold weather. I was committed to commuting to work, but there were definitely days when that 5.2-mile round trip with a bitterly cold wind blowing in my face and snow settling on the roads wasn't much fun at all. The odd DLR day crept in when it was just *too cold* to bike it and I'd always feel a tiny pang of guilt ... but you know what? There is nothing wrong with needing to ditch the bike on occasion and in my first cold-winter commuting experience; I had to listen to my body on that one. Hard.

I've been living with asthma since I was seven years old. It used to be quite bad when I was younger, and at one stage I was taking my inhalers every day to manage it. As I got older it calmed down, but all it would take was a common cold to kick it back into action and knock me off my feet. I knew that being out on a bike in the colder months could be a bit of a risk – even though I'd wear enough layers to look like a duvet on wheels. I was still powering my way through cycling in the winter, but after one chilly commute too many (yes, Mamma V – I really should have listened to you that day) I could feel the sniffles coming on. Uh-oh. With me, a cold will last for the usual two to three days before morphing into the most gross chest infection. The routine to combat it is steroids, antibiotics, sessions on my nebuliser and *lots* of bed rest. This combination will usually do the trick, but this time, after a week of meds and plenty of sleep, I still couldn't walk from my bedroom to the bathroom without getting breathless, so it was straight back to the doctor.

Being given another course of stronger antibiotics should have shifted the infection. Unfortunately, this was how I discovered that I'm allergic to penicillin. One trip to A&E and an overnight stay in Newham General later, I'd been signed off work by my GP for the rest of the month, meaning that getting out on my Pashley was a total no-no. Even though I was struggling to breathe without sounding like a set of deflating bagpipes and it was absolutely freezing cold outside, all I wanted to do was go for one tiny, little ride. Instead I was staring at four walls, trapped indoors by my own wretched body. I was desperate to be outside cycling – even in the snow!

It turned into a *long* winter of cycling discontent. All of December was a write-off. I'd never been signed off work for that long before, which was a revelation: both at how frustrating it was doing nothing and at how much daytime television I could actually consume. Never before did I realise that I could miss being on my bike so much. Cycling friends I'd made via blogging and social media during that year were keeping me sane – although I couldn't ride with them myself, I was able to cycle vicariously through their Instagram accounts and blogs, while I had nothing to put on my own! Come January, when I was fit and well enough to get back out there and prove I'd not forgotten how to ride a bike, I felt more alive than I ever had before. It was time to ride into a new year full of life on two wheels.

Sparks

Sometimes I concoct 'happily ever after' endings in my head. Yes, I know that as an adult I should probably know better, but the thing is, I need to do it from time to time. I suppose you could call it a defence mechanism – especially when I sense the presence of a particular something lurking in the background, ready to pounce and prey on whatever is making me happy at the time.

March 2011: I'd arrived at my first cycling milestone – a year of being on the saddle. I'd made it. Even with the odd ups and downs that came with learning how to ride all over again, that whole period and everything bike-related that had happened during it was such an awesome learning curve. Everything that came with being on a bike and the places it took me to both physically and mentally all carried the promise of a 'happy ever after'. I was clinging on to that desperately, as in between all of those glorious highs I was experiencing on two wheels, some rather shitty stuff was going on at the same time. There was my job at UEL, which I was becoming increasingly disillusioned with. It paid well, was close to home and I really liked the team of people that I worked with. But that wasn't enough to warrant me staying there. I'd never had proper itchy feet in a job before, but it had all become stale and I needed to do something else. It was really hitting me that being an admissions officer had never actually been my plan, and that I just kind of fell into it.

I'd achieved a degree in Politics with Law from Greenwich, had dressed up in the gown and thrown my cap in the air for the photos. I was the first one in the family to go to university, so it was a big deal as was the expectation for me to end up in a job related to my degree. When the position at UEL came along, I grabbed it as something to tide me over while working out what I was really going to do post-degree. I ended up enjoying it ... and sticking with it ... and then getting bored with it ... and panicking.

Outside of the office walls and a professional meltdown, my personal life was weighing on me too. Mamma V's deteriorating health was at the very top of that list. You never really imagine your parents getting older, the tables slowly turning between the roles of carer and child, and there was nothing sudden about Mum becoming unwell – her illnesses didn't just turn up out of the blue one day in 2011, but that year all the health issues that had been gradually developing all seemed to get in chorus with each other and started singing very badly from the same hymn sheet.

I had taken on the role of carer, and found myself suppressing my own fears and anxieties about my mother being ill, so that I could be strong for her. The last thing she needed was me falling apart. The phrase she comes out with when things get bad is, 'Just put me out to pasture, Jools, or send me to the glue factory.' Gallows humour has become her forte over the years.

I was also trying to keep my own personal demons at bay. I felt so much guilt about needing self-care in the middle of everything else that was going on and with Ian and I living in different cities, it was easy for me to start feeling isolated. I didn't want to talk about any of the bad stuff when he came to London. It was nothing against him at all – the pressure of maintaining a long-distance relationship was heavy enough without 'ruining' the precious time that we did have together with the sour contents of my head. And I most certainly didn't want to do that on my blog. Where once before I'd have maybe done that on BlackBarbieExperience, VéloCityGirl was not the place for it. That would mean acknowledging that something was wrong.

If we just totally gloss over those rubbish bits, for the first time in ages, the rest of my life was really good. I was enjoying stage two of my new relationship with cycling – a whole year of unparalleled bliss in the honeymoon period. That's when Sparks reappeared on the horizon. They were not the kind of sparks that you'd normally associate with the magic of romance; they were at the very opposite end of that spectrum.

Many, many years ago when I couldn't and didn't want to say it as I saw it, I called my depression something else – something that best described what it felt like. Mamma V lives with depression too, so I wasn't a stranger to the symptoms, having grown up around them. Picture an electric spark: an abrupt and sharp little explosion of electricity, emitting blinding white light in random directions. They're kind of stunning to look at, aren't they? Now, picture those electric sparks – hundreds of them – this time all going off inside your head at weird intervals for weeks, or sometimes months at a time, their blinding flashes of light laced with negative thoughts. Totally confined in that tiny space, with no hope of release. That's what my depression feels like. 'Sparks' sounded so much nicer than the D word, and didn't conjure up the social stigma that comes with being labelled as being depressed. It was a label I didn't fancy carrying around as a small child or when I hit my teens.

I knew that it had come back. Truthfully it had never gone away, instead lurking about in the background like an old secret or that slightly dodgy relative that no one in the family wants to talk about. But I thought I'd done a good, if not bloody excellent, job of keeping those sparks at bay, much better than any of my previous attempts. I was handling it and this new relationship with cycling was supposed to be helping me handle it too.

Instead of fizzling out (which is what sometimes happens after the honeymoon stage), my love for cycling and being on Frankie was getting stronger. The joy increased every single time I plonked my bum on a saddle, and getting sucked deeper into the vortex of bike-related happiness meant I was riding further away from my problems. It was there that the rub started. Cycling was supposed to be a welcome distraction from depression and the ultimate escape. Sharing all those firsts with Frankie, they were all so exciting, and it felt like the buzz was never going to end. We'd hit a super-sweet spot, those 'Oh shit – what the hell am I getting into with you?' moments occurred less and less, and were being replaced with more 'Hell yeah, let's get into this!' moments.

People could see how ludicrously happy I was, which I took as a sure-fire sign that I'd come out of the other side of one of my Sparks episodes. There I was, revelling in twelve months of radiance so bright everyone around me could have been blinded by it. Because all the love and serotonin I was riding through was so damned good, it blocked out all the other crap that was going on. I was doing a fantastic job of keeping up this pretence on VéloCityGirl too – partly because I felt like I was under some kind of weird pressure to keep it nothing but 'positive vibes only' for my readers. I didn't want to let any of them down. In a way, I'd presented cycling as some kind of magic fix-all, so suddenly declaring that it wasn't really didn't feel like an option.

I knew it couldn't last for ever, but on the surface it was easier to pretend that it would. I know I'm not the only person on the planet who does that – sweeps the crap under the carpet in the hope that it'll go away, and I've spent more years than I care to admit doing that. I felt like I had finally found a good place with cycling, so Sparks weren't supposed to be able to get in anywhere. I thought that cycling had made me immune.

I was in a strange position as I'd witnessed the same thing happen to Mamma V, time and time again. I could see, physically, how that poisonous feeling would manifest: her horrendous migraines would land her in a darkened bedroom for a couple of days, chronic upper back and shoulder problems that would leave her unable to turn her neck and the arthritis would flare up in both her knees. We didn't have the same physical symptoms, but hers acted as a sort of 'depressive's reference guide' allowing me to work out when my own were manifesting. Those panic attacks on my commute: they were a sign. The mornings where, even after having eight or more hours' sleep, my body felt knackered and I'd cry at the thought of getting out of bed: they were a sign too.

Other than these physical flare-ups, there were the more internal ones that would crop up too. No matter what the situation, if something was bad, it was *really bad* and if something was absolutely great, well it was *still really bad*. At my lowest ebbs, nothing was ever good. My life was *never* defined by the good things. The good bits were just the random intervals that happened in between the ongoing hell that was trying to get through each day. The most mundane task or the most joyous thing would be totally blown out of proportion.

And it started to get in the way of my cycling. Of course it did. Sparks were slowly burning away at my mind and claiming every good thing in their path. It felt like cycling and I had done everything we possibly could together and then BANG – the entire relationship had come to a screeching halt. Depression was applying the brakes to this ride. I felt I couldn't really turn around and say to anyone I was having some dark days, days when getting out of bed and hopping on Frankie were impossible. Cycling and running my blog – two of the things in my life that I was enjoying the most – started to feel like a chore. I was no stranger to this feeling though – it was anhedonia; the inability to feel pleasure in normally pleasurable activities. A teenage me had experienced this while life at home was falling to pieces.

The catalyst to getting help was a broken wine glass on a Sunday afternoon. Ian and I were doing the washing-up together, and I accidentally dropped a glass that I was drying. As it shattered into a thousand pieces, I shattered too in tears of despair. Ian had to literally pick up the crumpled and crying heap of Jools off the kitchen floor along with those pieces of glass ... that bloody well got everywhere, btw. I was still finding tiny splinters a week later. After he'd scooped me up off the kitchen floor, I poured my heart out to Ian. Opening up was hard, but such a release. In truly explaining how I was feeling, I had to explain how I was feeling about cycling too. I'd become so defined by it that the thought of saying it out loud terrified me: 'I'm not enjoying anything about cycling any more.'

Cycling was something everyone I knew associated with me. So to say that I didn't like it any more, and that it was an almighty struggle to find the enthusiasm for it felt like giving up part of my identity, like I was a traitor to my cycling family. But if I didn't talk, I stood the risk of imploding. Ian listened. He understood, he didn't judge, and he also didn't believe that anyone else would be judging me either.

'People will be more concerned about your well-being than they will about your bikes. They know cycling makes you happy – but you also need to make YOU happy and healthy too,' was his advice.

The following week I plucked up the courage and made an appointment with my GP to talk about how rotten I'd been feeling. I was ready to acknowledge the elephant in the room (or the one who'd been living in Frankie's basket for a while), and braced myself for a potentially uncomfortable conversation. The moment he asked me what I was there to see him for, I burst into tears all over again. It was a tough conversation to have but I talked about how I was feeling, and, at his request, did an NHS depression self-assessment form. The questions were not easy to stomach:

Q1: Have you found little pleasure or interest in doing things?

☐ No, not at all

☐ On some days

☐ On more than half the days

☑ Nearly every day ('yes, including almost zero interest in riding my bike')

Then, five questions later, this came along:

Q6: Have you felt that you're a failure or let yourself or your family down?

☐ No, not at all

☐ On some days

☐ On more than half the days

☑ Nearly every day ('yes, including my cycling family')

I was linking those questions to my bike life. Interest in it was waning, and I was convinced I was letting so many people down by allowing that to happen.

'Out of interest, Jools, how much exercise do you get, beyond your commute to work you've told me about?' the doctor asked. I glanced up from the form; was he reading my mind about my answers to Q1 and Q6?

'Ermm, not much more outside of that, really. I'm often too tired by the weekend to do more. And I don't feel like it.'

'And what about seeing people – other colleagues or friends on or off your bike – do you do that much?'

'No, no one else in my office commutes by bike. I do try to meet up with my friends on the weekends when I head out though.'

I knew I wasn't seeing enough of my friends. Becoming insular and withdrawing from seeing people, which included avoiding cycling with anybody? Guilty as charged. I could sense what my doctor was alluding to here (aside from straight-up talking to me about starting on anti-depressants): encouraging me to socialise more and get more exercise for the natural endorphins ... which of course meant spending a bit more time on the saddle. I listened to and could appreciate what my doctor was saying to me about getting those endorphins flowing, but I also took it with a pinch of salt. Exercise can be a huge help for a lot of people when it comes to mental health, but I've never been a believer in it being a fix-all. Perhaps that sounds strange coming from me – someone who evangelises the benefits of being on a bike – but I'm very wary of touting exercise as a 'one size fits all' cure for depression.

There have been so many times where I wanted to use cycling – one of my biggest passions – to make me feel better, but when I found myself crying my eyes out at the thought of getting out of bed and straight on to a saddle, it made me feel even sadder. It's incredibly difficult to get yourself motivated when you're depressed, and even harder to muster up the motivation for exercise when you're mentally exhausted. It felt like a vicious circle: I'd punish myself with the guilt of not riding my bike so force myself to do it, only for it to end up feeling like another dreadful tool I was punishing myself with. Exercise can of course be a help to mental health. I've had many a moment during and after a bike ride where I feel happier, which is bloody brilliant! Anything that's a boon to your brain is something to be celebrated, but I think it's so important to always keep in mind the 'not one size fits all' theory. We're all different, and that's okay. And going at a pace that works for you – that's always okay too.

Two weeks into the course of citalopram I was prescribed, I started to notice a change – mainly how woozy and tired I was becoming. The medication was working its way into my system, and the side effects had me wondering how on earth I'd be up for *more* cycling on a weekend. I was already struggling to maintain my energy levels, and these tablets were sapping more out of me. But there wasn't going to be a quick fix – getting some tablets doesn't just make depression go away. I'd accepted that this was going to be with me for the rest of my life, but it was up to me not to allow it to define who I am, or what I could achieve.

As the fog of the medication lifted after six weeks of taking it, I began to start making plans. Some serious re-assessments were in order. Too much of my life was being spent in the office – to be honest, there was nothing I could do about that for the time being, but that didn't mean the office had to be my life. Remembering to mentally clock out was essential to my survival.

One of the things I had stopped doing as often was commuting to work on Frankie. This was having an impact on my mood as instead of riding I had reverted back to getting on the DLR again – heaving with commuters and a trigger for my panic attacks, which wasn't exactly motivational. I had the idea of changing my commute route to work to freshen things up a bit. I plotted a longer but more picturesque and chilled route from Canning Town to the Docklands Campus. Leaving home earlier meant I could take more time, and perhaps some different scenery would inject some joy into my working day. Every week I planned something a little bit different: cycle past the allotments, take the path that runs alongside the river, stop and have a look at the planes taking off from London City Airport. Just simple tweaks to the everyday journey stopped it from being mundane – both the physical view and for my mentality too. Switching up the routes and noticing something new in my surroundings felt like it was waking me up. Things didn't feel so stale and I didn't feel so trapped any more. Just a little change like that – gentle and nothing too rash provided the stabilisers I needed to regain balance.

I started enjoying cycling again. It was no longer feeling like a chore or a tool for punishment. My attitude started to pick up, and for the first time in a long time I started to feel alive again. The next step was applying this to my weekends with Ian and with our friends. I wasn't quite ready to join a cycling club but I was ready to start committing myself to regular

weekend rides. It was about finding balance – I find that anything too strict and regimented has me running a mile and
although I was enjoying being on a bike again, I wasn't 100
per cent out of my cycling funk. I needed to make sure that if
I had a shaky start to a weekend, it wasn't going to be an issue
for me not to turn up.

From this, a new coping mechanism was born:
#CoffeeCycleSaturday. It's exactly what it says it is: cycling
on a Saturday and stopping for coffee along the route. It was
relaxed, with no pressure – just a gentle ride through the city, or
wherever we wanted to go. Ian and I would head off into town
and invite close friends of ours to join us for the day.

I really grappled with the idea of making #CoffeeCycleSaturday
a more public event on the blog – perhaps holding it as a social
ride for any followers who were up for joining us. They were
proving to be so much fun that I got carried away with the idea
of making them a VCG 'thing'. Even though I was on the road to
recovery, the pressure of turning something gentle into a bigger
social ride would probably have been a setback to the state I was
in. I accepted that it was okay not to make everything huge, and
just quite literally enjoy the ride. Soon, it wasn't a Saturday if
there wasn't a #CoffeeCycleSaturday going on. And it didn't feel
like a chore – so long as I was pedalling at my own pace, I was in
a good space again.

Being so low that you can't even bear the idea of getting
up and riding can be one of the hardest feelings to deal with.
I understand because I have been there, and come out of the
other side of it. I came off citalopram in 2012, and there have
been some spells since that have taken me back a few steps.
Perhaps one day, I may end up back on my meds again – I never
say never when it comes to that.

It's been great to reconnect with cycling and exercise as a
coping mechanism that works for me when Sparks creep in. But

like I said before, it's not a fix for everybody and believe me, I *really* understand that. I can't promise that it will work for you, but giving it a try (only if you're up for it) is worth a go. Getting out there for a ride around the block can be so liberating if the exercise frees your mind. Go at the pace that you feel happy with, and don't ever forget to listen to yourself, whether on the bike or off it.

You've Got This

I think we have our own preconceptions of what we're capable of doing and the fact that cycling challenges you in that way – be it your bravery, overcoming fear, or overcoming mechanical stuff – that's what brings us back because it's building you as a person. And there are times when things happen to me. Today, I did actually think to myself, 'You have ridden to the point of exhaustion and you have it in you to carry on. You could have given up at any point Adele, but you didn't … you do have something in you that is going to drive you through this.'

Adele Mitchell

I can totally understand where Adele is coming from when she talks about having preconceptions of what we're capable of on a bike and discovering what we can actually do. I still remember the surge of nerves that came over me while stood by the side of the indoor BMX track. It was around 11 a.m. on a Monday morning – I'd just spent the last three hours riding around the Velodrome in the National Cycling Centre, and the adrenaline high from doing that for the first time ever was still rushing through my veins. Before I'd wheeled my borrowed track bike on to those wooden boards, which had once been cycled on by the likes of Victoria Pendleton and Sir Chris Hoy, that same surge of nerves was lingering over me. 'If you don't think you're up to it, Jools, you can always sit this session out and take photos for your blog and write up?' said one of the organisers of the day. They were being kind, considerate: sensing that I was looking green about riding at speed around a track that looked like it defied gravity, they offered me the opportunity to give it a hard pass and just watch – 'You'll still have the experience of being in the Velodrome.' But that wasn't enough. I'd travelled all the way up to Manchester from East London the night before to do this – there was no way that I was going to let this chance pass me by … or at the very least, give it a spin and find out for myself if I had *it* in me or not.

I needed to apply that same 'Let's do this!' pattern of thought to the BMX track. It had been years since I'd last been on a BMX, and I'd never actually stepped foot on a proper BMX track. Before doing anything, Quillan Isidore (a full-time BMX athlete for Team GB) gave me a one-on-one practice session on his own BMX, adjusting the saddle height so I could get used to being on one again. It felt all right having a little ride on the flat path next to the track. Deep breaths. Knee and elbow pads strapped on … plus full-face helmet that made me look like a Transformer. It was time to face my fears and give the track a go.

I could feel my heart beating in my throat as I lined up with the other riders to do a lap, even though we were not setting off from the higher start hill or starter gates. In comparison, the descent was pretty small, but big enough to get my blood racing. Quillan and the track coaches signalled for us to go, so I set off, carried by the speed of the BMX wheels taking me down the hill and towards the little bumps that I'd need to pump my bike over.

Perhaps it was sheer adrenaline that got me around that track. Perhaps it was the joy I felt while I was doing it that powered me on. But something inside of me clicked – and all that fear I had standing by the trackside vanished when I got on the bike and gave it a whirl. I may not have spent three hours on the BMX like I did on the Velodrome, but I came away from that session feeling stronger and proud of what I'd challenged myself to do. I'd found out that I was indeed capable of many more things on two wheels than I'd thought.

I'm lucky enough to be able to call Adele Mitchell one of the greatest friends I've made in cycling and definitely part of my cycling family. We first met back in 2013; a bloggers' event at a branch of Sweaty Betty (a women's activewear brand) on the Kings Road brought us together. We were both selected to be part of an initiative they were running called 'The Fit Crowd' – a collective of like-minded sporty women working with the brand to inspire new communities of fitness-focused women around the UK. When it came to us getting ready to take part in the exercise classes they laid on (along with free clothing to wear) for us that evening, we soon discovered there were not enough changing rooms in the store. Somehow the two of us ended up huddled together in their cramped and stuffy basement, struggling to get out of our civvies and into the luxury activewear we'd be exercising in that night. I think anyone who you've never met before in your life, but can instantly laugh with while hopping around in your knickers and bra together is set to become a friend for life.

An award-winning freelance beauty and fashion editor and copywriter by trade, Adele also writes about women's cycling – specifically MTB (Mountain Biking) and road cycling – on her blog and for other cycling publications, including dedicated MTB magazine *Singletrack World* and *TWC* (Total Women's Cycling). I've yet to go MTB riding with Adele (well, at this stage, I've yet to do any MTB at all – another one for the list) but I have been road cycling with her. She was the first person I ever rode clipped-in with … like I said; she's a great friend.

Adele's transition from writing about beauty and fashion (Adele was beauty editor at *Just Seventeen* – a fortnightly magazine aimed at teenage girls – when it was one of the biggest-selling titles in the UK) to writing about and getting into life on two wheels is one of my favourite 'how I got into cycling' stories. It all came about when she flicked through an in-flight magazine while going on holiday. This came at a time when she was at a crossroads in her life. Adele explains: 'I have three children – I think they were all under five at that point when we were going on that skiing holiday and, although I was *very happy*, working as freelance journalist and having three children under the age of five is intense. I didn't feel I had an awful lot else in my life at that point – I felt it was time to find something for *me* but I didn't know what that *something* was.'

Adele had an incredible and exciting career, and had 'done the having children thing, which was quite an intense period where you're just focused on them' but needed to re-find herself. While sat on her EasyJet flight, Adele picked up the magazine to have a read. 'It was left open on a page advertising the London Triathlon, showing people taking part in it, and it was a female participant in that ad which caught my eye. There was a man swimming, another man running and a woman riding a bike …

and I looked at it and I just thought well I can run, not very far, but I know how to run. I can swim – I've definitely done that before. And I can ride a bike and I just thought to myself, "I'm going to enter that!" And I did!'

Triathlons provide a substantial challenge of endurance, strength and mental toughness – something that Adele, who was looking for a challenge at the time, could really get her teeth into. When she got back from her skiing holiday, she signed up for the sprint distance London Triathlon. She trained hard for the six months leading up to the event, using every spare moment that she could grab: getting laps in the pool at her local leisure centre, running on the lanes and trails close to home and of course cycling. The thing is, when Adele was training for the Triathlon, she didn't actually own a bike, but had a husband who did. 'He's a keen cyclist and very kindly said I could have one of his bikes – so I took him up on it, even though it was a bit too big for me ... and was a mountain bike.' Traditionally, the cycling part of a triathlon is done either on a tri-bike or a standard road bike (the difference between the two is the frame geometry – a tri-bike is designed so that your upper body is lower and further forwards when sat on it to make you more aerodynamic, and also opens your hip-leg angle making it easier to run off the bike). Thanks to her husband being a mountain biker, Adele ended up with a much beefier machine to train on, but even though it was the 'wrong' type of bike for the event, it still worked for her: living in an area of Surrey where there is a lot of mounting biking on her doorstep, she incorporated this into her training regime: 'When I trained, I trained on the mountain bike, so I trained off road ... even though the triathlon was actually a road event.' The seeds were starting to be sown for the love of mountain biking that she's known for today.

Six months and a lot of training later, Adele completed her

first triathlon in an impressive 59 minutes and 59 seconds, which she was pleased with – although not so pleased about swimming in London's Victoria Dock, as she tells me with a laugh: 'The water is green and it smells of diesel – you put your hand out to swim and you can't see your fingertips ... so you're just thinking what on earth is underneath me!'

It's refreshing to listen to Adele Mitchell – now one of the most respected voices on the women's MTB scene – talking honestly about her limited knowledge of the bike she used for the event. The cycling part of the triathlon is always going to be a fond memory that stands out for Adele – even though it was her awakening to the world of MTB, she can still see the humour in doing a triathlon on one: 'I was so over-biked at the triathlon doing it on that thing, it was ridiculous! I didn't know anything about it!' she says with a smile. 'I just got on it and rode it. It was a titanium mountain bike from America. I remember a bloke in the park before the event saying, "Wow, that's an amazing bike!" and me saying, "Is it?! It's not mine," and he's asking me, "Who lent you that then?" and I'm going "My husband" and that's all I could tell him – I knew nothing, nothing at all about bikes.'

Although Adele didn't have loads of MTB knowledge, she did discover that she could tackle climbs on them – really well. While other participants floundered around her on the ascents, she was way ahead, tearing them up with ease. 'There was a hill on the course and I think that was the only place I overtook anyone, maybe because I had easier gears on the mountain bike ... but then it registered in my head – I'm really enjoying this and I can *really* do hills on this thing!' That 'something for me' Adele was looking for in her life appeared at the end of the triathlon. She no longer felt like 'just a mum', but the kind of woman who does sport, cycling in particular, and for her that was an amazing feeling.

Doing another triathlon definitely wasn't on the cards for Adele but getting back on a mountain bike was. As she puts it, 'Swimming is okay but I can take it or leave it, running is good, but the cycling was addictive – and best off-road.' That year, Adele took it up a gear and got her own mountain bike for her birthday, and then started riding with other women in her community. An avid mountain biker, Adele's husband rides with a group of men every weekend, and has done for around twenty years. It turned out that some of the wives of these men fancied giving mountain biking a go too, and soon enough Adele found herself forming a cycling group with them. 'We all happened to have Friday as the day we could all take the morning off work, so I started to ride with four women who were the partners of these men. We started our women's ride, which is still – and this was 12 years ago – going on every Friday morning.'

One of the brilliant things about having a group or friends to ride with is that it's great for keeping your motivation up. This is something that I've learned over the years and something that Adele really appreciates too: 'We were always going out together, and doing that really kept us all on track.' Their group rides went beyond the off-road trails of Surrey and took Adele back on a plane again, this time going on a cycling break instead of reading about bikes in an in-flight magazine: 'We go on mountain biking holidays! We went to Menorca once. You're thinking to yourself how lovely it'll be to ride around the coast there … but the coast of Menorca is ROCKS! Lots of it is very steep and right on the cliff edge, so it's really challenging.' Pushing herself to this new kind of cycling challenge didn't surprise just Adele, but other people around her too, who perhaps didn't expect her and her group of girlfriends – average age, forty-five – to totally smash a route that demands fitness and skill to complete. 'We had a guide but he didn't ride with us: instead he would deliver our overnight bags to the next hotel every day, and then brief us each evening on where to go and what to expect on the next day's ride – all of which were long and, in places, tricky. On the last night of our stay, our guide joined us for a celebratory dinner. We were so proud of ourselves and at one point I cheekily suggested, "You didn't think we were going to manage those rides, did you?" We all laughed about it but I'm sure he had initially thought, "Oh my god, who *are* these women?!"'

Empowerment – one of the recurring terms I use in this book – springs to mind when listening to Adele telling her cycling story. A group of women – older women at that too – decided to get together and start riding mountain bikes for fun, which resulted in new adventures, discovering what they were capable of and exceeding expectations that they and others outside of their group had about them. This was another incredible feeling for Adele, which also made her question what she was doing while working in the beauty industry. While her MTB adventures were kicking off, she was still working in that sector, but the light was starting to dim on it for her: 'When I was working on a teen magazine in the early days, it was very empowering – you were helping people find themselves. It was all "girl power" and finding yourself and being feisty.' But as she grew up with the beauty world, it became more and more about how you have a problem – and that problem is age. 'I didn't feel like I had a problem,' Adele says, going on to explain, 'and if I did, I didn't want to be telling everyone else it was all doom and gloom unless you rubbed *this* cream or *that* serum into your face, knowing perfectly well that it was not going to make that much difference.' It started to feel like a cruel industry, and Adele no longer wanted to be part of it. 'That's the part I didn't like. I think it's changed a little bit now. It's caught up and it is a bit more empowering. But you are still saying that unless you look a certain way you're not acceptable. And we all know that's not healthy or nice.'

The wheels were in motion once again for Adele to change the direction her life was going in. Disillusioned with the beauty industry, she was moving away from it, and looking for something else. Already down with the digital, Adele had a Twitter feed, but it was all about the sector she was in. 'I was working mainly for beauty titles, so of course that's what my feed was filled with.' One day she wrote a tweet about going out riding – 'I wrote something like "been for a great mountain bike ride today" and then put "sorry to be talking about mountain biking when you're expecting beauty but it's my day off"'. Then somebody responded to her post: 'It's not your mountain bike tweets you want to worry about, it's all the beauty stuff we have to put up with for the rest of the week!' This took Adele by happy surprise, leading her to think: 'Maybe people do want to read about me and my cycling after all.'

Adele decided to test the waters and start to write more about mountain biking. And then she had what she calls 'a bit of an issue'. Adele posted something on Twitter about a cycling promotion that she thought was sexist: 'What I was looking at didn't represent women's cycling as I knew it, which is about enjoying the challenge – not what you look like in a bra.' The editor of *DIRT* (an online mountain bike magazine) spotted Adele's comment and got in touch with her. 'They commissioned me to write a piece on women in mountain biking. Women in MTB was such a small area at that point but I knew I could write a whole feature on it.' At the time, Adele says that writing that piece was an 'Oh gosh, women in mountain biking' moment, like it was a novelty, but now it's become much more diverse – she goes on to explain: 'There are so many levels and achievements that people want to get out of it. But at that point it was a feature on women in mountain biking which was largely me, talking about my experiences of being out on the trails, how it was a really nice place to be and people being really friendly – wanting to know more about what bike you've got than whether you're a man or a woman.' When Adele looked at the media and how women in MTB were being reflected in that, all she saw were women being objectified: 'It was the media who were totally out of kilter with what was happening on the trails.' This is another sector Adele believes has caught up a little bit now.

Other cycling publications began to notice Adele's writing – from talking about her own experiences, to what she was seeing in the media – and they started to pay serious attention to her words too. When *TWC Magazine* launched, Adele ended up being approached and then commissioned by them to write pieces ... and before she knew it, she was being hailed as a 'cycling influencer' and her cycling journalism career was born.

Adele was a voice which was missing and so desperately needed on the MTB scene, but the 'influencer' tag is something that Adele shakes off a bit. 'I'm just someone who rides a bike and talks about it,' as she modestly puts it. 'I'm a better writer than I am cyclist, or I hope I am! And I'm aware of how the media works, so I could see that social media was important to me for my career anyway. I was also trying to be informed about it [MTB, cycling media, the history of it all] rather than just giving a knee-jerk reaction so I could back up any argument really.'

Authenticity and learning more about bikes was another avenue Adele was going down. It was important to her to be authentic, which included having an understanding of the mechanics of the bike. Just like me, when she started out in cycling, the maintenance side of things was a bit challenging for Adele. 'I started to think, "Right – I need to understand what's going on with the bike. And I need to know this stuff." I wanted to engage with it fully, in order to be able to be authentic, really. You have some responsibility to know what you're talking about if you end up in that position. And it's interesting. And I do find the mechanical stuff really challenging because ... y'know I'm not or ever have been a mechanics kind of person. When you start to do it, it's quite simple, but also when you start to do it, you're like, "I don't know if I can do that."'

It can be frightening to openly admit to not knowing everything – not being as knowledgeable as people assume you are with maintenance or being afraid of other things in cycling altogether. I think about those fears and nerves I experienced staring at both the Velodrome and the BMX track that morning, but how empowering it was to admit to myself that I was scared, and then work through and control that fear to have an amazing morning of riding. Being more open about fear in cycling (especially MTB) and talking about it is something that Adele advocates a lot. Around the time I interviewed Adele for the book, she had written an incredible piece on fear and mountain biking. You don't have to be into MTB to be able to relate to it. Telling me about it, Adele talks about bottling stuff up and the impact it can have: 'I've just written some things about managing fear and putting myself out there because you're not supposed to say you're frightened, are you?'

Adele expressed her own MTB fears – from a gnarly tree-root on one of the trails she rides which she has trouble clearing, to fears about hurting herself, messing up technical sections of rides and not being as good a rider as she thinks she should be. Of course, the narratives given on social media can add fuel to that fire too – as she highlights, 'It seems that while one half of the Internet is leaping over jumps and getting air like a badass, many riders are really struggling with fear.' The responses that she had from people were lovely and highlighted the importance of it only taking just one person to say, 'You know what, I'm just going to say out loud: "I'm a bit shit at this and it frightens me sometimes,"' and how that can open up dialogue. Being the person to start that conversation led to other women sending their own stories to Adele to share on her blog, in the hope that it will encourage other women to feel less alone and confront their cycling fears.

Although she rarely refers to herself as one, Adele Mitchell is one of the greatest influencers I've met in my time in the industry. From encouraging me to take on Box Hill, to speaking with her online (or when we get to share panel stages together), I can't help but be inspired by what a cycling badass she is. It's that frank and honest nature – putting herself out there and being a voice for older women in cycling who are under-represented is pretty incredible too.

She knows it comes with risks, and they're ones she's willing to take, as she says: 'I'm not very good at this and sometimes it frightens me, and I'm going to think about why that is and say it. And actually the thing I feared most was other people's judgement. And I then had to put myself out there, do that really basic thing of, you know what, I'm going to say this and I'm going to risk the fact the people might not like me for it and I'm going to see what happens. And then see if people decide they don't like me, does it matter? How will I react to that? And actually what happened is a lot of people came forward and said, "That's how I feel too."'

A Tourist in Your Own City

Cycling on a weekend had become a firm fixture in my diary. While commuting to work on Frankie was always a pleasure, it was nothing like getting on my bike and seeing where a #CoffeeCycleSaturday would take me – both physically and mentally. They had become the highlight of my entire cycling week, as they were something that both helped me cope and encouraged me to keep on going on my bike.

I have such fond memories of Saturday 28 May 2011 – the first 'official' #CoffeeCycleSaturday which I did with Ian. The plan was to cycle across the river from East to South London and spend the day around Bermondsey – at least that's what Ian told me. You see, as cheeky (or lazy) as it might sound, Ian was tasked with plotting our route for the day. Although I've lived in London all my life, I will freely admit that my navigation skills around the city can be *terrible* at times, especially compared to his, so with him being a total caffeine fiend and foodie, getting him to plot the route meant it would be guaranteed to be lined with plenty of coffee and delicious sustenance stops ... and no dead-end streets.

The initial plan for the day was to cycle across the river from East London to Bermondsey, then back east to Shoreditch and then loop back home. I knew that the cycling adventurer in Ian would probably have a bit more than that in store, but I was happy enough with this jaunt. The thought of being on Frankie for most of Saturday afternoon was exciting enough for me – this was a feeling that I was missing! We cycled the Cycle Super Highway (CS3) all the way to Tower Gateway, with a leisurely cycle over Tower Bridge. In all my years being a Londoner, I had never crossed that bridge by foot or by car. It wasn't until I started cycling that I actually went on it. Mad, isn't it? Usually when I travelled south of the river, it would always be on the Tube – hidden underground and never via one of the most iconic bridges in the world. That's another wonderful thing about riding a bike – all the new discoveries you can make about things in your city that are right under your nose, and that you sometimes take for granted.

One of the best moments of our ride was being held up while Tower Bridge was raised to let a boat on the river underneath sail through. Just as we were approaching the north-side tower, we came to a stop. The traffic lights had turned red, and two of the wrought-iron turquoise gates came together from opposite sides of the tower and closed. Crowds of people started to gather on either side of the road – they were leaning over the railings as far as possible, pointing their smart phones and Go-Pro's on selfie sticks towards the archway. The anticipation and excitement of what was coming was thick in the air – and even though I'd figured out what was going to happen next, I was happily swept away in the wonder of fellow Londoners and tourists all waiting for the big moment. I pulled my phone out of my track-top pocket to grab a picture of this spectacle and, along with the crowd, gasped in childlike wonder as the bridge began to lift. The road that was once ahead of me – paved with uncharted cycling adventures – was rising towards the sky in one majestic movement. Something about that moment – watching it going up and coming back down again – felt so apt: regaining that sense of wonder while regaining my love and energy for cycling seemed to just click into place. The road was open, and I was ready for what it had ahead for me.

After the incredible scene of Tower Bridge in action, we snaked our way south to Bermondsey for the first stop on our #CoffeeCycleSaturday: Maltby Street Market. We'd been there plenty of times by Tube and foot, but Maltby always feels like a bit of a hidden gem. Tucked away under railway arches, you'll find market stalls and traders selling a variety of foods – ranging from farm-fresh fruit and veg in a rainbow of colours and seasonal flavours to mini-bakeries, coffee roasters, butchers and dairies.

Our first stops at Maltby Street had to be St John Bakery and Monmouth Coffee. We'd skipped breakfast in order to stuff our faces with food and drink from both places. We went into the bakery and bought two of their famous vanilla custard doughnuts. Along with buying a loaf of sourdough ... and six of their freshly baked madeleines to take home. It would have been rude not to show our appreciation of all that early morning baking they had done – plus my basket had plenty of space for extras. Then it was a tiny cycle over to Monmouth Coffee (who roast their beans on site, which is a smell to savour) to grab two flat whites to go. By a stroke of luck, Ian and I managed to nab a free table outside their shop, propped our bikes up against it and tucked into our American-style breakfast of coffee and doughnuts – the perfect reward for an early morning cycle.

With enough sugar in our systems to keep us on the road for a good while yet, we moved on to the next part of our #CoffeeCycleSaturday: cycling to Shoreditch through the almost silent City of London. I absolutely love the City when it's like that – when you're out early enough, the streets are silent compared to the mania of a weekday. It's not quite as vacant as *28 Days Later* London, but it's a fantastic chance to cruise around on a bike and enjoy the quiet roads, so I 100-per-cent recommend getting out as early as possible if you can.

Ian had chosen this different route so we could continue our adventure around London. He'd mapped out a cycle that took us over *actual* London Bridge (I say 'actual' because of the easy mistake people make in thinking that Tower Bridge is London Bridge ... something I still catch myself doing). We weaved through the financial heart of the city, taking in architectural delights like the Lloyd's Building along the way – another landmark that I had glanced at from the top deck of a bus but never really paid proper attention to. It's so stunning up close. As we continued on our way to Shoreditch another unusual building caught my eye – 30 St Mary Axe, more commonly known as The Gherkin. 'I need to have a proper look at this!' I shouted to Ian as he was riding slightly ahead. I signalled to stop and we turned into 1 Great St Helen's and walked our bikes over to the building. Standing right underneath, The Gherkin was almost overwhelming to stare at for two reasons: 1) the sheer humungous nature of the building, both tall and wide, and 2) the memorial at the base of it – The Tomb of the Unknown Roman Girl. This was an education for me: in 1995 when The Gherkin was being built the remains of a teenage girl who was buried in keeping with Roman traditions were discovered on the site. While construction continued, her body was housed in the Museum of London. When the skyscraper was completed twelve years later, she was returned to the site for reburial, after a service was held for her at St Botolph's Church.

That sense of childlike wonder returned as I gestured to Ian to join me in what I was about to do next: lie down on the floor to get a proper look up at The Gherkin. Ian looked at me, seeming puzzled. 'Are you sure? That's not like you!' he laughed, which may be fair. I was known as someone who gets pissy when their box-fresh trainers get scuffed outdoors for the first time. But this wasn't the old Jools any more. 'Totally sure!' I said, laughing at his reaction as we lay on the floor, both transfixed by the rays of sunshine bouncing off thousands of diamond-shaped panes of glass (7,429 to be exact). We daydreamed under that skyscraper for what seemed like hours – probably getting odd stares from folks walking past, but I didn't care. This bike ride was bringing out the best in me, and I'd re-found a connection with Frankie that I was worried I was losing, and a sense of adventure in cycling which I'd forgotten about.

When we slow-rolled to Shoreditch via another coffee stop (this time Nude Espresso), Ian had plotted a surprise detour knowing that it would make me happy. He'd included a sneaky but very sweet stop at the Tatty Devine jewellery shop, who were having a mega sale! Their Brick Lane store was only a few minutes away from Nude Espresso. It was absolutely lovely to pop into Tatty Devine and catch up with some of the Team Tatty ladies ... and come away with some acrylic delights to add to my collection back at home.

Powered by coffee more than food – and the adrenaline hit from the Tatty Devine sale – at this point, brunch needed to happen. Our very last stop on the route was Broadway Market – a gorgeous old shopping street (and one of the very few left like it in East London) that's nestled away in the heart of Hackney. Something always draws me back to that part of London, old family history with the place, I guess. It was another short ride by bike to get there, but there was so much to see along the way. We were weaving down more cobbled side streets, looking at the beautiful old houses near to Columbia Road Flower Market, blissfully quiet compared to the usual Sunday rush there. Arriving at Broadway Market, you're instantly greeted with a plethora of stalls, heaving with all kinds of items – clothing, jewellery, arts and crafts, fresh produce and street food. I found myself checking the capacity of my basket! We spotted one of the food traders making and selling croque monsieurs. The smell of the melted cheese and hot ham was too hard to resist, so we bought two, stuck them in my not-quite-full basket and cycled over to London Fields to sit and eat and people watch. After that it was time to wend our way back to Canning Town, refreshed and re-energised, counting the days until I got to do it all again the next week.

That ride may not have been the most challenging I've been on, but *that* was the absolute joy of it – the pleasure of just getting to know my city in a way I never had before – and reconnect with the joy of being on a bike. There was no rushing around, or getting stuck in Saturday morning shopper traffic, or missing bits of the city by being on the Underground. This was seeing things for the very first time like Tower Bridge in action, learning the back streets and secret routes into the city, and discovering little hidden gems along the way.

As time went on, I would get more adventurous on the #CoffeeCycleSaturday routes, going further than south of the river – like cycling over to Chelsea and back, for no other reason than to see what was around there and how it all looked from the saddle. And that was what made those rides so special – getting to know my city, and getting to know myself. And of course a good cup of coffee and the best doughnuts in town were a bit of a bonus too.

In February 2011, I made a decision that seemed completely at odds with the sparks bouncing around in my head: I decided to take part in a massive cycling event with hundreds of other people around me. That's the same me who was questioning whether I wanted to be on a bike any more and not wanting to spend that much time around other people.

The event in question was the Tweed Run – an annual sportive that takes place in and around Central London. Although 'sportive' (meaning a short-to-long-distance organised mass-participation cycling event) doesn't sound like the right definition for it, the Tweed Run does fall into that category. There isn't anything remotely 'sporty' about the event: a 'metropolitan bicycle ride with a bit of style', which sees hundreds of people cycling around London in their finest traditional cycling clothing. I'd first heard about it back in 2010 through my cycling friend Mark Ames, who I'd met via VéloCityGirl. He was the man behind iBikeLondon, one of the early cycle-chic blogs I worshipped, and he was also one of the first bike bloggers who welcomed me into the online cycling community when I launched VCG. Realising that the Tweed Run would be 'a Lady Vélo' kind of ride, Mark suggested Ian and I apply for the 2011 run. Even though it was described as a gently paced day, I was nervous about taking part in my first mass-participation bike ride.

Mark's blog post and photos from the 2010 ride were amazing: a sea of people cycling through the roads of Central London on bicycles like my Frankie, massive smiles on their faces and clad in the finest tweed attire. That post was enough to convince me to try my luck for tickets, though I had to brace myself for potential disappointment as the Tweed Run sells out very quickly.

That said, in the weeks before the tickets went on sale, instead of planning my outfit and the military precision I'd polish Frankie with, I was questioning if I really wanted to apply after all. I had to keep quiet about those doubts though: I was still not talking publicly about struggling with sparks on my blog. I felt I had a front to maintain on VéloCityGirl, an obligation to keep 'positive vibes only' for my readers. In an effort to try and shake off my fears, I revisited Mark's previous post on iBikeLondon, reminding myself that the Tweed Run looked like ridiculous amounts of fun. This was the kind of happy that I needed to inject back into my life, so why not throw caution to the wind and just go for it?

The very heart of the Tweed Run was about encouraging more people to ride bikes simply for the love of cycling. Created by Ted Young-Ing in 2009, he organised the first one via London Fixed Gear and Single Speed (LFGSS), an online cycling forum. I do love a good Internet forum that brings people together! Ted put together that first event with a dual purpose: to get people riding again during the cold weather (the first Tweed Run was held on 24 January) and because he had bought some tweed plus fours and was looking for an excuse to wear them. As Ted said in a 2013 interview, one of the aims of the ride was to 'show people that cycling doesn't take special outfits at all – one doesn't need fluoro clothes or Superman outfits to enjoy a day out on a bike'. A fantastic plus about that first event is that it raised money for a nominated charity. That year, Ted held a tombola prize-draw that benefitted Bikes4Africa; an organisation that refurbishes donated second-hand bikes and delivers them from the UK to African schools, enabling children living further away from the schools to get there safely and on time. It's a key part of the run: every year proceeds from the sale of the tickets go to a nominated cycling charity.

Fast-forward a few years from that chilly January ride with a handful of attendees, and the London Tweed Run had grown so much that the numbers of participants ran into the five hundreds and then on into waiting list territory. Ted had started working with other cities, including New York and Tokyo, who wanted to host their own Tweed Runs.

Everything about the Tweed Run looked and sounded like my perfect cycling event, as well as being the most stylish one I had ever seen. The only way I would find out if it was for me was to actually take part in it.

26 February 2011 – 11:45 a.m.: ticket-sale day. Thankfully it was a Saturday, so I didn't have to worry about any distractions (like being at work and having to do my actual job) getting in my way. I was glued to my laptop with the tweedrun.com tickets holding page on my screen, fifteen minutes before the official sale launch. I was clicking the 'reload this page' icon on my browser every couple of minutes – you know ... just in case there was a sneaky early release. Ian was back in London for the weekend, so to stand a bit more of a chance he'd loaded up the Tweed Run website too. We were both camped out on the sofa armed with tea, biscuits and eager fingers on our keyboards.

The pre-hype for the ride had really kicked in, and it wasn't just me getting carried away in it. In between refreshing the website, I kept on checking the tweedrun hashtag over on Twitter: loads of people were tweeting about the event, anxious and eager to get places. Seeing just how popular demand for it was, I kept my fingers crossed that we stood a chance of getting lucky. I refreshed the web page again at 11.57: the ticket sales were open three minutes earlier than expected, which was a surprise. 'Ian!' I yelped at him from my end of the sofa – 'I'm in, I'm in for tickets!' Poor bloke – I probably half deafened him with how loudly I shouted. It felt like I was the only person online who could see this, so without hesitation, I got on with completing registration for the two of us! I was glad I did: by 12:03 *all* of the tickets had sold out. I couldn't believe that we'd just got two places on the Tweed Run. I was going to do my first sportive in style.

The two-month period between the euphoria of getting our golden tickets and the day of the ride was the strangest wait. This was especially apparent as my Sparks had come to a head in March – a month before the Tweed Run. All the anxiety and mental health issues I'd been juggling had just come to a head, and although it was a relief to muster up the courage to go to my GP and get some help, the timing felt so rotten. I had hoped that the buzz I was syphoning off other people's excitement about the Tweed Run and the thrill of nabbing two places would be enough to keep my cycle demons at bay. But they were still there, lurking in the background, questioning my decision: 'Why are you doing this, Jools? This is the last thing you need right now.' I was lapsing back into spending less time on the saddle, so I had to do something to make those doubtful voices stop, and remind myself why 9 April 2011, the date of the Tweed Run, was going to be one of my best days on a bike in a long time.

I love organisation. Making sure things are in order and everything is in place is something that makes me happy. Perhaps that's why I did so well at being an admissions officer and operations manager. Anyway – as good levels of organisation are something that gives me an almost perverse sense of happiness, I figured that being set for the Tweed Run would do the same thing and banish those fears I was grappling with. Other than having a bike, one of the most important requirements for taking part in the Tweed Run is wearing some form of tweed clothing – of which I had *none* in my wardrobe. Safe in the knowledge that we had places on the ride, I got on with planning and organising our attire for the day. It was a welcome and wonderful distraction from my worries to focus on how we were going to look. It may sound superficial but clothing is such an integral part of the Tweed Run. Researching traditional cycling outfits for the event was so much fun – it was like getting sucked into a bicycle, fabric and textile black hole that I wasn't even trying to escape!

Ian's outfit was a lot quicker to put together in comparison to mine. The top half was a white shirt (which he already owned), a grey V-neck jumper to wear over it (another wardrobe win) and a grey tweed flat cap that he picked up in Burton on his way to work one morning (bonus!). For the bottom half, and to keep up the grey-toned theme, we tried to get hold of a pair of grey plus fours for him to wear. Plus fours are trousers that started life as traditional baggy knee pants – also known as knickerbockers – often worn in the nineteenth century. Originally they fastened tight around the knee with buckle adjusters, but were later extended four inches below the knee – hence the name – giving the wearers more freedom of movement. Between us, we hunted on eBay, scoured charity shops and even tried specialist hunting shops who sold plus fours, but where the first two were fruitless the latter were asking almost £200 for a pair. Yikes. Top tip: if you're ever stuck for a pair of plus fours then do what we did and tuck the bottoms of a pair of straight-leg trousers into a pair of nice socks (Argyle if you can) and wear some smart shoes to get that traditional gentleman look on a budget!

The high street and eBay were kinder to me for my outfit. Honestly, I had *nothing* in my wardrobe that was remotely close to suitable for the day. As much as I pride myself on having a pretty decent and varied selection of clothing, almost everything I owned was way too modern and far too loud. I used this as a perfect excuse to treat myself to a tiny bit of retail therapy – after all, I was going through a hard time and shopping can be a bit of a pick-me-up – but there were two rules I had to stick to: 1) Anything that I bought had to come within a strict budget (if Ian wasn't going to be spending £200 on a pair of trousers, I certainly didn't want to go wild in the aisles either) and 2) I must be able to wear any items beyond the Tweed Run – wardrobe recycling all the way.

I wanted to cycle in a pair of trousers or smart shorts. I *love* a good dress, and there were some incredible gowns on display at previous rides, from Victorian steampunk-style, big-bustled dresses with extravagant bustiers, lace-up boots and mini-top hats and aviation goggles to more traditional clothing: A-line frocks and tea dresses with padded shoulders in patriotic colours, worn with T-bar or peep-toe heels. They looked great – they really did – but I found myself drawn to the outfits on the Tweed Run that were a bit different. Like a crisp, white shirt tucked into 1940s high-waisted, wide-leg trousers with masculine tailoring or high-waisted shorts with a button-up front panel. I decided that was the kind of look I wanted to go for.

As with Ian, I came across some beautiful items of clothing that fell quite a bit outside of the budget I had in mind, but luckily eBay and the high street (and Mamma Vélo's accessories collection) were kinder to me with alternatives. I wanted a good look from the top all the way to the bottom – and one that would complement Frankie too, my biggest and best accessory for the day!

I found an amazing 1940s-style cloche on eBay from a milliner called Anna Chocola. Similar to bonnets, a cloche is a bell-shaped fitted hat, worn low on the forehead with a little brim around the front. They're usually made of felt so that they form to the shape of your head – which was perfect for the cornrows that I had in at the time. Anna had one in her online shop that was brown houndstooth, with a wide black ribbon going around it. Teaming it with a pheasant feather brooch I'd bought previously was a perfect combination. Next came the shirt – a white pintuck ruffle-front blouse, with gold buttons and strong puffy shoulders from ASOS. Getting the exact high-waisted trousers of my dreams was out of the question – they were way more expensive than I realised at the time, so smart shorts was the next best thing, and on that score it was Mango who came up with the goods! I wasn't going to wear heels for the day – I still wanted to maintain that slightly masculine look all the way down to my feet. Topshop had a magnificent pair of two-tone brown-leather wingtip brogues and a small brown-leather bag that set the whole outfit off a treat. Mamma Vélo provided the finishing touches to my outfit by letting me borrow her vintage Louis Vuitton silk scarf and gold locket and chain to wear for the day. Carrying pieces of her with me on the day would be just perfect. I guess those days of being that child who went into work with Mamma Vélo at Progressive were more formative that I could have ever imagined.

The day had finally come. After weeks of on and off doubts and wardrobe researching and planning, it was time to do my first ever Tweed Run. Riding towards the starting point of the ride in the splendid sunshine and with Ian by my side, I was filled with excitement – a feeling that I was determined to hang on to for the duration of the day. Every so often Ian and me would encounter other participants (it really wasn't that hard to spot other people who were going to be on the Tweed Run) who dinged their bells at us in acknowledgement and waved hello. Wave upon wave of tweed-clad bike lovers gathered in Paternoster Square next to St Paul's Cathedral – the rider registration and starting point for the ride and also where the traditional group photocall would be. Even though I knew that it was going to be a big event, nothing prepared me for how breath-taking it would be to be in such a grand venue and see so many bike lovers gathered together, dressed in every variant of tweed you could imagine. And I was going to be riding with all of these people – something that I'd never imagined possible in the middle of London!

The route took in some of the most iconic landmarks and areas of the city. It went down from St Paul's over the South Bank, then over Westminster Bridge. From there we all cycled through Hyde Park, around Trafalgar Square and stopped on Savile Row in Mayfair, famous for traditional bespoke tailoring, so of course the Tweed Run had to give a nod to the place! It was also where the 'Best Moustache' competition for the day would be judged – Ian attempted to enter the comp with my Tatty Devine moustache necklace, but strangely enough he didn't win ...

We continued down Regent Street, where plenty of cars were honking their horns at our group. At first I thought we had pissed off almost every driver in that area, but it turned out they were mainly beeping to say hello! Arriving at High Holborn for the ride's tea and sandwiches stop, tourists flocked over to take photos of us. I was happy to stop and pose for anyone who wanted a picture, as I was so pleased with the outfit I'd put together. I was having too much fun to give a damn about how bizarre the whole thing may have seemed to onlookers – it was all about celebrating the joy of being on a bike. Post-posing, it was the home stretch, which was on super-familiar ground. The route took us along Clerkenwell Road, through Old Street Roundabout and then to Bethnal Green for a massive knees-up at the Bethnal Green Working Men's Club.

Everybody really let their hair down at the party – there was 1940s-style swing dancing, barbershop quartet singing, and cocktails and ales flowing, and the opportunity to have a proper chat with people I'd met en route. The whole day from start to finish was a brilliant opportunity to really get to know people. I'd surprised myself by being brave enough to break away from riding with Ian and cycled alongside strangers to make new friends. I'd found that when you just rocked up and cycled beside someone on the ride, conversation was struck up almost instantly.

At one point on that first ride after I broke off from riding with Ian, I gravitated towards a bloke on a Pashley Guv'nor who looked interesting. He had a pipe hanging out of his mouth, and a teddy bear dressed in tweed in the front basket of his bike. As I got chatting to him, I thought I recognised him from somewhere in London before. His face and voice were *so* familiar, but for the life of me I was completely stumped about how I knew him. He cycled off after our brief chat to ride ahead, and I didn't realise who it was until another person cycled up next to me to ask what it was like chatting and riding with Ewan McGregor!

The Tweed Run set the wheels in motion for me to take part in more sportives. I guess I had preconceptions about what that word means. Although I have gone on to do more 'sporty' ones, that's *not* what they are all about and they go beyond just being on a bike. If you're thinking about riding your first sportive – whether it's something laid-back like a tour of a city or a bit harder like the Tour of Flanders – there are a few things that you can do to get yourself prepared for it. Picking the right event for the first time is a must. Finding a mass ride that suits your ability is a gentle way to ease yourself into it. There could be local events in your area to check out, for example. Thinking about the kind of distance you can cycle is always good too! Cycling twenty-five miles a week on my commute to work, I knew that riding ten very flat miles in London at a *very* leisurely pace would be doable ... but if it was taking part in riding 800 kilometres across a week on the Haute Route through the Alps, my daily regime wouldn't be enough to cut it! Getting used to riding in a group before taking part in a big ride will also be a massive help: although I was nervous about riding with 500 people, I hadn't considered that the smaller group rides I'd been doing with Ian and some of our cycling buddies would actually help prepare me for doing something like the Tweed Run. Riding in groups is one of the most sociable and enjoyable aspects of being on a bike, especially when you start to feel relaxed around other riders. It's also a great way to pick up on the etiquette of cycling in a group, as well as meeting other people. You should also make sure your bike is fully prepped for the day and you're ready for any potential hiccups that might happen. I admit, for my first sportive, my puncture-repair kit was actually Ian – I didn't have a clue how to DIY it at that point. One of the biggest tips I can give you about doing a mass ride is stay safe and ENJOY IT! Listening to and following the guidance of the marshals on the Tweed Run was so important as we were riding on open roads. This was another thing that set me up for how to ride safely and listen to instructions in other sportives in the future. They're a ride, not a race – so go at your own pace, don't feel the need to stick any pressure on yourself and just enjoy the sensation of the ride and the people with you! It really will be one of the best things you'll ever do on two wheels ... and you might get to hang with the odd Hollywood A-lister too.

One of the most surreal parts of that day (other than the spectacle of 500 people dressed in tweed, riding vintage-style bikes through the streets of Central London) was being interviewed by a freelance journalist who knew who I was. During one of the tea stops, they came over to me for a quick chat about taking part in the Tweed Run ... and let me know they recognised me as Lady Vélo from VéloCityGirl. I'd only been running the blog for a year at that point, and still regarded it as my tiny corner of the Internet that was probably only getting a handful of hits. I really didn't expect anyone would know who I was at the event. That was the first time it properly hit me how much VCG had taken off, and it struck me just how much people were actually looking at it, reading it and paying attention.

This moment, and subsequently seeing myself featured in the finished article in print a couple of months later in *Cycling Weekly* and the now defunct *Cycling Active*, was a good reminder of why I started the blog in the first place and why it was so important to keep it going: visibility and accessibility. Seeing my grinning brown face in that magazine, talking about doing the Tweed Run for the first time, how I felt about it and what I was wearing was a big deal. Not because it was the first ever bit of press VCG got – but because it was a place that I didn't think a face like mine would inhabit. Deep in my heart, that's how I felt about doing the Tweed Run: I was going against the grain taking part in an event like that. Jumbled up in all those emotions I was feeling – in amongst all that positive adrenaline and the negatives of Sparks – I was also feeling conscious of entering a cycling space that was predominantly white. I'd kept on pushing that to the back of my mind, as I had every right to be there: no one was telling me that I couldn't, but when you're not seeing it, you're not feeling that this could be 'your world'. But it was – it was my world that I felt so exhilarated to be a part of, and I wanted to pass that on to anyone else who might be looking at the Tweed Run or any other mass-participation bike ride and thinking 'I'd quite fancy a go doing that.' So I had to keep on going out there and doing it and happily smile for the cameras and let them stick my photo out there as many times as they wanted to. It was more than a picture and more than a one-off event. It was the start of something much bigger than that.

There was also something so fitting about discussing my outfit from head to foot in that interview. As Ted started the Tweed Run to show people that you don't have to don hi-vis clothing to enjoy a day out on a bicycle, I was more than happy to evangelise the beauty of that ... and how empowering it felt to be in that particular kind of attire and cycle through the streets of my city and feel so damned free.

Cycle Style and Suffragettes

You know, people say to me when they know that I've got this brand, 'So do you actually ride a bike?' almost like they want to catch me out because I don't look like I cycle. And I'm just like ... errr ... yeah!

Jacqui Ma

I didn't know I was a *cyclist* and that there was a specific look that I as a *cyclist* was supposed to adhere to until I was twenty-eight. The moment I made known my intention to get back on two wheels, two types of response started to come my way: there were the roaring and joyous words of encouragement I got, telling me to just enjoy being back on a bike, and there were sage words of old wisdom on the kind of clothing I would need to ditch and what I would have to start wearing once I was cycling on the roads of London again.

It was time to forget about the stuff that I wore *all the time*; like what I'd have on when commuting to work by train, or if I was heading out for the day (or night). If I was going to be travelling by bike, I'd best put the skirts and wide-leg pants aside and replace them with something like a pair of water-resistant cycling trousers, or if I wasn't willing to do that, as a compromise – a pair of jeans with some reflective bands clipped around the ankles. No more wearing the kind of clothes I was wearing when I went to check out my potential Pashley back in March 2010. Forget that purple felt double-breasted dress coat and vintage leather saddlebag slung across your body, Jools! You've gotta replace those with a hi-vis waterproof jacket and a sturdy rucksack ... preferably a cycling-specific one or at the very least put a yellow day-glo cover over it. Let's not even talk about those metallic-pink winkle-picker shoes on the pedals.

I loved my extensive wardrobe and vast collection of accessories, and didn't understand why, suddenly, people were whispering in my ears about how all of that had to go if I was to become a '*cyclist*'. Sacrificing my normal everyday garb was apparently part of the deal. I didn't remember it being like that when I was younger. I didn't own or wear any cycling-specific gear when I was a teenager and certainly didn't when I was a kid either. But that day when I walked into On Your Bike with my CycleScheme paperwork, I felt obliged to get 'cycling apparel' ticked off the list because it was the 'proper thing' to do ... no matter how utilitarian and unlike *me* that clothing felt.

Cycling, women's clothing and the women's emancipation movements of the nineteenth century all have an interwoven relationship with each other, which might come as a bit of a surprise. Much has been documented about the role the bicycle played in women's liberation. Once you've moved around the circles of women's cycling for long enough, you're bound to come across the 1896 quote from famed American social reformer and women's rights activist Susan B. Anthony, who played a pivotal role in the women's suffrage movement: 'Let me tell you what I think of bicycling. I think it has done more to emancipate women than anything else in the world. It gives women a feeling of freedom and self-reliance. I stand and rejoice every time I see a woman ride by on a wheel ... the picture of free, untrammelled womanhood.'

Closer to home, there was Alice Hawkins: a suffragette from Leicester, who was also a member of the Clarion Cycling Club, which was a socialist recreational group. In 1902, Alice cycled around the city to promote the women's rights movement and did so while wearing a pair of bloomers – a style of trouser created by Amelia Bloomer – another famous women's rights advocate of the nineteenth century (who herself had been inspired by the pants worn by fashionable Turkish ladies in Istanbul). Bloomer promoted a change in dress standards for women, believing the full-length skirts and dresses of the 1800s to be restrictive. A woman in a long skirt or dress could not easily ride a bicycle, and a woman who could not ride a bicycle was inhibited. Alice did this at a time when it was risky to be both a female campaigner *and* a bike rider, and was accused of 'outraging public decency' by cycling in such attire. The image of a woman in bloomers back then was regarded as scandalous, so seeing one riding around in trousers AND campaigning would have blown the minds of many who were keen to keep the status quo in place. By dictating the styles of women's clothing, they had in turn continued to repress women from free movement and limit their independence.

You're probably wondering how on earth that little history lesson is relevant to feeling pressurised into wearing today's cycling-specific clothing. Women back then on a bicycle in garments of their choice that had been designed by women for women represented changing times. And that's still relevant for women in cycling today – designing the clothing, accessories *and* riding the bikes. Cycling has traditionally been a male-dominated industry, but there are women out there who are actively redefining that perspective and smashing the patriarchy that holds the primary power. One of those women is Jacqui Ma – a mother, entrepreneur and the designer and founder of Goodordering, an independent company based in East London which makes cycling bags and accessories.

Jacqui is no stranger to the world of bag production, having previously designed for big names including Puma, Virgin Atlantic, Microsoft and Tripp Luggage on behalf of Debenhams. A keen bike lover herself, after witnessing the cycling boom of 2012 at close proximity, Jacqui identified a gap in the market for colourful bike bags that didn't compromise style in favour of functionality and practicality. The seed for a new project was planted: 'I live above an independent bike shop in East London, and I'm a bike commuter too. Every day I would hear all the bikes in the unit downstairs being moved around or being fixed. There's a really romantic vibe about the bikes and the sounds that come from them.'

At the time, Jacqui was also living with a flatmate who was trying to get into commuting to work by bike on a weekly basis but was constantly running into the issue of not finding a cycling bag that worked for her – both practically and style-wise. Jacqui was encountering the same problem too, but it took her a while to see that the solution was right under her nose: 'She [Jacqui's flatmate] had been trying to find a decent pannier for ages – but there was nothing on the market that was talking to her and didn't scream "CYCLING!" One day she said to me, "You're in the same boat and really know a lot about this stuff ... why don't you just design one!"' Jacqui had noticed how much cycling had started to pick up in the area of

East London she was based in, and how stylish the activity had become. She started secretly sketching some bike-bag ideas, wanting to 'design something that women cyclists would appreciate', as Jacqui noticed that most other bags on the market were 'either high-tech, serious cycling kit or covered in flowers'. Eventually her business Goodordering was born.

Jacqui has since branched out beyond multi-functional commuter bags, and her company now produces children's school bags, baby-buggy bags (which double up as bike-handlebar bags), eyewear and even collaborated with TfL (Transport for London) on a limited-edition bag that slotted perfectly into the small luggage rack on the publicly available Santander cycles. Jacqui is no stranger to the world of bag production and has more than just a lucky knack for knowing what's going to be the next big thing – she worked at leading trend-forecasting company WGSN for several years.

Taking the leap to start her business on a full-time basis whilst juggling motherhood was huge. There was also the risk of getting lost in the vast competition. The bike-bag market is saturated with thousands of designs and giant brands that dominate the field. From panniers to backpacks to courier bags, the competition is *fierce*, especially from huge retailers who are able to mass-produce their product at a fast rate. Jacqui realised she had to put something out there on the market that would stand out from the rest. 'After working on those sketches, I knew how they [the bags] had to be,' Jacqui explains. 'I wanted them to be different to all the other bikes bags that are out there – I wanted them to be identifiable.'

One of the things that had struck me the most about the cycling bags available on the market when I got back on a bike again was their utilitarian aesthetic. A lot of the designs followed a similar pattern: super-practical designs in waxed cotton or canvas in muted, khaki colours, with plenty of pockets, zips and an overall look of going off for a lengthy cycle-tour expedition. Of course there is nothing *wrong* with that (even I have a few bags like that in my collection) but that's not what everybody is in the market for, or what I wanted to be using every day. Practical doesn't have to mean boring – it can also be fun and scream 'excitement' rather than just 'this is for your bike, and your bike only'. This was something that Jacqui was more than aware of too when she set out to create her brand: 'Goodordering bags couldn't be the same as all the others. They had to be unique because that's the only way to cut through all these other big brands. I was competing against players like Herschel and Eastpak, so I knew if I was going to make a go of it, they had to be really special – something *really* different.'

Jacqui's first range embraced the fun side of things: inspired by Japanese school bags and retro airline bags from the 70s and 80s, the references also gave her designs a dash of personal nostalgia from her Japanese heritage. Anything with a good story behind it is usually a winner, and in her next round of designs Jacqui took it even further with her buggy/cycling bag. As an entrepreneurial working mum who was always on the move, Jacqui started to consider the issues of mobility she faced, and how that must feel for other parents out there having to travel with more than perhaps a laptop and mobile phone in tow. Although not a parent to a small child myself, Jacqui and her buggy/bike bag concept got me thinking about the women's liberation movement and bicycles: the importance of having that freedom to get around, and not be restricted in doing so. This was a brilliant example of women designing with other women in mind – another thing that Jacqui had also noticed was missing from the cycling bag market.

As a female-led cycling brand, (although Goodordering design and make unisex bike bags and accessories), Jacqui is one of the women in the industry who is turning that patriarchal system on its head. Jacqui doing this is an example of women creating change which they're in charge of – it's not her doing this range for another company, it's her creating her own platform.

I believe that *any* device in cycling that gives the freedom to travel outside with your own power is something to be celebrated, and the normalisation of cycling via clothing and accessories is a big deal. It's not that far-fetched to compare the importance of the Victorian dress reform movement to the changes in cycling fashion today.

As Jacqui points out: 'Fashion is underrated in the sense of the impact it can really have. Some people just say it's a bag to put stuff in. When I see people who don't have a bike who tell *me*, "I'm going to get myself on a bike so I can have one of your bags" – I take that as a huge compliment. Their ultimate aim is to start cycling, and if my bags make them feel that empowered? That's really wonderful.'

Community Links

17 April 2011

'So … are we actually going in?' asked Amy, nervously. We were both stood on the pavement, staring through the massive open gates of Look Mum No Hands!, focusing on the entrance just beyond the bicycle-filled courtyard. We'd made it this far – all we had to do was walk through the gates and enter a cyclist's mecca.

'I guess so … I mean, yeah – why not?' I replied, her nervousness matching my own while I tried to maintain my cool.

Breaking off her stare from the courtyard, Amy turned her head and looked at me. 'Even though we don't have bikes with us?'

'Oh yes, Amy,' I said, mustering up the nerve to take the first step over the threshold. 'Even though we don't have bikes.'

Regarded as London's original cycling café to serve the needs of the city's cycling-mad inhabitants, Look Mum No Hands!

(or LMNH as it's also known) is the ultimate one-stop-shop for any bike lover. Under one roof, you'll find food, a bar, cycling clothing, bike accessories *and* an in-house repair shop. Its excellent reputation as one of the coolest and friendliest bike cafés reaches way beyond London. You can find social media posts from bike-heads around the globe who have paid a cycling pilgrimage to the place and loved it.

Located on Old Street (an area of East London that seems to have some kind of gravitational pull on my life) LMNH is sandwiched between the hipster hive of Shoreditch and the designer heaven of Clerkenwell. I'd cycled past the café-bar-workshop a few times during my first year on Frankie; LMNH opened in April 2010 – a month after I started cycling again. Any trips towards Barbican or into Central London by bike (usually with Ian) went along the route LMNH is on. It's in the perfect location to catch the attention of the hundreds of trendy bike commuters riding through the area ... and you can't really miss the place either. Sprawling across the ground floor of a seven-storey post-war office block, it boasts colourful outdoor seating underneath large front windows – usually filled with towering cheese plants, bicycles and bike art on display. And of course there are the huge black fortress-like front gates emblazoned with *Look Mum No Hands!* on them in white paint. The gates that Anna and I were about to walk through.

It had taken me a whole year (and a bit) of owning Frankie and a whole year of LMNH being open before I felt ready to set foot in there. I'd not read or heard a single bad word about the place from the online cycling community. If anything I had folks singing the praises of the venue to me, asking why I hadn't visited as soon as it had opened: 'This place would be right up your street, Jools!' was the kind of positive vibe I was picking up. But between getting those good vibes, there were those destructive down moments with Sparks, yet again, getting in the way of my thinking … and I felt kind of intimidated by the whole package.

Everything that was so appealing about LMNH was also intimidating me at the same time. It feels so strange to say that now especially as it is such a big part of my cycling life today, but the doubts had crept in. Like, was I a 'proper' (that word that I don't like using) enough cyclist to hang out somewhere like that? Would it be okay to turn up on a Pashley if most of the bicycles locked up in the courtyard were stripped-back fixed-gear or super-light road bikes? Would I get laughed out the place because I didn't really know my shit about bike mechanics? ARGH!

While the anxiety about visiting wasn't completely banished as we went *sans vélos* (of course you don't *have* to own a bike to go there), buddying up with Amy, a wonderful friend of mine from before the days of VCG, to check out LMNH was a good idea. We both had our reasons for wanting and needing to see the cycle café in real life. I felt that visiting the place was part of my ongoing cycling journey as Lady Vélo, and Amy was toying with the idea of commuting to work by bike and wondered if a little injection of London cycling culture would convince her. Her route (which would have been Chalk Farm to King's Cross via Regent's Canal Towpath) would be a beautiful one – especially in the summer. We both needed a bit of pedal-powered encouragement, so getting together and supporting each other to do this visit was ace.

As Amy and I walked through the huge gates, we were greeted by the sight of bike upon bike, locked up on the LMNH courtyard railings. They were in all different shapes and sizes, ranging from expensive-looking road bikes to simplistic fixed-gear and single-speed machines, with a few town bikes thrown in for good measure. There was even a battered Dutch-style sit-up-and-beg that looked like a rather weathered version of Frankie. This array of bicycles helped put our minds at ease. The knowing look we gave one another was the unspoken mental note we'd both made: 'Our kind of bikes would be all right here.'

The front door to LMNH was already wedged open, and as we turned to go inside, it was nothing but people ... *loads* of people. Cycling past the joint I'd always noticed that the shop never looked quiet, but it never looked *this* busy either.

'Errr, Jools ... did we miss something?' asked Amy as she scanned the room, doing a quick headcount. All those heads were looking up at something on the big screen on the back wall.

'Ahhh ...' I said to Amy, pointing at the *Eurosport* channel, which was on the TV screen. 'One of the Classics is happening today, isn't it?'

On the very Sunday we chose to pop our cycle-café cherries, thinking that it was going to be a chilled day to break ourselves in at LMNH, the Amstel Gold Race was being shown on their big screen. This race is one of several that make up the Spring Classics: a series of professional one-day cycling races held in March and April throughout Western Europe. Incredibly popular amongst cycling fans, the Spring Classics are some of the most prestigious and oldest races in the history of professional cycling, with some dating back to the nineteenth century. That year, the seven which made up the Spring Classics were:

Milan–San Remo (Italy)
Gent–Wevelgem (Belgium)
Tour of Flanders (Belgium)
Paris–Roubaix (France)
Amstel Gold Race (Netherlands)
La Fleche Wallone (Belgium)
Liège–Bastogne–Liège (Belgium)

At that point, my knowledge of the Classics and their schedule wasn't as ingrained in my mind as it is now. I love the spring cycling season – for me it's the marker that a long and sunny summer filled with bikes is on the horizon. But back then, it didn't cross my mind that Look Mum No Hands! would be showing the races. *Of course* they would be – just like a decent pub would stick a major football, rugby or tennis tournament on their big telly, why wouldn't a cycling café do the same with cycling races?

Stood there in that moment, watching everyone else in the shop watching the Amstel Gold, I wondered if we'd made an error. Amy and I had come to LMNH on a day like this with no bikes and no real clue about the race. I was worried I'd go right back to feeling like an out-of-place newbie again and that I'd possibly put Amy right off her bike commuting idea by doing this visit. There was a free table near to where we were stood: in the initial rabbit-caught-in-headlights moment we hadn't noticed it, so we slid over and nabbed it, and instinctively picked up the two menus on the tables to peruse, almost hiding behind them. It felt like a relief to be sat down. I know the whole shop wasn't staring at us, but paranoia can make your brain do funny things.

As we sat there, scanning the menus in silence, Amy shot me a look over the top of hers, which set us off both off laughing. We'd realised the ridiculousness of how nerves had almost got the better of us!

'Well, we've made it this far and survived, right?' I said, feeling more at ease about the whole thing. Amy smiled back, nodding in agreement and I offered to go get us some drinks from the bar.

While paying I got chatting to the staff behind the till. We talked briefly about it being my first time in LMNH, me getting into cycling a year ago, and that I'd left my bike at home. I know part of me was shoe-horning 'I do ride a bike, really!' into the chat, like I was still trying to justify my being in the café. Before walking back to our table I stopped and looked around me – everything suddenly felt very different. I actually started to *see* LMNH for the first time. All that apprehension, which had been clouding my thoughts and vision about the place, had started to lift.

I now saw groups of friends getting passionately animated about the big race on the big screen – not a scary group of people who I was convinced were all judging me and Amy as outsiders. And who says that they had all arrived by bike, or were into cycling in the first place? I was jumping to conclusions, which was a bit short-sighted of me. Reading the room again, I saw folks there who were not even paying attention to the Amstel Gold Race: there were people working on laptops, a group of girlfriends having a spot of lunch and some with headphones on, reading books. There were different-sized bike frames and wheels, suspended by metal hooks from the high ceiling like works of abstract art and shelves and bookcases stuffed with bike books, manuals and magazines.

I felt like I belonged there, one of the aims of the café. I now know that the three founders of LMNH – Matt Harper, Lewin Chalkley and Sam Humpheson – wanted the café to be as inclusive a space as possible, starting with the name they gave it. Understanding that bike shops in general can be male-dominated spaces, the trio decided on Look Mum No Hands! – a name that they've said in interviews they felt everyone could identify with.

Amy and I stayed in LMNH well after the Amstel Gold Race had ended as we were having such a wonderful time hatching plans for her to start cycling to work, and how we'd both definitely be making a return to the place at some point with bikes (and probably our cycling-keen boyfriends in tow).

I felt so connected after that visit, and with every visit to LMNH since – which has included things that I never imagined doing there like hosting Q&A events with inspirational female cyclists and moderating panel talks on sexism and misogyny in the cycling industry – that connection just gets stronger and stronger with the team and the community there.

There is a lot more to the bike-like than just hopping on the saddle and riding. I will always be grateful to places like Look Mum No Hands! and the community that comes with it as things that have further enriched my life on two wheels.

If you'd asked me when I started VéloCityGirl where I thought the blog would be after a year, my answer would probably have been, 'I hope it's still going,' not 'I have just interviewed Olympic gold-winning track cyclist Victoria Pendleton on how to encourage more women to take up cycling.'

I had to double-check it wasn't a wind-up when the request came in May 2011. I'd been invited to take part in a bloggers' conference to interview Victoria about Cycletta – a new series of women-only 20-kilometre cycling events, created with involvement from British Cycling, to encourage more women to take up riding, have fun doing so and build up their confidence on two wheels. Victoria was announced as the scheme's ambassador and, as the key spokeswoman for the initiative, would be holding a series of phone interviews.

Being one of the bloggers invited to speak to her was a huge deal for me – I said yes in a heartbeat. Victoria had been one of my cycling sheroes since watching her win gold in Beijing 2008. Witnessing her take gold and silver that year (and she would repeat the feat in 2012) were huge inspirations for me. Her strength, grit and determination were something to be respected and admired. She was a professional track cyclist, but she wasn't only seen on the tracks of a velodrome. She was also an everyday bike rider, and at that stage was on the cusp of releasing her own 'Pendleton' bike range with Halfords (it launched a year later in 2012). Her range of ladies' bikes was a far cry from her competitive background – they were sit-up-and-begs like Frankie, a stylish mix of classic and contemporary components. Being asked if I wanted to interview her was another mind-blowing moment for my tiny little corner of the Internet. The request to do this also highlighted how VéloCityGirl was gathering traction and reaching people far and wide.

I had a week to put together questions I wanted to ask her. I wasn't a journalist by trade, and had *never* interviewed someone like her before, but I really wanted to get it right – and ask some questions of my own that were not directly related to the Cycletta programme.

The day of the interview, I was a bundle of nerves – excited, yes, but definitely a bundle of nerves. I was still in a state of disbelief that I was going to be interviewing Victoria Pendleton ... and worrying if the questions I had for her were utterly terrible. Granted, I wasn't actually going to be face to face with Victoria, but this was probably as close as I'd ever get. I'd booked the day off work so was able to do the phone interview in peace at home with no distractions.

At 9.45 a.m. I was perched on the edge of my seat at the kitchen table – staring at the clock on my iPhone waiting for the 10 a.m. call from the PR company to dial me into the conference. At 10 a.m. on the dot my phone rang – my nerves and excitement made me jump in my seat! This was it – time to talk to one of my cycling sheroes in real life. I answered, and after a quick rebrief from the woman at the PR company she said:

'Okay, so we're going to put Victoria on the line for you now' – putting her on the line *for me* – OMG! – 'I hope the two of you have a wonderful chat!'

Part of me was convinced dry mouth was going to take over and I'd not be able to get my words out, but before I could say anything Victoria sprung into happy verbal action on the line. She introduced herself and then immediately asked me questions about VéloCityGirl – how long I'd been blogging for and how long I'd been cycling for. *What?* Seriously – I was thinking to myself, *how on earth* does Victoria Pendleton know about my blog? I'm sure Victoria had been briefed by the PR team but it didn't feel forced when she asked me questions about myself, and then continued to ask more off the back of what I was telling her about my own cycling journey. In those 'getting to know you' moments at the beginning of our interview Victoria managed to put me at ease, which gave me the confidence to get stuck into my questions for her ... and push the thought of them being utter pants out of my head.

Victoria had been named by *Red* magazine as one of the most influential women of 2011 so, with the launch of Cycletta, I wanted to know how she hoped to inspire more women into cycling. Victoria explained that the idea behind the organised rides was to 'give women the opportunity to cycle on traffic-free roads, and to make it as appealing as possible' and that she wanted to lend her celebrity cycling status to the Cycletta initiative to encourage more women to get involved.

It was great to hear Victoria acknowledging the position of power she holds and how her profile could be used for the greater good of encouraging more women and young girls into cycling. But there can also be a bit of backlash when it comes to 'women only' cycling events. Questions have been raised if there is actually a need for them – especially recreational and leisure rides – to be split along gender lines. It's a hot topic in the cycling industry that has rolled on for some time. Some believe that women-only rides are a fantastic catalyst to boost the confidence of those who feel intimated cycling with men, while others believe it's a patronising step backwards for women on bikes and is as anti-inclusivity and as sexist as having men-only rides.

During the interview I really felt like I could open up to Victoria about my reasons for getting off a bike at eighteen, including the catcalling and jeering I would be subjected to by men – ranging from guys on the street or in their cars shouting at me to other male cyclists riding the same roads as me. When I asked her about the slightly competitive nature that cycling on the roads can take on (such as when I've been jeered at for wobbling or hesitating by aggressive bike bros), Victoria said although she could be quite competitive herself (in her field she would be), she could relate to how distressing situations like that on the road for a woman – new rider or seasoned cyclist – could be. She hoped that removing any competitive element or atmosphere would make the event more approachable and encourage more women to come along.

The mixed-abilities thing was something that I brought up with Victoria, as Cycletta had different levels of riding groups you could join. Of the rides that Cycletta was offering, the one that would have appealed to me and my Pashley at the time was the 'Leisure/Commuter' rides, but even then I was concerned that I could end up being one of the slowest in that group! Her advice to me and other women who could be worried about the same thing was that, as it was such a relaxed environment, there would be no pressure and that the groups themselves would 'probably split out naturally', so those who want to go faster end up at the front, medium-pace riders in the middle and so on. She added, 'I say give yourself plenty of space and ride within your limits and don't force yourself to go beyond your own personal comfort zone. It's one of the best things that you can do, especially on a ride like this.'

It was coming towards the end of my allocated time slot for the interview, and I realised I'd not asked Victoria any questions about cycle style yet! Fashion-talk was one of the biggest draws on VéloCityGirl, so it would have been criminal to not ask Victoria about hers.

Outside of the skintight Lycra she wore for competitions or training, you would see images of Victoria in glossy magazines taking part in fashion shoots that involved bikes and 'everyday' clothing. Well, when you're a star, posing in a glamorous Wayne Hemmingway green Union Jack dress as Victoria did in 2009 is probably 'everyday' clothing. Anyway, what I'm saying is she doesn't live on the track and ride in skin suits or bib shorts alone! I had to know what kind of bike she rode outside of competitive sport and what her typical cycle-style wardrobe would be. Her answer didn't disappoint at all:

'I'm usually training six days a week on my bike, but when I'm not, I have an old shopper ... I don't even know how old it is! It's a proper old black frame with fat pedals, massive handlebars and panniers!' And she went on to explain what you'd be likely to see her wearing on that. 'When I do cycle into town, I'd probably be wearing flat ballet pumps, a nice little blouse and some skinny jeans and probably my mac – there is never a situation when a mac is not appropriate to cycle in!'

I knew that I had *totally* gone over my time-slot speaking to Victoria, but I didn't know when or even if I'd get a chance like that again. She was an absolute joy to chat with – definitely not just the competitive, gold medal-winning Olympian that you see on the television. She was keen to connect with everyone and get more women on bikes. For a while after the interview, I kept on thinking about that part: *connecting with everyone and getting more women on bikes.*

I could fully appreciate the need for women-only cycling groups. I know how unnerving it can be cycling alone or feeling intimidated on the road, and how riding with groups of other women with mixed abilities can boost your confidence. They can also provide a safe space to ask questions, be it gender-specific ones or for help with mechanical queries, without feeling like you're under pressure to know it all. But there was another group that was at the forefront of my mind that I couldn't discuss with Victoria: groups for people of colour who wanted to get into cycling, or were already into it, and needed to have that support network.

Listening to Victoria talk about Cycletta and evangelising what the project had set out to do was fantastic. As a woman, *of course* it was heart-warming to hear their plans and Victoria's passion for it, which was evident by the excitement in her voice. But for me, it highlighted that this kind of project for women of colour in cycling was still missing, and that there was still much more work to be done.

I've always been a strong believer that cycling is for *everybody*, but there is no denying that many barriers to entry still exist for women of colour wanting to get on a bike. I know from my own experiences that one of the biggest barriers was not seeing anyone I could identify with in a lot of the standard advertising, marketing and campaigning that exists for the activity. A source of frustration for me is that huge governing bodies and cycling organisations don't recognise the need to incorporate WoC (women of colour) who ride into their initiatives, and therefore fail to push for inclusivity. I mean, how amazing would it be for women like me to see a project like this for us get the green light, and be promoted with the same amount of gusto?

In a lot of the panel discussions and debates I've taken part in about cycling, a recurring theme that pops up is the importance of organisations 'at the top' actually stopping to think about the positive changes they could be making, and then actually working *with* people from marginalised backgrounds to start putting those plans into action. In order to navigate out of the frustrations of the 'you can't be what you can't see' narrative, more than often it's women of colour at the grass-roots level of cycling who create and run those groups. An example of this is Black Girls Do Bike (BGDB) – an American organisation created by Monica Garrison in 2013. When Garrison got back into cycling as an adult, she noticed the low numbers of other African American women cycling around her and felt compelled to do something about it. She created BGDB with the mission of growing and supporting a community of African American women who share a passion for cycling. Still running the organisation today, the group membership online has grown to 13,500 people.

I haven't found an organisation on the scale of BGDB in the UK, though I hope a movement like that will happen here. Trying to make something like that happen has been on my mind for a long time. I've had conversations with some of the inspiring WoC friends I have that are into cycling about creating a platform ourselves. It's something that I've wanted to do for longer than you can imagine. Lots of factors get in the way of that happening: time, lack of resources and fear. Despite growing up with other black girls who were into cycling like my sister and my childhood friends, fear is a barrier to entry that still exists. Speaking to my sister about why she hasn't ventured back into cycling as an adult, Michele tells me that worry of it not being a space for her holds her back. Her school friends that she's still in contact with feel the same way too – and they also don't feel comfortable or confident enough to start together all over again, which is a shame.

There is a real importance to creating spaces for marginalised groups, but the fear of getting attacked about it is real. I've had conversations with people who have told me that creating a safe space for WoC in cycling is a regressive and racist step to take. I don't see it that way – I see it as trying to make something positive – something that encourages other women of colour to feel like they can get on a bike and ride, and that cycling is a space for them!

Creating such groups as a response to the lack of representation of WoC in cycling is not a bad thing – it's a powerful movement that could change lives. That wasn't a conversation I could have with Victoria that day on the phone, but doing that interview gave me a lot to think about regarding the changes that still need to be made within the cycling industry. Fundamentally, it's about making sure the industry is indeed encouraging and enabling everyone to get on a bike.

Within my first year of blogging about my bike life on VCG, I had made some brilliant connections with like-minded bike lovers. One of the most exciting and unexpected of those was working with Bikeminded; a community project created by the Royal Borough of Kensington & Chelsea (RBKC) to promote cycling amongst its residents. Through a variety of campaigns and events, Bikeminded aims to get as many people as possible cycling in the borough, and experience more of their area and what it has to offer.

It started with an email in late July 2011, which came via my blog. It's always lovely when someone sends an email to VCG, but this one was really something else. The Road Safety and Travel Plan Manager at Kensington & Chelsea Council,

Kathryn King, had been following VéloCityGirl online. An avid coffee drinker, cycle-chic fan and cyclist herself, Kathryn found my blog – especially the #CoffeeCycleSaturday entries – useful for her own personal travels by bike to discover more of London ... and approached me about working with her and the council on the Bikeminded project, to create a Royal Borough cake tour.

I couldn't believe it – the #CoffeeCycleSaturday adventures that had started as a way of pedalling myself out of a cycling black hole had caught the attention of RBKC, inspiring them to want to create a similar event *and* ask me to work with them on it! After picking my jaw up off my keyboard, the answer to Kathryn was of course yes – despite the fact I didn't have a council-planning bone in my body. Absolutely my *'I'm not the right person to do this, surely?!'* vibes were creeping in – but the answer *had* to be yes. I may not have the experience in some areas, but clearly I *did* qualify through my love and enthusiasm for cycling (and cakes). This was a cycling victory that I had to grab by the handlebars and proudly acknowledge!

My excitement for the project meant I wasted no time – a week later, I met up with Kathryn to discuss ideas for the cake tour. She cycled to East London to meet me in Shoreditch for lunch at Nude Espresso. She'd never been there before and was keen to try it after my blogging about it.

Kathryn was even lovelier in real life than in the emails we had been exchanging – and her cycle style was on point too. Kathryn arrived at Hanbury Street on a bright yellow Electra Cruiser – also known as beach cruisers, they have an upright seating posture, very straightforward steel construction, and usually large balloon tyres, meaning they're super stable and very easy to ride. Kathryn's also had red roses painted on the frame and skirt-guard. Wearing a fabulous pair of gold-beaded sandals, and cobalt-blue turn-up trousers teamed with a white tailored peplum top with gold embroidery, I simply *had* to take a picture of her amazing summer cycle style for my blog!

Style compliments exchanged, we discussed our ideas for the ride over blueberry pancakes and flat whites. It was awesome to be sat there bouncing thoughts off each other and getting so excited about it. It was hard to believe that a few months prior, I had serious doubts about my desire to get on a bike, and there I was, hatching plans for a group bike ride with a like-minded bike lover.

Learning more about the demographic of the RBKC during this meeting with Kathryn was an eye-opener. I had my own ideas about what that area of London was like – and what the cycling culture must have been like there too. My preconceptions were fuelled by what I saw in the media and having 'big days out' in the posh bits of London, and by its postcode: Kensington and Chelsea is the borough that has *royal* status and boasts luxury department stores like Harrods and Harvey Nichols. My view was that everyone who lived in the area would have easy access to cycling because surely they all must be minted, but that wasn't the case. RBKC is one of London's richest boroughs, but it has areas of both great affluence and of poverty. As documented in a study by Trust for London and the New Policy Institute, Kensington & Chelsea has the greatest income inequality of any London borough. Private rents for low earners have been found to be the least affordable in London, and according to a recent report by local Labour MP Emma Dent Coad, in the World's End council estate residents have an average income of £15,000 a year, while owners of nearby homes on the other side of the King's Road have average earnings of £100,000.

This ride wasn't just about all the fancy cake shops, gorgeous shopping avenues and famous landmarks in the area that we could include in the route – it was about inclusivity and enablement and accessibility. Bikeminded wanted to give all residents, no matter their financial situation, access to cycling, and to have the freedom to enjoy an activity that should be readily available to everyone. It would also be a great way for residents to meet their neighbours, allowing them to make connections and build a less fragmented local community.

After our meet-up in Shoreditch, the pinging of emails back and forth between Kathryn and me continued for weeks, filled with more ideas and suggestions. If you were to look at my computer screen while I was at the office, you'd think I worked for both Google Maps and the baking industry rather than in university admissions.

Organising a public ride alongside my day job was a huge task, one which gave me even more respect for Ted organising the Tweed Run. With me juggling UEL work and VCG stuff as well as the ride, and Kathryn working on other projects too, the event – which was officially named the Kensington & Chelsea Cake and Coffee Cruise – wasn't going to happen until October, some months away.

Although I knew of some fabulous cake shops and patisseries dotted around the area, mainly thanks to Ian, I didn't know the layout of the area that well, so Kathryn and the Bikeminded team worked on a route. They even managed to get the owners of the shops on board to provide the cakes and coffees on the stops – result!

Of course, we had to know if the whole thing would actually *work*. We needed to bring together my suggested coffee and cake stops alongside the route that Kathryn and the Bikeminded team were plotting and make sure this would be possible with a large group of people of different riding abilities taking part. In wanting to get it right we realised the best way to find out was to put on a closed test version of the Kensington & Chelsea Cake and Coffee Cruise.

My immediate thought was that the best people to have as testers of the ride would be some of the cycling bloggers that I had got to know online in the last twelve months of running VCG. From a purely selfish standpoint, it was also a perfect excuse for me to meet some of these bloggers in real life who had welcomed me into the cycling community. It was my way of saying a huge 'thank you' for their warm virtual hospitality. Kathryn and I worked hard to squeeze the test ride into September – doing it at least a month before the official ride would give us a chance to iron out any problems that might have cropped up and, thankfully, some of the bloggers that I invited were able to make the date we'd set aside.

From the list of bloggers I had invited to come, those who were able to make to our reconnaissance mission were:

Mark Ames of ibikelondon
Jemma Leahy of Help! My chain came off!
Andreas Kambanis of London Cyclist
Tillie of Tillie & Coco
Mina Zaher of Kings Road Rocks!
And, of course, Ian was on the ride too, representing
    VéloCityGirl

The day of the test ride was wonderful, and all went completely according to plan. The September summer sunshine was lingering over London, adding to the fantastic mood we were all in.

Still, I'm glad we did the test ride, as it put me in such a confident frame of mind for the public ride. Comparing the two was so pleasing: both went perfectly! Pulling out all the stops, for the public ride the Bikeminded team organised Royal Borough bike valets to look after all the bikes at the various intervals en route so everyone could pop into the shops and enjoy a coffee and cake, and get to meet their fellow cruisers and people from the borough. They also laid on Royal Borough marshals throughout the cruise to ensure everyone's safety and give advice to less confident cyclists.

On the test version there were eight of us doing this ... on the public version, twenty people attended! That may not be up there with Tweed Run numbers, but for us, that was an incredible turn-out.

We started by meeting at 1:30 in Notting Hill at a coffee shop appropriately named Pedlars, where everyone had the chance to meet and mingle. We set off at 2 p.m. sharp for the two-hour cruise on a route going through the borough. Our stops included Buttercup (a lovely little independent bakery that focuses on mainly on cupcakes), Pierre Hermé (one of the world's best macaroon boutiques – French *Vogue* once dubbed Pierre 'The Picasso of Pastry'), Cocomaya (a beautiful artisan bakery which could lure you in just with the aromas wafting from the shop) and then on to our final stop, The Chelsea Teapot. Located towards the end of Kings Road, this beautiful shop had the perfect ambience for a group of happy cyclists who all needed a cup of tea after a ride.

At the end of public ride day, I couldn't get over the joy I found in seeing the variety of ages, backgrounds and bikes of the riders who came along. It brought home to me once again how important and diverse the cycling community is, and why it's crucial that something so simple should be available for everyone. Cycling had pulled so many people together, and my biggest hope was that those who had come along would keep on riding.

It meant a lot to be one of the people that facilitated the ride. Using any kind of power to bring people together and to ride bikes is incredible. No matter how small or large your platform is, if you have one to use, then use it.

May 2012: my favourite event of my cycling calendar had swung back round again – the Tweed Run. After that first ride in 2011 there was no way I wouldn't be signing up for tickets that next year.

However, this would actually be the *third* time I'd be doing the Tweed Run. In November 2011, a special edition of the event, sponsored by designer Ralph Lauren's diffusion line 'Rugby', was put on, and I was lucky enough to attend. This time round, instead of the mad panic to get tickets online (and after building up a great cycling friendship with the Tweed Run team), Ian and I were invited by Ted to the event as 'Press'. Ian was on photography duties and I would chat with fellow Tweed Runners for the write-up on VCG, as well as documenting the day on social media, of course.

Experience had taught me that one of the best opportunities to get chatting with people is during the picnic or tea stops or when the group photo is about to be taken – not that it's a problem chatting to people when you're riding (hey, Mr McGregor, if you're reading this) – but it's much easier to dart around the almost stationary crowds to get photos, soundbites and details. As everyone was being herded towards the steps of the Royal Albert Hall for the traditional group photo, Ian and I were scooting around with our bikes, looking for something to prop them up against. We got so distracted getting photos and interviews for the blog, we neglected to grab a space so that we could join the group photo. It's always taken without the bikes – the logistics of getting more than five hundred people all in the same spot to pose plus their bicycles would be a space nightmare.

All of the available wall space was snaffled while Ian and I were doing our blog thing in the crowd and we didn't want to leave our bikes lying on the ground for some poor soul to trip over. Eventually, we found a massive twig on the grass that we wedged into Frankie as a makeshift stand, and leaned Ian's bike against her. The twig couldn't hold the weight – pretty soon it snapped, sending both our bikes clattering to the floor. 'This is silly,' I grumbled at Ian, as we were fiddling with our impromptu creation, trying to make it work again. 'I'd have been able to stand Frankie up if she actually came with a kick-stand.'

This was something that had cropped up many times before when I'd been out with my Pashley. If I needed to stop somewhere for a moment, I had to make sure I could find something to lean her against, which was always a bit frustrating. I needed to sort out buying a kick-stand, but I could never understand why the model of Princess above mine came with a kick-stand as standard. Pashleys are heavy bikes, so trying to lean them against something that wasn't a solid wall or a tree would usually end in disaster. The stick gave up again – my bike alone was way too heavy to be supported by it, so I let Ian use it for his and decided it was the floor for Frankie. Overhearing me griping about it, a man came walking over to us from the crowd.

'Would you like me to park your Pashley against mine over by that tree? I can make a bit of space for you if you want?'

'That's very kind – thanks!' I replied. I wheeled Frankie towards the tree that his immaculate Pashley Guv'nor was leaning against, along with a couple of Pashley Poppy models.

'That's the one of the annoying downsides with the Princess Classic,' I moaned. 'I love it, but I don't understand why they never make them with a kick-stand like the Sovereign or have them across the entire range.' I said that in a kind of 'Pashley owner solidarity' and felt validated when the man silently nodded in agreement with me.

'Hmmm, quite,' he said, looking Frankie up and down, as he leant her against his bike. 'We really must sort out a kick-stand for you and your bike.'

We. *We?* He looked at me and a massive smile grew across his face. Out came his hand now that it was free, to shake mine.

'Allow me to introduce myself. I'm Adrian Williams, MD of Pashley Cycles.'

Oh god. I'd just slagged off my bike to the person who ran the company that made them. The company that made the bikes I was in love with. The ground could have swallowed me up then and there. Also – *how could I not know this*?! Pashley were one of the sponsors of the Tweed Run. This was my third time taking part in the event, but I had *never* clocked who the 'People from Pashley' were on the ride! Even though the logical thought would have been, 'They're probably the ones riding around in a group on Pashley bikes, Jools,' in my defence *lots* of people were riding around on Pashley bikes at the Tweed Run. Thankfully Adrian could see the funny side (as did I after getting over my mortification) and reassured me that what I said about the lack of a kick-stand on the Classic wasn't an insult, but 'good feedback to consider'. I guess this was the ultimate ice-breaker to speak to another person you seriously respected in cycling – having a whinge about the brand to the MD and then spending some of the day cycling side by side. At the end of the ride, he caught up with me at the after party, asking for my details so he could send me a little present.

Two weeks later, a brand-new kick-stand with instructions on how to attach it to a Princess Classic arrived in the post. I spent a happy Saturday afternoon out in the back garden attaching it to Frankie myself – it kind of reminded me of all those times that I'd watched my brother tinkering with my Burner but had never got involved. This time, I decided that I was going to be the technical one and give it a go.

Me giving 'constructive feedback' to the MD of Pashley could have been one of the worst things I'd ever done. Instead it was the beginning of one of the best friendships I've made in cycling. Adrian is an MD with a difference – accessible, incredibly friendly and willing to connect with his fan base on their love of all things Pashley. I started going to other Pashley events, and ended up connecting with other Pashley enthusiasts that I never even knew were out there. That's the power of cycling – its ability to bring people together, even if you start off on the wrong foot. Or kick-stand.

It was a sweltering summer day in July 2012 and my heart was pounding out my chest with nerves, intensifying the closer I got to Look Mum No Hands! I pulled into their courtyard with Ian just behind me on his bike – we couldn't quite get to the parking bays as there was a hive of activity going on: camera crews scurrying about and boom mics looming. The second episode of *The Cycle Show* — ITV's brand-new TV programme dedicated to all things bike — was being filmed at LMNH, and I was there to be a guest on it.

Just a week before, I was perched on the sofa, eyes glued to the TV screen to watch the very first episode. I was filled with hope and high expectations: I'd never seen a magazine-style series that was solely dedicated to cycling. There was *Top Gear* for all the petrolheads, but as far as I was aware, there was nothing like that for bike lovers or anyone who just fancied knowing a bit more about riding and bike culture.

The very start was promising: presenter Graham Little, buzzing with enthusiasm, burst on to the screen in the middle of LMNH, introducing *The Cycle Show* as something that 'celebrates bicycles of all shapes and sizes and the people of all shapes and sizes who ride them'. Reeling off all the different types of cyclist he could think of – BMXers, mountain bikers, commuters, roadies and casual riders – he declared that if you were one of those, 'this is the show for you'.

Based on that promising line, I was ready to feast on a pick'n'mix of cycling delights for the next thirty minutes! Graham's piece to camera segued into a Video Tape (VT) montage of high-octane riding. There was road cycling, mountain biking and BMX, all whizzing (and crashing) across my TV screen. Then it was back to Graham in LMNH to introduce the studio guests: ex F1 World Champion Nigel Mansell and Scottish racing cyclist Graeme Obree – who famously broke the world hour record twice in 1993 and 1994. They were both interesting people to have on – I knew of Mansell from my days of watching Formula One with my dad in the early 90s, and he was the owner of Team UK Youth, who were a cycling team for the under-24s, with a focus on kids from disadvantaged backgrounds. Although my knowledge on Obree was limited, I knew he was the famed 'Flying Scotsman' known for his unusual riding positions and for the 'Old Faithful' bicycle he built which included parts from an old washing machine. On the sofa they discussed Bradley Wiggins' recent win of the Tour de France and what this meant for British cycling.

I continued to hang on, telling myself that the content and direction of the show would change lanes. When Wayne Hemmingway (remember I mentioned him dressing Victoria Pendleton in that Union Jack dress earlier?) rolled on to my screen on a sit-up-and-beg bike in the next piece of VT, my fashion heart skipped a beat! Were they about to discuss cycle-chic? Was Wayne going to stop the most stylish cyclist he could find in London and chat with them about what they were wearing? No. It was a piece on cycling safety and how to ride with caution through a busy city. *Wasn't expecting that, but fair enough*, I thought to myself.

The final segments of the show followed the same pattern. That's when I realised there wasn't going to be a shift in gear. There was a group of eight roadies testing out the Olympic Road Race route on Box Hill in Surrey (three women were in that group, though), then back to the studio with the guys chatting on the sofa again (this time joined by Gary Fisher – the founding father of Mountain Biking), rounded off with the Rollapaluza cycling challenge (where participants battle it out on static bikes over a sprint distance at speeds in excess of 50 mph) between Obree and Fisher. Viewers were welcomed to share their thoughts about the show on *The Cycle Show* Facebook page or Twitter and invited to tune in again the following week.

Wondering if anyone else in the cycling community had any thoughts on the first episode, because I certainly did, I went straight on to Twitter and searched *The Cycle Show* hashtag and their @ mentions, looking for other opinions. I found quite a few – many were applauding the show, talking about how much they'd enjoyed it and loved the guests. Others were saying that they were keen to see what was coming in the next episode as that wasn't revealed at the end of the show. Then I checked out my Twitter feed, which would contain tweets from people I followed directly on there. As I suspected, there were tweets from people I knew – especially fellow female cyclists – who had watched the show and were not that sure on the content, and I shared some of my thoughts as well. I had mixed emotions about the first episode – I was pleased to see a show that was dedicated to cycling had actually happened, but I wanted to share how important I felt it was to see more women (beyond the three that were riding up Box Hill) and more diverse groups on the show. That first episode just felt so ... well, male and MAMILish.

I considered doing a blog post on VCG about it, but I also wanted to give the show a chance before doing anything that seemed like a scathing review. For all I knew the producers could have more plans up their sleeves for the rest of the series that would blow my socks off – but as I'd learned from the Pashley kick-stand incident, feedback is key! What I didn't expect was to actually end up becoming part of those plans. The next day, off the back of my tweets, I received an email from the producers of *The Cycle Show* inviting me to join them as a guest on the next episode to chat about the changing cycling culture in the UK – and to do a bit of presenting. To be asked to have a chat on the sofa was one thing, but to do a segment on the show was something else. I'd been on TV before – in the audience at MTV's London Studios watching Liberty X perform when I was twenty – but this was going to be *slightly* different.

I was incredibly excited but almost as soon as I'd replied with my enthusiastic yes to their offer, Imposter Syndrome started to kick in. I'd been back on a bike for two years at this point, did that really mean I was qualified to talk about cycling culture? Answer: Yes. I knew that in my heart, I just needed to remember it. And luckily LMNH was going to be the location, which was a home from home for me now. Though it wouldn't be your average Sunday at the café, which would be filled with an audience, crew, cameras and other guests, the location would definitely put me at ease. There was of course the other thing I could do that would put me at ease: go shopping for a new outfit. If an invite to be a guest and guest presenter on a TV show all about cycling wasn't a perfect excuse to flex my cycle-style muscles, then I don't know what is! Only a couple of weeks before all of this, I had seen a beautiful bicycle-print dress in Anthropologie. It was a white floaty voile, with red and blue bicycles all over it. That dress was a proper 'you'd need to be going somewhere special to buy that, Jools' affair. And now the perfect reason had come up.

I had a rough idea of what to expect – the producers had sent me a brief about the kinds of questions I'd get asked on the sofa and some information on the cycling group I'd be interviewing, so that I could prep some questions. However, I realised when I was cycling over to Old Street that morning, I didn't actually know who the other guests would be. Perhaps I'd missed it in the email, but my mind was blank as to who I'd be spending the day with and potentially having a chin-wag with on the sofa. As Ian and I locked our bikes up, there was a bit of a pushing and shoving in the crowd forming outside.

'I didn't realise it was like this behind the scenes,' I said to Ian, wondering if the place was going to go beyond capacity. 'It's usually this level of busy when one of the big races is on or something.'

There wasn't a big race on – but there was something big. And that something big was the legendary Eddy Merckx. I had ZERO CLUE that The Cannibal (a nickname Eddy got because of his insatiable appetite for victory and how he devoured *everything and everyone* around him in a race) was going to be there.

Before I got back into bikes, I didn't know a hell of a lot about Merckx. My days of watching cycling coverage with my dad on a Sunday afternoon on Channel 4 (what is it about dads watching every bit of sport on the TV?) came long after Merckx had retired from competitive riding. It wasn't until I got together with Ian and started to express my interest in getting a bike again that the 'cycling legends' conversations started.

When I got Frankie in 2010, one of the first big educations I was given by Ian was to watch what he called 'the best film about professional racing' that he thought I would enjoy – *A*

Sunday in Hell. This Danish documentary film was made in 1976 by Jørgen Leth and covers the gruelling 1976 Paris–Roubaix bicycle race – one of those Spring Classics I mentioned earlier. Ian knows my taste in films and was totally correct to assume that I would love it. *A Sunday in Hell* is a gritty and honest documentary, told from the perspective of organizers, spectators and participants … including one Eddy Merckx.

Winner of over five hundred races, including an unequalled eleven Grand Tours (five Tours of France, five Tours of Italy, and a Tour of Spain), Merckx is regarded as one of the best professional male cyclists of all time – and one of the most stylish. After watching him in that documentary and learning so much about his triumphs, skill and determination, I felt inspired by him. And now he was going to be right there in Look Mum No Hands! I'm not quite sure how I missed the memo as the throngs of fans who had arrived for the filming certainly hadn't!

We weren't going to be on the same segment as each other (Eddy was going to record his interview earlier as he had another public appearance to shoot off to that day) but I *had* to speak to him before he left. Who knew if I would ever be as close to Eddy Merckx – an actual cycling legend and cycling hero of mine – again?

It quite often takes people by surprise when I say that Eddy's a hero of mine – like they're surprised I know who he is and what he's achieved, maybe because I didn't grow up in a cycling-mad household, or maybe because I was riding around on a Pashley and not a beautiful, old, steel road bike … who knows. But it just goes to show that your heroes *really* can be quite different from you.

My moment came when I was ushered over to the section of Look Mum No Hands! that had been cordoned off for the recording. I had to get my microphone and sound pack fitted and tested – and Eddy was sat in that section, chatting with a producer. Obviously much older than the man I watched in that documentary, I knew instantly that it was Eddy. There was no mistaking Merckx: he's still one of the most notable and recognisable professional cyclists after all these years ... and I am not embarrassed to say I also knew it had to be him because he was a handsome young man with drop-dead gorgeous dark hair and swagger ... and still carried that flare and cheeky side-eye look with him, well into his silver years. I grabbed my chance. With my heart making its way up into my throat, I walked over to Eddy to say hello. As I got closer, I started to hesitate with my steps: so what that I was there as a guest as well – what if he doesn't like being bothered by people all the time and this is just as annoying? I wanted to back out, but it was too late – he caught my eye and gestured for me to come over for a chat!

Did I freak out a bit about meeting Eddy? Of course I did! I managed to do a good job of holding that down though. Although we didn't speak for long (I could sense the producer needed to snatch him back for the interview with Graham), he gave me such a warm greeting! I introduced myself, said that I was into cycling and that I really respected and admired him and his cycling and his style (yes, as in his fashion sense from back in the day).

It was lovely that he took the time to say a quick hello. Being beckoned over by Eddy Merckx meant a lot as a) I was getting ready to bolt out of talking to him and b) there was part me of that could feel that ol' devil Imposter Syndrome tapping on my shoulder and telling me that I wasn't supposed to bother this cycling icon. And that I wasn't supposed to be on *The Cycle Show* either.

But I bloody well did belong in that space alongside Eddy and every other guest who was going to be on the show. I had to remind myself of this and not listen to that pest on my shoulder telling me otherwise. And of course always remind myself of the significance of visibility. Starting up VéloCityGirl is what got me there in the first place ... keep it all up, Jools! It meant so much when Eddy was happy to pose for a few pictures with me and sign a LMNH cap for me too – moments that I'll treasure for a very long time indeed.

After that whirlwind meeting and getting mic'd and briefed by the producers for the running order of filming, it was down to business. During our chat on the sofa, Graham asked me questions about how I got back into riding a bike, and what it felt like cycling in London from my perspective, which I was more than happy to talk about. Even though my heart had managed to lodge itself back in my throat with nerves, it was an enjoyable experience, as was having a chat with the guest I was sharing the sofa with – singer and actor Gary Kemp! If you're of a certain vintage, you'll know who Spandau Ballet are and probably remember him and his brother Martin playing the Kray twins back in 1990. Anyway, it turns out that aside from making some of the best pop hits of the 80s, Gary is well into his road cycling!

Once my sofa segment was done, it was off to sit with the cycling group of the week I'd be interviewing: Team Near Naked. They were certainly were not your standard weekend group riders. As I walked into the garden to get set up for filming, the sight of four men – all dressed in white flesh-tone skin suits laid over with anatomical sketches and a fig leaf covering the genital area – greeted me. That was a surprise. There was a very good reason behind the interesting choice of cycling attire: Team Near Naked is a charity dedicated to fighting male cancers. They cycle in that kit to raise awareness and reduce the embarrassment associated with men going to the doctor. Even though what they stood for was something very serious, they were an absolute laugh to chat with. From seeing the funny side of their skin suits to the kind of reactions they get while they're out cycling, it was ace to hear more about them, and be able to share their story and mission on national television.

After all my nerves, I was on top of the world by the end of the morning's recording. It was something I couldn't have dreamed of doing and I was ready to add it to the list of incredible experiences Frankie and VéloCityGirl had opened up for me. I couldn't wait to do a write-up about it on my blog – what an experience to talk about! The absolute whirlwind of going on a prime-time TV show to talk about my cycling journey, getting to meet The Cannibal (and fangirling over him), getting to meet Gary Kemp (and also fangirling over him) and doing a spot of TV presenting too? It was all so unreal. The feedback I got from friends of mine both online and IRL who had watched the first episode blew me away. The nicest comment I got on the blog was from a woman called Annabel:

'I have been following your blog for a couple of months and it was wonderful to see you on TV. You came across very well and I think there is a career there for you! I have been so inspired by blogs like yours that I am going to start my own looking at stylish cyclists in the Leamington Spa area!'

What I *didn't* expect was an email to drop into my inbox the next day asking me to join *The Cycle Show* team as a guest presenter for the rest of the season (and I would subsequently carry on with *The Cycle Show* until it came to an end in 2015). This girl from Canning Town was going to be a TV presenter! This brown face that used to get excited as a child when another brown face appeared on the TV in a positive role (like in *EastEnders* when the Tavernier family moved on to Albert Square in 1990 – that was a BIG deal, man). It was confirmation that what I was doing with VéloCityGirl was making a difference in cycling culture. I was actually making a change and I had to own that with pride and not let my own self-doubts and the doubts from others ruin that.

November 2012: once upon a time I couldn't imagine being in a job where four weeks in I'd wake with my heart racing with excitement every morning; my mind bursting with new information and ideas, feeling more fired-up than I had for seven working years of my life.

That's what my first month at Vulpine – a start-up online cycling apparel company that specialised in high-end casual clothing for life on and off the bike – felt like. This wasn't a dream. Through the power of VéloCityGirl and my blogging about cycling, I was finally in a career that got my blood pumping ... and I was working with people who were so unbelievably passionate about cycling and style – my two loves! I threw myself into it all. Less than two weeks after I'd started, Vulpine held their second Cycling Fete. Their fetes were a day of celebrating all that was good about cycling: they'd invite independent cycling brands from around the country to have their own stall at the fete, where they could sell and display their goods. Family entertainment would be put on during the event too. My role was to arrange the Vulpine stall and make sure everything we needed was there, as well as being the first point of contact for all the brilliant stall-holders taking part. I was determined not to cock the whole thing up before my boss arrived.

I was finally in a role where I felt like I could be truly creative, and not be shot down for thinking aloud at work. The way that I got the position of sales and operations manager for Vulpine was a far cry from any previous jobs I'd applied for. It had all happened via VCG and social media. The MD of the company was a keen cyclist who had been following me online. We became friends on Twitter via a shared love of cycling and fashion. After months of speaking online, we finally met up in real life over a drink in a pub called The Garrison in Bermondsey. Getting on like a house on fire, I didn't realise that this was the beginning of a job interview. When we met up again a few weeks later for dinner, I was asked if I'd be interested in joining the start-up as the first official employee as the sales and operations manager. It was a huge risk – I had a secure job working in admissions at UEL – and there was no guarantee that Vulpine was going to survive through its first twelve months. But I just knew in my heart that I had to do this – I had to take this chance. It was the dream job – working in cycling and fashion and being able to make my mark on that world? That was an opportunity I couldn't miss. I'd be changing the cycling landscape, which excited me. Shaking up the old guard of what cycling is, all via the power of my tiny corner of the Internet seemed crazy! But it was true – my little digital home was having an influence and I had to run with it.

Getting to know new cycling-mad people was awesome: from meeting and answering queries from customers, talking to journalists and working with the stockists – it was a lot of work but a lot of fun. I also shared another passion with my new colleagues: changing the face of cycling. When I started my blog, I talked about a cycle revolution. At Vulpine, I was working with a team who were singing from the same hymn sheet: it doesn't matter what you ride and how you ride it. No cliques, no snobbery – none of that. Friendliness, all-encompassing, welcoming, passionate cycling was the thing.

I couldn't wait to see what the next year had up its sleeve. 2012 had been a whirlwind for me in cycling – stepping back and looking at it all, I couldn't believe how far I'd come. Two years prior, I'd started a blog. It was all about getting back on a bike after a ten-year absence from cycling, getting that sense of freedom back and keeping it chic on two wheels. Now here I was, the 'new girl' in the office for the first time in a long time and a whole new woman to the one I'd been before. 2013 had a lot to live up to ...

The Bike Life for Me

Nine months into my cycling-life change, everything on the surface was going incredibly well: VéloCityGirl was going from strength to strength and professionally I was thriving in my role at Vulpine. But something else that had lain almost dormant in my brain started ticking over. When all of this positive stuff started kicking off, I found myself really thinking about certain things around me – or rather becoming more conscious of the lack of certain things that I wasn't seeing on my 'fabulous' cycling journey, especially when I started working within the industry. I'd kind of clocked them before, but these things became even more obvious when I was looking from the inside, out. It's not that I was socially unconscious during my teenage years on a bike, but the groups I was now rolling with as an adult were completely different, which was no bad thing at all. The friendships and connections I started making now were much more diverse, and went way beyond the 'traditional'

images of what cycling is and who supposedly does it. As a woman and as a black woman working within that industry, I became a lot more aware of the social and cultural differences that existed, and began to feel there were many more missing stories from that mix. Some of the other spaces that I started to occupy were opening my eyes even wider to this.

A space I never expected to be in was on BBC *Newsnight*. Certainly not twice. *Newsnight* was that serious current affairs programme my dad always watched when he wasn't on the night shift at Ford. Going on *Newsnight* always looked like a terrifying position to be in: sat across a desk from Jeremy Paxman, being mercilessly grilled on whatever the current affairs hot topic was. Thankfully when I went on for the first time it wasn't with him, nor was it live in the studio. In the summer of 2013, BBC The Hague correspondent Anna Holligan asked if she could interview me as she was cycling the two-hundred-mile journey from The Hague to Westminster to examine the differences between cycling culture in the Netherlands and London. My first thought when I read her email was W*TF? Did she actually mean me?!*

It was a year after Team GB's Olympic success at the Velodrome – a time when cycling was hitting peak popularity in the UK. That local Olympic buzz even rubbed off on me and I was already two years into riding, so of course I was up for evangelising the gospel about the beauty of biking it in my home city.

We met on a sunny Saturday afternoon at Broadway Market in Hackney, one of my favourite destinations to ride to in London. It was also a lovely setting to show off some of the best of East London. With the bonus of cycling café Lock 7 located there, we could film part of the interview in relevant surroundings too. The piece was pretty relaxed: a tiny crew filmed us riding our bikes and chatting and then continuing the interview over lunch, both scenarios allowing me the luxury of not being a total bag of nerves.

The following Wednesday, I watched the show with my mum from behind a cushion on my sofa, waiting for the cycling feature to appear like it was the monster in a horror movie. Although it was all pre-recorded and would be heavily edited, I was still scared of looking and sounding like an absolute tit on the telly. The feature finally came up and for the first five minutes the joys of cycling culture in the Netherlands were broadcast to homes all around the country: parents riding with their children in baby-seats on the backs of their bikes or in big, beautiful 'bakfiets' (cargo bikes); commuters riding with one hand on the handlebars and the other feeding apples into their faces. Then there was a focus on the Netherlands' dedicated cycling infrastructure and bike lanes, which took riders past old, romantic-looking windmills; how cycling worked so well alongside public transport – including the fact that most of the trains have low-step access on the platforms and spaces to stick your bike – and how riding a bike was an ordinary, everyday part of life for the people of the country. It was glorious and reminded me of how much I loved riding in Berlin ... and why heading to the Netherlands was something I desperately needed to do.

How the hell was this going to measure up against riding in London and what I'd said about it? All I could recall about what I'd said was something vague about a cycling revolution happening in the city and how it's not all doom and gloom riding here.

Then Anna and her Omafiets – a hand-built Dutch utility bicycle, also known as a 'Dutch Granny-style bike' with back-pedal brakes (also known as 'coaster brakes' – these are a special rear hub which performs two functions: it allows the bicycle to roll without forcing the pedals to turn and it's also a brake, operated by turning the pedals backwards) – arrived at

Harwich International Ferry Port in Essex. Her adventure from there towards the Houses of Parliament was a world away from the previous narrative: hoisting her heavy bike up on to a train, where the step was too high and the carriage had no dedicated spaces for cycles, then arriving at Stratford Station and cycling straight into horrendous traffic and the notorious CS2 Cycle Superhighway in Bow, and finally almost getting edged out of the blue lane by a flatbed recovery truck coming towards her.

My heart sank. If she was riding the CS2, that meant she was on her way to meet me – so perhaps I'd not been edited out of the whole thing.

'Oh shit,' I thought to myself, waiting for the sofa to swallow me whole, 'I'm actually going to be in this, aren't I?' The 'Anna-in-busy-London-traffic' clip then cut to a pre-recorded interview with then Mayor of London, Boris Johnson, at a press conference for the inaugural RideLondon–Surrey Classic. He gave a soundbite about his plans to get London to not be a 'great fleet of people with their heads down, wearing Lycra, who feel that they've got to get from A to B as fast as they can' and instead adopt the same relaxed attitudes, cycling culture, and infrastructure as the Dutch.

There was of course a slight irony to him talking about this while promoting a one-day men's professional road-race event.

And then, came a, 'Whoooo! Oh gosh, look nah, Julie, it's you!' from Mamma Vélo. I peered from behind the cushion. The Boris piece segued into me riding across the screen with Anna, laughing and smiling on our Dutch-style bikes, with a vibrant and busy Broadway Market as our backdrop. Then I appeared on screen sat in Lock 7, credited as 'Lady Vélo – Cycling Blogger', giving my best 'cycling is great, it's not all bad but needs some changes' vox pop.

I breathed a sigh of relief when the segment came to an end. Mum was still proudly beaming about the whole thing. Ian texted me the moment it was over to tell me how brilliantly I'd come across. I breathed out again.

It was then that everything else we'd discussed that afternoon of filming flooded back to me. What *hadn't* been shown was when I had talked about this cycling revolution not just being about physical city changes and money being put into building better infrastructure to get more people using their bikes. I'd talked about the social and cultural changes that were needed *within* cycling to get, or at the very least encourage, people from marginalised backgrounds on bikes, especially considering how culturally diverse somewhere London and the United Kingdom is as a whole. You can't really shoe-horn all of that into a short segment like that, especially if it doesn't quite fit the narrative of the feature. It was so disappointing that it had been cut out though. Those elements were so important to the picture of cycling as a whole, but it was a part of the story that didn't get the space that it deserved so badly. I knew that I needed to find more spaces in which to really talk about those issues.

After that segment ended, I was able to put down my protective sofa-cushion shield and my phone pinged with a notification from Twitter. And then it pinged again with another . . . and another . . . and another . . . and another. This continued for what seemed like an eternity, and I found myself wanting to reach for that plush sofa shield once more. I'd realised the moment I saw 'Lady Vélo' and not 'Jools Walker' flash up as my name on screen that my social media handle had just been exposed to a much bigger audience than I could have ever imagined – including keyboard warriors and online trolls.

I'd come across some of them before when I did my first stint on *The Cycle Show*: 'Why doesn't she just cock-off on her Pashley and take her London-fashion-cycling shit with her?' was the funniest and cleanest of the abuse I'd found in a thread about my appearance on the show. There was also the fact I had the 'audacity' to be on the same episode as cycling legend Eddy Merckx, and that I'd dared to talk about 'pretend cycling'. I'm not going to lie – I was bloody gutted when I read that. I had to resist the knee-jerk urge to create an account on that forum so I could retort with a killer comeback. That wouldn't have solved anything – feeding the trolls never does. I knew I needed to develop a thicker skin and conserve my energy for bigger and better things, and use comments like that as the fuel to propel myself higher.

I was expecting abuse along those lines all over again; especially given the wider audience this had gone out to. I picked up my phone, and started to scroll through the notifications, preparing myself for the onslaught of Twitter-nasty, but there wasn't any, not that evening, anyway. Unbeknown to me, the next day, Anna's piece was published on the BBC *News Magazine* website as a stand-alone article, with the whole film of us talking included. More people kept on seeing it so the audience kept on getting wider – people who may not have caught *Newsnight* could still pick up the film. Days later, warm and kind messages were still coming in, either through Twitter or people emailing me via the blog. Messages about the love of cycling and other people's stories of how they got into it made my heart glow.

It was about representation, showing that cycling really isn't just an activity for the super-serious, middle-aged, speedy-cycling-dude-kitted-head-to-toe-in-Lycra. There I was, proving that us lovers of a slow cycle were out there too. There were other messages coming though which were hitting me pretty hard, messages from other women of colour saying what a positive impact it was to see a young black woman on a platform like the BBC talking about being into cycling and enjoying it. Those messages had a recurring theme that I could identify with all too well. There were women who were thinking about getting on a bike but were unsure if it would be a space for them; there were others who were already riding and had been questioning if they wanted to continue; others had stopped and were unsure about taking the steps to getting back on the saddle. And then there were those who were straight-up hyped to just see another woman of colour out there. New connections were made, new friendships were forged, and I was given even more food for thought on stuff that had been lurking in my mind from the moment I had swung my leg over Frankie in 2010.

It's not that I had ideas above my station – I couldn't quite see myself as a one-woman revolutionary who was going to single-handedly turn the whole cycling industry on its head, but having seen that impact I wanted more than ever to use any platforms I owned, or any bigger ones I was given access to, to speak up and help amplify the voices of others who felt like they didn't have the arena for their stories. VéloCityGirl came with the absolute fear of exposing myself to bad vibes and negative feedback, but my heart was telling me that disruption is what makes progress and being visible was a positive-disruptor step to take. The faces I didn't see cycling during my teenage years almost certainly contributed to me getting off a bike at eighteen and I didn't want that for the next generation of cyclists.

#BlackGirlMagic

If you can't see yourself in this industry and you can't see yourself in that world, why in the world would you magically have this idea that you can be a part of it?

Ayesha McGowan

Visibility is key. As Marie C. Wilson says: 'you can't be what you can't see.' Seeing someone like you showing you what's possible can make a world of difference. Ayesha McGowan is an amazing example in action of why visibility is so important. I first came across Ayesha via Twitter and her powerful blog 'A Quick Brown Fox', which she launched in 2015 to chart her mission to 'add colour and numbers to women's cycling'. Ayesha embarked on a journey to become the first female professional African-American competitive road cyclist. At the time of writing this, there still isn't one in the United States. Or the rest of the world. There hasn't been one in the history of the sport. That should have you shaking your head in disbelief.

Ayesha's drive to become the first came from having an amazing time in her first amateur racing season in 2014, while trying to find *anyone* who looked like her.

'I was trying to figure out who looks like me, who had done this before and how far have they gone, and what had been accomplished, because you don't really hear so much about bike racing in the regular world. It's just not something I felt like I could talk about so I was just curious,' she said when I spoke to her in 2017.

While asking around and doing her research, Ayesha couldn't find a single African-American woman who had gone pro. This understandably took her aback. 'It was 2014 and I just didn't understand . . . almost everybody rides a bike, and at some point in the history of cycling this must have already been done. And it hadn't.'

Ayesha had reached a point in her life where she decided that she could be the change to the status quo that she was looking for. Deciding to fill that role was a decision that came to her quickly, and something to this day that she has never regretted, feeling compelled to do it. For Ayesha, representation is super important and this was an area where she felt she could make an impact and create representation where there wasn't any. As she puts it, this was 'literally like an overnight decision'.

This knee-jerk feeling was something that I could relate to from my own experiences of getting back into cycling. I was fully aware that while I was looking within the cycling community in relation to marketing, branding and even at elite level, the impact of not seeing anyone you could identify with or anyone you could recognise yourself in was devastating. I could appreciate what a shock to the system it could be going into cycling professionally – albeit at a totally different level to Ayesha – and not seeing any representation. Ayesha had also noticed this in the melting pot that is New York: 'That city is *very* diverse. There are all kinds of people everywhere and I could not understand why this little pocket of NYC that I was living and cycling in was pretty much untouched. There were maybe one or two other black women that raced – that was it. And there were quite a few women racing.'

It's impossible not to feel empowered by Ayesha and what she's doing. Following her blog and social media channels where she keeps a running record of her pursuit is like watching one of the most kick-ass cycling documentaries ever. And it's not just everyday people like me whose attention she's captured. Big brands have noticed Ayesha, her following, and the influence she possesses. She calls out bullshit where she sees it, and is open about the highs and lows she encounters on her mission.

'I've had companies ask to work with me, and literally the words they used were "What do you need to work with us?" The top thing I asked for was a voice, a seat at the table, an opportunity to be in the room when you're making these decisions for your branding, your marketing, your women … *your women of colour.* And they came back to me, completely ignoring that part. They offered money but no seat at the table or a voice and I turned it down because that's not why I'm doing this. There's not a lot of money in bike racing – it's just not something you do if you want to be a wealthy person! I'm doing this because I care about it and it matters to me. Yeah, I need money to live and eat and pay the bills but I'm not going to sell my integrity because someone wants to pay me to do that. That's not something that I'm OK with.'

It isn't always like that though, as Ayesha points out: 'For the most part everyone's been super encouraging – I've spoken to and get messages from people all the time that are like, "You got me to get on a bike," which is amazing!' Ayesha even got a message from another woman of colour, telling her she was the inspiration behind this person doing a swim across the English Channel – completely removed from the world of two wheels, but stuff like that embodies the importance of representation.

While being vocal and visible is essential to changing the system, it undoubtedly comes with its own pitfalls, like those Internet trolls I mentioned before, or being labelled the 'angry black woman' – something I've encountered on a few occasions when all I'm trying to do is open up dialogue.

'I feel like if you're black and you have an opinion that's *always* going to be the reason you have that opinion ... forget the fact that maybe *something is just wrong* and you're speaking up because maybe something should just be done about it. It's not that I'm angry and frustrated – I am *also* those things – but being a black woman is not the sole basis of my frustrations.'

There is no denying that it can be exhausting and hard to cut above that kind of noise and get someone to really hear you. As Ayesha highlights, 'If they have already decided that you're just an angry person and whatever is coming out of your mouth is completely irrational, they have also already decided that they shouldn't waste their time with it. That is what makes people angry, that is what makes me angry.'

As well as being labelled the 'angry black women' in conversations about change in cycling, there is also the curse of tokenism – yet another thing we've both witnessed and had similar experiences of. Tokenism instead of representation is something that intersects across different groups in cycling. It's easy to spot brands bringing in 'that black woman who rides bikes' or 'that older woman who blogs about cycling' and slotting them into the place that suits their messaging at the time and leaving it as that, instead of actually offering a seat at the table to have real conversations and help make changes. This frustrating phenomenon is something that still desperately needs to be addressed properly in cycling.

Wheeling out diversity for diversity's sake doesn't make for a positive or a legacy change – what *does* affect change is normalising inclusivity. When you're a 'face' being used in various campaigns or when brands reach out to you to be involved in a superficial way without offering you and others the chance to *be* a fundamental part of what they are doing – this is another barrier to entry to potential change.

'Wanting to be part of whatever they're actually doing is what I would like – to have a voice *in* there, to have a say in how it's done and what is portrayed and not just be the token black person for your marketing campaign, which I feel like is a very fine line to walk,' says Ayesha. Because to some extent there isn't a lot of representation in the industry, it can be easy to end up being *that* token black person for that moment (and looking back at some of the projects I've been involved with, I can recognise myself as having walked that fine line between opportunity and exploitation). But along with Ayesha, I can also find humour in the madness of it all and joke about it: 'You open a magazine or you open any website and you'll see *maybe one black person* in a picture or maybe you'll see another black person, but ... *it's the same black person* ... I've checked! I check all the damned time and I feel like there are so many black people in the world that at this point I don't care if you just find someone else and get them to ride a bike! Stick them in some of your clothes! I just want to see that representation and that makes such an impact.'

After we shared similar experiences with each other about being *that person*, something she said stuck with me. She says that flipping that kind of situation on its head can be done for the greater good. 'If I can at all be a voice and direct the company into a space where eventually it won't be tokenising, that is what I'm going to do. I feel like my biggest asset is my voice. My biggest asset is my understanding of both worlds: the cycling world and the non-cycling world and how those two can merge.'

Tokenism most certainly doesn't equate to representation, and even though so much power emanates from marginalised groups creating spaces for ourselves in cycling, I still believe that change has to come from higher up. Perhaps some would disagree with me saying that or find it a bit of a contradiction, as I champion the mantra, 'If you're not seeing it, go out and be it!' a lot. But as much as we can create these spaces, recognition for the need of change must come from higher up the cycling food chain, so it actually starts trickling down.

One of the most common ways companies try to reach out to wider audiences is through the use of brand ambassadors. These are people who are hired by a company to represent their brand in a positive and 'welcoming' light and by doing so, help to increase brand awareness and essentially sales (everything always boils down to sales!). As an ambassador is meant to embody the identity of the company in demeanour and appearance, if a company happens to be set in its ways and continues to follow the same tropes about what a 'traditional cyclist' looks like, they'll inevitably run into the problems of lack of representation and exclude the very people they should be reaching out to. What's even more alarming than this unconscious bias is first-hand experience of knowing that some companies consciously won't venture outside of their standard demographic for fear of damaging their brand. This was yet another experience Ayesha and I both had in common – companies wanting to 'tap into' a minority audience but not have anyone who represented it on their actual platforms. I'll never forget the time a company wanted me to work with them on a cycling project and asked if I had any other cycling friends who could be part of it too – only to be told by the project manager that some of my suggestions would make their campaign 'look a bit too urban'.

Ayesha continued this theme: 'It seems like sometimes companies are afraid to use their own platforms to amplify these voices … so they reach out to folks like us and have us do it for them: use their products and have us running the competitions, giveaways and stuff like that on our blogs – but they aren't also representing us in their marketing and branding. They're like, "We're just going to see how *your* audience reacts to us supporting you from a distance and *then* we'll see what happens from there."'

Of course there are cycling brands out there who are recognising the issue, and on occasion you do see some of them doing it differently and shaking up the usual aesthetic in advertising, but as Ayesha points out, it still has a way to go. She makes the important point that *equity*, not just equality, is the key: 'There's been a lot of new promising [advertising] campaigns coming out, and I strongly believe that the change will happen from within the industry – the industry has the power. They need to do it, but I don't think that "equality" is going to just appear one day. I think equity is the answer *and* the driving force.'

With equality, it's assumed that everyone will benefit from the same support framework – so, essentially this means treating everyone the same. Although it aims to promote fairness, equality can only work if everyone starts from the same place. Equity actively moves everyone closer to success by levelling the playing field – this may seem unfair, but without equity, patterns of discrimination are difficult to see, making it harder for the causes of inequity (the systemic barriers) to be removed.

On how the industry can address equality versus equity,

Ayesha explains, 'I think the industry needs to hire more people of colour, more women of colour and have them in the room making these decisions on a company level, so it's not just a bunch of middle-aged white men looking around trying to figure it out! Why not just *ask the people you're trying to reach*? Unless you're *not* trying to reach them ...'

Amongst all the highs and lows Ayesha encounters on her journey, something that is always guaranteed is her dedication to her mission. As she explains, it hasn't been easy and she has made plenty of sacrifices. 'This [journey] has required a lot of life changes. Lots of talking to myself in self-reflective moments about what I can and cannot do – be that having to not do social things and having to say no to going out with family and friends, or *really* forcing myself to get out of bed even if I'm not a morning person.'

But what is it that makes the journey so worth it for her? Spurring her to keep going even when the going gets tough? For Ayesha, it's far more than just her professional achievements giving her that boost. 'I'm mostly inspired by the people that are impacted by what I'm doing – people that feel like they're being represented and that something is happening for *them*. Those folks who decide, "Oh ... I'm going to get on a bike!" or are like, "I saw you doing your thing and that made me want to do X or Y" – I think that's really cool and it encourages me to keep going! I think to myself, if I reached that person, how many more people can I reach? I've had high school friends that I haven't spoken to in years hit me up on Facebook and they're like "Hey! I bought a bike because of you!" and I'm like "YES!" And it's a great feeling – that's such a big drive for me.'

Ayesha's determination and enthusiasm is contagious (and I defy you *not* to feel that energy while following her incredible journey). What she is doing and attempting to achieve is uplifting, and gives me real hope for change. It's still shocking and disappointing to be saying the words 'hope for change' in 2019 when it comes to women of colour within the cycling industry. There will be a day when seeing a black woman in a professional peloton isn't considered an anomaly. There will be a day when the gate-keepers are not all middle-aged white men, and equality and equity is a universal standard. It may be years before this happens, but Ayesha is committed to inspiring as many women as possible and disrupting the homogenous status quo with her own brand of black girl magic. 'My biggest mission is representation. It's happening, but I'm still on this journey. I'm not a pro *yet*, but if I can show the image of a female African-American pro racer and open the doors, then others can do it too.'

Something Old, Something New

Once upon a time one bike was more than enough. But then I *needed* to get an old runaround for spending time in Southsea. And then, three years later, I fell hard for another beauty of a bike. There was no reasoning this time – I just *had* to have it. Perhaps I could get away with laying the blame squarely at the feet of the industry I was now working in; I was exposed to different kinds of bikes all day, every day. It was making the thirst I had for bikes even worse and frequently had me looking around my house thinking, 'I'm sure I've got space for just one more in here.'

I'd first laid eyes on my latest obsession at Bespoked – a bike show in Bristol that features frame builders from around the world and beautiful hand-built bicycles. I was working there with Vulpine, and even before I left London I knew I'd end up drooling over all the bikes on display. But there was one brand in particular that got my attention from the moment we got there, and it wasn't just because they were setting their stand up right opposite ours. I'd never come across the brand before but their bikes were so unusual. ColourBolt was the name of the brand. They specialised in urban bikes with an understated design.

I finally got to quiz Jay Pond-Jones, the founder of the brand and a total bike enthusiast, during one of my tea breaks. He explained that each one of their bikes was designed with a specific aesthetic or practical purpose in mind. Take their 'Scarred Black': a black mirror-polished steel frame with silvery scratches all over it that will scratch more as you ride, making the design and your ride aesthetic come together. The one I had my eye on, though, was the 'Ratty Black'. Aside from being a step-through it was nothing like the other two bikes I owned, or what I assumed I'd usually go for.

First up, it was a single speed. I'd not owned a single-speed bike since the days of the Burner and I was so used to riding with gears, I couldn't imagine how my legs would cope going up hills or even the Canning Town Flyover (*if* this bike was going to become mine). But of course there are benefits that come with having a single-speed bike – like the simplicity of it all. As it has no gears, you don't need to think about changing any when you're riding. I often get moments of panic on road bikes when it comes to shifting gears for a climb or descent and worry about getting it wrong. There is also the element of relatively easy maintenance on a bike with no gears. With less moving parts than a multi-speed bike, it's got less stuff to potentially go wrong on it: no derailleurs (the system commonly used on bikes, consisting of a chain, multiple sprockets of different sizes, and a mechanism to move the chain from one sprocket to another) and no gear shifters. Perhaps my old Burner was better than Stephanie's fancy Falcon after all.

The black Ratty was super low-key in design, but stunning

with it. The frame was a Columbus Spirit tube set that had been finished in a rough, hammered black texture (it looked a bit like those old battered wrought-iron railings you'd see around London). Columbus is the biggest and most famous steel-tubing manufacturer in Italy, known worldwide for their extremely light and well-manufactured products. Even though carbon-fibre frames are some of the lightest you can get, steel frames are well renowned and still loved for the responsive ride feel that they give. If you spend enough time around cyclists and hear them using the term 'steel is real', it's a bit of a nod to that. The black front fork was a Columbus Minimal – a carbon-fibre fork that was a perfect match to the light-weight Columbus frame. Carbon also has more flex, so improves comfort over the stiffer and heavier aluminium forks.

There were no decals either. Aside from the classic red and white Columbus dove logo on the fork, the single red chain-ring bolt (hence the name 'Colourbolt'), and the silver Exustar BMX Pedals (which look a bit like the Givenchy logo and that *really* pleases me), there was nothing loud on this otherwise monochrome build. For someone who usually lives for loud, the beauty of the understated design really got me.

I didn't get a chance to take Ratty out for a test ride. No – scratch that – I didn't *take the chance* to take Ratty out for a test ride. I didn't dare, in case it resulted in a little something extra in the back of the van on our way back to London. I mean, what was I going to do with a third bike anyway? I didn't actually *need* it, I told myself, while the devil on my shoulder whispered that having something lighter than Frankie when riding around London when not needing to carry a load of stuff with me would be nice (Frankie has always been my pack-horse of a bike thanks to her big front basket and panniers). I *already* had one large bike in the house (again, that little voice mentioned that Frankie lived in the downstairs cupboard, totally out of the way, and there was probably enough space in the spare bedroom for a sleek little bike to slot into). Maybe it wouldn't be that mad after all to get another one. Maybe.

Three weeks later, I was working at SpinLDN, another four-day bike show, with Vulpine and was back in the company of Colourbolt. Ratty was still with them. It hadn't been sold in that space of time. Orders for versions of it to be made may have been taken – usually at events like Bespoked the bikes on show are either custom builds that have been made for clients or are sample models for potential customers to view and place orders from seeing the build and spec – but *that* bike hadn't been bought. I was (not so secretly) thrilled to see it was still around. I managed to resist for two days, but Jay knew I was itching to have a go on that bike. SpinLDN had actually incorporated a mini-track area into the show for visitors to have a ride on the bikes, and Jay handed Ratty over to me so I could go for a spin. I couldn't believe how much lighter and faster it was compared to my other two-wheeled companions. Ratty felt so good and the size of the frame was a perfect fit. Of course it was. I reluctantly handed the bike back to Jay and thanked him for the chance to whizz around the track.

On the final day of the show, I went over to see Jay and his team for one last chat and to admire Ratty. That would be the last time I'd see her gleaming on the Colourbolt stand before everything got packed away. We compared stories of how our trading weekends had gone: we'd made brilliant sales on our stand, and Jay had taken a few bespoke orders and actually made a physical sale at the show. Of course, it was Ratty. A bike that gorgeous, who wasn't going to take that home with them? If you lived in the city, it would be the perfect light, zippy number to ride home on. I glanced over at Ratty every now and then on that Sunday, with the brown 'SOLD' ticket swinging from her handlebars.

Final checks and tweaks needed to be done to Ratty before the new owner could cycle off on her. Handlebars and saddle height at exactly the right level. Tyres fully pumped and wheels checked. Brakes in full working order. The simplicity of a single speed and not having to check lots of moving parts at its finest.

'It's all perfect – you all set to go?' I heard Jay say.

'Yeah, I'm looking forward to see how my legs survive climbing up the Canning Town Flyover on this!' I replied, sat atop my new baby with a ridiculously massive grin on my face.

It was now summer 2014 and I'd been blogging as Lady Vélo for four years. In that time, I was immersed further into cycling culture, and was hearing more about events that happened in the cycling calendar. There was one that kept cropping up in conversation: Eroica Britannia. It was hard *not* to have heard about it now I was in the industry and I was running in circles of friends who loved taking part in a good old sportive.

It was a ride that sounded like no other. Founded in 1997, L'Eroica is an Italian sportive with various routes – the shortest being 46 kilometres and the longest coming in at 209 kilometres – which takes place every October across the Strade Bianchi (the white gravel roads) of Tuscany. The event harks back to a vintage age of cycling. Think of the old days of road races on non-asphalt surfaces: nothing but miles of uneven cobbles, gnarly gravel and relentless hard-packed stone. Riding across roads like that on a steel bicycle with no let-up for hours was a struggle. But if you toughed it out and completed it, that made you a hero – hence the name. L'Eroica's big pull is that it is *strictly vintage*: no Lycra and definitely no modern road bikes. The intention of the sportive is to celebrate a golden era of cycling and raise awareness of the traditional Strade Bianchi, keeping it as close as possible to the style of the time is a respectful nod to its history, and you get a real feel for what that era was like. Out go the technical Lycra bib shorts and super-geared carbon-fibre bikes, and in come the woollen jersey and shorts combos and vintage steel road-racing bikes (specifically, models built up to 1987).

Granted, it sounds kinda hellish on your legs and arse from the 'lack of modern comforts' perspective, but L'Eroica quickly grew in popularity: what began as a ride of just ninety-two people has mushroomed into one of the most popular sportives ever. In 2014 five thousand people from around the world subscribed to take part. Four years into my cycling life, my interest in doing it was certainly piqued, but I didn't quite feel up to taking on the Tuscan hills just yet.

The team behind L'Eroica had announced they would be launching a British version of the sportive – 'Eroica Britannia' – in the Peak District, with three different routes. As part of their big launch, they invited me to take part in the inaugural ride and cover it on VCG. I'd never done a ride on that scale or even tried climbing 'proper hills' and I damn well knew the Peak District wasn't going to be a #CoffeeCycleSaturday or a gentle ride in the park. The only mass participation ride I'd done was the Tweed Run but that was on the pretty-much-flat London roads, with similar riders at a relatively sedate pace. But the whole thing had piqued my interest. I was learning more about the wider sport all the time, and had marvelled at the daring nature of other cyclists I knew who took part in large-scale events and sportives. Although Eroica Britannia wasn't a race, it would see me riding at a big sportive as a relative newbie with potentially thousands of other people who knew exactly what they were doing. To add to that I wouldn't have Ian as my 'support bike'. Was it a challenge? Was it an absolutely massive one? Yes. What was my answer? A big fat *yes*. I knew there would be quite a bit of work to do for this one, and that's what made taking part in Eroica Britannia so much more appealing. I wanted to see if I could do a 30-mile sportive over the hills of the Peak District. Saying 'yes' to doing Eroica Britannia straight away was an indication of how much my confidence on a bike had grown, and I wanted to run with that feeling for ever.

I upped my daily cycling intake (longer rides to work, and riding almost everywhere I possibly could – the shops, #CoffeeCycleSaturdays, errands for Mum – you name it, I did it) as my way of training as I was not mentally ready to suddenly try and take on Richmond Park or the Box Hill Olympic Road Race route! I just needed to ride more to build up and be ready for the day.

The event was a weekend affair, so I headed up to Derbyshire on the Friday for the start of my 'Great British Adventure', filled with excitement for Eroica Britannia. On my solo train journey up, I was still pondering how completely different the actual bike ride would be for me. There is no denying it – cycling thirty miles over terrain I'd never experienced before on a bike that wasn't mine did excite me, but it also had my brain ticking over like mad. I was eager to get on the trails and do it!

There was word on Twitter that fellow cycling friends of mine would be riding Eroica Britannia, so it was brilliant to start bumping into familiar faces on the connecting train before I'd even arrived in Bakewell. Good friends of mine Jenni Gwiazdowski (founder of London Bike Kitchen), Caren Hartley (the frame builder behind Hartley Cycles) and Kelly Miller (originally a fellow cycle-style blogger and now a high-end luxury leather jacket designer in Paris) were all taking part. They had formed Team CTC and were cycling on behalf of Cycling UK. Seeing them all and talking about how exciting it was to be taking part in the first ever Eroica Britannia got me even more hyped. Their enthusiasm for the weekend was infectious! We went our separate ways at Matlock as they had their own bikes with them and were going to cycle to the campsite. Part of me wished I was doing that too, but without a suitable bike for the event that wasn't going to happen.

Eroica Britannia wasn't just about the big ride on the Sunday – there was a three-day family-friendly festival that accompanied the sportive, which I would be checking out to report on for *The Cycle Show*. When I arrived at the venue and hopped out of the cab, it was like stepping into the biggest and most magical fairground I'd ever seen. The festival was based in the Bakewell Showground, which was surrounded by the lush rolling hills of the Peak District. The grounds had been transformed from a great big green field into an outdoor arena of pure fun. There were big top tents dotted all around, in a multitude of colours, all bursting with activities and talks to check out. Lights and bunting trailed between each tent, and of course there were bikes everywhere. Stalls selling almost everything 'vintage bike' that you could imagine: beautiful, old, steel road bicycles, woollen jerseys and cycling shorts, metal bidons to carry your water in, and more bike parts and components than I dared count. So many people were there too – all happily buzzing around the stalls, checking out what the festival had to offer. And the vintage style that was on display from almost everyone was breathtakingly beautiful to watch.

Getting sucked into the amazing atmosphere of the festival was also a welcome distraction from the nerves that were setting in about the ride. I started thinking about Team CTC – the mini-cycling team that Jenni had formed – and wondered if I should have made plans to be part of a group of riders instead of going it alone. Although I was as excited as hell about taking part, I was also pondering how completely different the actual bike ride would be for me. However, I was still eager to get on the trails of the Peak District – the challenge of pushing myself to try something like this would surely be part of the fun of it all.

I had never been to the Peak District before, so getting to know that part of the country and why L'Eroica had chosen it was high on my agenda. In the Italian L'Eroica, the riders sample the local food and drink on the mountainous routes, with stops featuring cheeses, cured meats and wines. It turned out the hilly Peak District was the perfect location to recreate the ride. With its beautiful terrain and a classic British twist on the food, the area was set to match Tuscany.

To kick things off on the Saturday, Gian Bohan – a Sheffield restaurateur who took part in L'Eroica in Italy and loved it so much he bought the licensing for it to the Peak District – held a Brooks England breakfast at The Old Original Bakewell Pudding Shop. There was a chance to sample some of the local delights that would feature on the route stops, which of course included the famous Bakewell pudding. I was fully schooled by the locals on the difference between a Bakewell pudding and a Bakewell tart (it's a highly contentious issue – the types of pastry and fillings used are key) and promised to never confuse the two again. I began to feel more confident about the ride and even dream that maybe one day I'd brave the Italian Job.

Festival fun aside, the first part of the serious business came on the Saturday afternoon: meeting and getting acquainted with the bike I'd be doing the ride on. I didn't own a suitable pre-1987 bike (the Raleigh Twenty definitely wasn't the one for a ride like this) and even though the rules were a little more relaxed than the Tuscan event, I wanted to keep with tradition, so didn't bring Frankie with me. I'd never been on a *really* old bicycle before, so was up for giving that a go and getting as close to the L'Eroica experience as possible. I'd also thought to myself, 'How different could it be?' It was just riding a bike, which I'd been doing for the last four years. The organisers hooked me up with an Italian gentleman called Stefano who was running one of the vintage bike stalls at the festival. He provided me with an old French road bike that would be my steed for the event. Along with that, he gave me a speedy lesson on how to ride it. And this is where the fun and games began.

His English was limited and my Italian non-existent, so we communicated via the universal language of cycling: pointing at components and making bike-related gestures in the hope that we understood each other. It was tricky at first, but I worked out Stefano was telling me that the brakes levers (the handles that you pull on to apply the brakes) on the bike were on opposite sides to what I was used to. In the UK, the left lever is the rear brake and the right lever is for the front brake; on this French bike, it was the other way round. A little bit of trivia for you – this is related to the country the bike is made in, which side of the road you drive on and hand signalling: for people in Continental Europe, North America and everywhere else that drives on the right, the brakes would be 'the other way round'.

I spent the rest of the afternoon practising how to ride the bike in the safety of the Bakewell Showground, trying to get acquainted with the feel of the bike, its European brake system and the metal toe-clips on the pedals. A toe-clip (sometimes called a cage) is a thin metal or plastic attachment to the front of a pedal. It gets its name from being shaped like a toe and is designed to stop your shoe from slipping off the pedal while cycling (they are especially good for climbing). For further security some have a strap (usually made of leather on the more old-skool ones) and buckle system on them which goes around or through both the pedal and the toe-clip, which you can tighten around your shoe.

I also had to get used to the gear-shift levers being located on the down tube rather than the handlebars, meaning I would have to take one of my hands off the bars and reach down and change my gears instead of just being able to do it on the handlebars. There was a hell of a lot to get used to! Although I couldn't do anything about the brakes or gears, I *could* get rid of the toe-clips – I'd noticed that they could be unscrewed from the pedals. I wasn't ready to start strapping my feet on to an unfamiliar bike and forget I'd need to unbuckle before coming to a stop – there *really* was enough to remember already on this thing. I wheeled the bike back to Stefano to stow for the evening and gestured to him for the cages to be removed. I could tell by the look on his face – and his animated gestures – that he was saying something along the lines of, 'You're mad to take these off, Jools!' but he did it, which was a relief. Much as I wanted to keep it 'real' for the ride, I also wanted to get through it without freaking out. I needed to relax for the rest of that evening and headed back to the comfort of the B&B I was staying in – after all, it was an early start the next morning and I had thirty miles of uncharted territory ahead of me. It might have been the 'short' route, but it was enough for me to feel a little bit apprehensive turning in that night.

Sunday morning. The day of the ride had come round and I was a bag of nerves getting ready for what was ahead. A strong believer in omens, I took getting '1942' as my rider number a lucky sign – it's my dad's year of birth. The moment I collected my registration pack and saw those digits I decided this ride *had* to be something good. Rolling out of the showground and over the start line, I had hope in my heart and my legs I would become my own hero on the Peaks. The first part of the ride was gentle enough – smooth roads, stunning countryside, and pretty much every person I ended up riding alongside was up for a chat. Which is when I realised what I had lost sight of while I was busy working myself into a panic about being the newbie.

This is a brand-new route! In that sense, we were *all* newbies getting swept up in the excitement of this sportive. And that spurred me on some more: so what if I'd never done a sportive like this before? Everyone has to have a first ride.

Eventually, the smooth asphalt roads of the Peak District started to run out, and the gnarly side of the ride kicked in. Around a quarter of the short route was off road, and the total ascent of that route was 2,825 feet. *Thousands of feet of elevation.* On this very old rickety steel bike with slightly temperamental gears and, at the worst moments, brake blocks that kept sticking to the rims.

My very new roadie and climbing legs were feeling it. I had my first ever experience of complete cramp in both my legs during one of the harder climbs. I'd had cycling-related cramps before – my first time was after doing my first Tweed Run, hours after we'd got home. Curled up on the sofa post-ride and your leg muscles deciding to go a bit bonkers is one thing, but while you're actually on a bike, climbing what feels like a seventy-degree angle? I thought my legs were going to fall off. There was no choice but to stop riding and get off the bike – that decision had been completely taken out of my hands by my muscles going into spasm. I moved to the side of the road, dragging the bike next to me to get it out of the way of other riders making their way up. Sat on the floor, I was trying to stretch my legs but it felt like I was trying to mould set concrete, my muscles were refusing to play nice. I was downing as much water from my bidon as I could without drowning myself. I knew that rehydrating was supposed to help with cramps and now know it would have been even more helpful if it was something like Diroalyte in my bottle. I kept yelping in this weird delirious mixture of laughter and pain. Every time someone signalled to me to ask if I was okay as they rode past, I gave a 'thumbs up' and gestured for them to continue on their climb even though I was beginning to feel slightly stranded. I guess it was a mixture of pride and also not wanting to break anyone's climb mid-flow.

Eventually a Pashley Tandem came into view, momentarily distracting me from my aching legs as I'd never seen one before: once a Pashley fanatic, always a Pashley fanatic. The wonderful couple on the tandem stopped to help me, refusing to take no for an answer. They stayed with me for five minutes and helped me back on my feet, and this saved my ride. I knew I didn't want to give up, but at that point I really wondered if I had it in me to complete Eroica.

'You can do this, just take your time!' were the encouraging words the couple called to me, before hopping back on their tandem and continuing up the hill.

'Take your time.' So I did. As my legs came back to life, I walked the next part of the climb then got back on without falling off at a weird angle, making my way to the top. Time was on my side, I reminded myself. This wasn't a race and the day was still ahead of me, so I decided to take a slow roll for the rest of the route, snaking my way around (and getting lost a bit when I didn't read the signs properly) to the finish line, hours later back at Bakewell Showground. That ride was hot and hard. But most of all, despite the agonising cramps and losing my way around the course, it was fun. The Peak District is an absolutely beautiful location – the railway tunnels of the Monsal Trail were a little slice of heaven, providing natural air conditioning when I was sweating buckets. The refreshment stops, filled with local food and manned by residents cheering you on while stamping your route card and offering encouragement, were such a boost too. I had not just challenged the rolling hills of the Peaks, I'd challenged myself to see what I was capable of on a bike, and even if I hadn't completed it, I'd have still relished the fact I gave it a try.

Saying 'yes' to Eroica Britannia had set something off in me, and not just in regard to wanting more cycling adventures – I was 100 per cent up for more of those – but also the desire to step outside of my comfort zone and jump into things that I would usually have been afraid of, or simply assumed weren't for me. That's the beauty of trying: opening up the possibilities of enjoying something new, the courage it can give you and the growth that comes with it. In the cycling world, I've found there tends to always be someone around the corner willing to take the time out to spur you on in a low moment. Even better if it's two riders on a tandem.

One for the Road

The first time I handled a road bike was at the end of a sunny Sunday afternoon ride at Look Mum No Hands. Locked up next to Frankie was a fancy-looking road bike that I couldn't take my eyes off. I had absolutely no clue about the tech and spec of it (build, components, gearing: nada) or what model it was beyond its brand name – *CANYON* – blazoned along the down tube in back-slanted uppercase letters that looked like the bottom of them had been clean sliced off. I'd never seen a bike like that before but it looked flashy and *fast*.

The owner of the Canyon clip-clopped over and caught me, mid-gawp. Instead of ignoring me, unlocking and leaving, he struck up a conversation. He was proud of his machine so when he asked me how long I'd been riding for and which bike was mine, I was suddenly convinced he was taking the piss. I felt it should have been glaringly obvious looking at what I was wearing (slip-on Birkenstocks, a pair of bootcut Levi's jeans, a loose-fitting T-shirt and a straw trilby) compared to his attire (shoes that seemed impossible to walk in, Lycra cycling-team kit that clung to every muscle, a sleek black road helmet, and visor glasses that wouldn't have been out of place in a Daft Punk video) that none of the stealth-looking bikes around us were mine. I wasn't ashamed of my Pashley, but I was bracing myself for the 'Oh, that's not really a proper bike though, is it' response when I pointed out Frankie to him.

'That's a lovely one!' he said, with a genuine smile spreading across his face, his eyes lighting up. 'My granddad had an old Dutch-style bike that looked a bit like yours.'

He seemed caught up in nostalgia having seen Frankie, bending over to have a proper look at the frame and examining her details.

'They're quite heavy those, aren't they?'

'Yeah', I said, shrugging it off, 'but I love it and the routes I ride in London are pretty flat anyway. Guessing yours doesn't weigh as much!' I joked, but I was thinking, 'God, please don't let this turn into a conversation where I'm schooled about performance and being more "aero" in the city or something.'

But my new cycle buddy surprised me again when he replied, 'Nah – both really different bikes, but they both get us where we need to go, right?'

I liked that. And with that, he gestured at me to pick his up. I lifted it up with *one hand*. I knew that it was going to be light, but not *that* light. Considering how tricky it could be to manoeuvre Frankie around, especially when it came to tackling steps, this was a revelation. I handed his Canyon over to him, we wished each other happy travels and he clipped in, riding off towards Clerkenwell. The Canyon looked stunning and the experience of lifting it up was a revelation as to how lightweight bikes could actually be.

Still, in those first cycling years, if you'd asked me if I had any interest at all in getting my own modern road bike or dabbling in road cycling in the future, I would have most probably given you a tentative 'maybe' as an answer. There would have been a combination of reasons behind that: other than the fact I was getting used to bike-commuting in the city and being on two wheels again, the thought of having both my feet clipped into a super-lightweight carbon-fibre frame, riding on skinny tyres, while still trying to maintain a sense of balance and control straight-up terrified me. I did have an interest in road cycling, but I didn't see myself ever *needing* to do it: my impression (or preconception) of road cycling was that it was a fast, mostly competitive sport where you had to belong to a club and be in peak physical fitness to do it. Fast-forward to 2013 and Baadgyal, my carbon-fibre road bike – or rather bike frame – joins the family.

I have to lay the blame for my desire to get into road cycling (and ending up with my fourth bike) squarely at the feet of the roadies I worked with on a daily basis as well as having a roadie-inclined boyfriend. Between working at Vulpine and working on all things VéloCityGirl, I made a lot of connections in the cycling industry, which in turn led to working on lots of exciting projects. One of the most amazing connections and friendships I made was with Phil Dempsey, a keen road cyclist and founder of Aprire Bicycles.

Phil was a friend of Vulpine and visited the office on a few occasions to chat with us about future projects we could collaborate on – stuff like our seasonal photo shoots in which some of his bikes could be used. Working in operations, I'd be involved in chats regarding the logistics side of things (which probably doesn't sound very glamorous but was a lot of fun), but soon enough the conversations steered away from organising the delivery of road bikes to our offices to me potentially taking delivery of one of Phil's bikes for myself.

Aprire bicycles are beautiful and incredibly well-made carbon-fibre machines – which is no surprise considering Phil's background. Phil, who founded the South London-based company in 2009, is a qualified engineer who specialises in carbon lay-up and stress analysis. He started his career in component and hydraulic-brake design in Taiwan, then suspension and frame design, spending over a decade designing for companies such as Hayes, FUNN, DMR and Banshee Bikes. Phil and his team design all Aprire bicycle frames in-house using methods that include FEA (Finite Element Analysis) to verify his hand calculations – it's all rather technical and precise, but that precision and attention to detail results in the solid, lightweight, performance bikes Aprire create.

After seeing his bikes up close and personal in the office and the many chats we had about cycling that didn't involve work, I started to express my interest in perhaps testing out a carbon-fibre road bike someday for my blog. Before seeing an Aprire, the closest I had really got to a carbon-fibre bike was that time in LMNH. That experience had piqued my interest a little in what being on a road bike would feel like. Getting to know Phil and Aprire only made that interest grow stronger. He really enjoyed what I did with VéloCityGirl and how the blog explored different elements of cycling culture, so the idea for Lady Vélo to dip her toe into the world of road cycling on an Aprire bike was born!

I said 'bike frame' earlier because that's how Baadgyal started out when she was first presented to me on Sunday, 9 December 2013 while I was running the Vulpine stand at the Cyclogames (one of the fetes we'd put on, called that because it was cycling-game themed). I didn't actually know that Phil was going to do that. The original plan was to get the bike in the New Year. I'd already chosen the model of Aprire frame I wanted, the Celeste, and also chosen the colour scheme – a black body with purple vinyl decals (the transfers or stickers which go on the bike and make up the pattern). Phil had taken my measurements to calculate the size of frame I'd need, but there wasn't the right size for me in stock at the workshop (all the bikes are designed in London and then the frames are made in Taiwan or Italy), so I'd have to wait until one was shipped over, he'd build it up for me at the Aprire workshop and then bring it to me at the Vulpine office.

I was busy working the stand, dealing with some customers and didn't see what was going on behind me. I felt a tap on my shoulder and turned, thinking it was a member of the team trying to get my attention. But it wasn't – there was Phil, with a massive smile on his face holding my brand-new Celeste frame! It was a lovely and overwhelming surprise – Phil had conspired with my colleagues at work to make this happen at the Cyclogames. The event was held the day before my birthday and as I would be on annual leave from the Monday for the rest of the year I wasn't going to see Phil or anyone until January – so he brought it to the event that day so I could see it, before taking it away to build it up for me. I didn't think the surprise could get any more amazing than it already was, until I saw one of the decals Phil had put on the top tube reading 'Lady Vélo'.

I know a couple of tears welled up in my eyes when I saw that – my online name on the top of that frame … which was going to become *my* road bike. Being Lady Vélo really was taking me on adventures further than I could ever have imagined. Whereas once upon a time I'd thought my Pashley was the only bike I'd ever want or ever be interested in riding, my cycling horizons were being broadened with every single spin of the wheels.

I didn't have wild fantasies about taking part in road races or becoming the next Marianne Vos when I got Baadgyal (although if that happened then I wasn't going to be complaining) but I was still getting myself in knots about it. Something about the term 'road cycling' seemed so loaded, like there were rules you had to follow in order to be doing it, you know ... 'properly'. Perhaps that feeling is a symptom of the kind of opinions and rhetoric we so often get exposed to in the advertising and marketing of sporting activities. The narrative of sports like road cycling is that it's a serious and hardcore sport, not one where it's totally fine to just have some fun doing it. There is an obsession with glorifying suffering, training, racing and winning. It's such an exclusionary message, one that is disconnected from the pure joy of diving into something and giving it a go for the first time, regardless of your level of ability or confidence. Doing those things on your own terms is key. Which in this instance meant that I didn't have to feel obliged to suddenly only wear Lycra, and didn't mean I had to be clipless every time I rode.

Okay, reader – we need to take a little diversion: allow me to give a you an explanation of the term 'clipless' as I'll be saying it a fair few times from this point onwards and because it's also quite a confusing term for what it is.

Clipless pedals are a two-part system for your bike. Part one is a small pedal that has a locking mechanism on it, and part two is a cleat that attaches to the bottom of your bike shoe. Your bike shoes clip *into* that locking mechanism on the pedals, connecting you securely to your bike. Riding a road bike using this system is supposed to improve your riding style, as it allows you to use or recruit more of the muscles in your legs more efficiently than flat pedals would. With flats, you get most drive when you push down, but with clipless pedals, you create forward propulsion when you pull up (as your shoe is still attached to the pedal).

Now – that name thing. Remember the toe-clips I got taken

off that old French bike I rode at Eroica Britannia? Those thin metal attachments on the front of pedals (to keep your feet in place and give you more propulsion when you cycle) were the precursor to today's clipless pedals. Toe-clips are still in use today alongside the more modern version. Both couldn't have the same name – the modern ones perform the same function, but don't have the clip at the front of the pedal, so were called the *clipless* version.

Going clipless straight away wasn't necessary considering the level of riding I was doing in the very early stages of owning Baadgyal. The thought of being in Central London and being unable to unclip at a set of traffic lights would leave me in a cold sweat. Everyday pedals that I could actually rest the soles of my Nikes on, while knowing I could lift my feet and release myself whenever I wanted to, would do me just fine for now.

I was still a newbie to all things 'road', and the equation as I saw it read:

diving straight into riding with my feet clamped on to a set of pedals

+

no clue and confidence about it

=

a road recipe for disaster

Another brand-new fact at this point: I had no idea that some road bikes are sold or supplied without pedals. It turns out that no matter whatever level of knowledge you *think* you've got nailed, every day in cycling can be a school day, my friends. I didn't discover this golden nugget of information until the day Baadgyal was delivered to me at work – fully built up, but minus pedals attached to her crank arms. At the time I was very perturbed, but as I discovered for myself further into my road-cycling journey, the pedal and cycling shoe systems for road bikes can be a very individual matter. Instead of the bike shop or manufacturer assuming what shoes and cleats suit you, it's always best to find out for yourself, especially with the many variations out there.

Admittedly going into the whole thing with a touch of cycling knowledge bravado, I didn't raise the subject of pedals with Aprire when they were taking measurements and discussing details of the bike. A combination of assumptions: them assuming I had pedals and shoes sorted out and me assuming it would come with pedals as standard just like my other bikes had, led to me being in that pedal-less predicament when she arrived. A bit late in the day to be panicking about how I was supposed to give her a test ride. It certainly wasn't the most mortifying thing to ever happen to me since I started cycling, but I did feel like a bit of a plum about it. There's a photo of me I posted on Instagram on the day she arrived, grinning wildly, and though I was thrilled behind that smile, I was feeling pretty embarrassed about falling at what seemed to be the simplest first hurdle of getting on a road bike.

While realising that cycling sure has some weird quirks, I was soon reminded of some of the more beneficial ones that came with working with obsessive bike-heads. Like random unwanted bike components lying around the office. I was soon handed a pair of bog-standard chrome-alloy flat bike pedals one of my colleagues didn't need any more, because they'd upgraded their set-up a few weeks beforehand. That act of one man's trash becoming another woman's treasure allowed Baadgyal and I to go out on our first spin the day she arrived. The world (or at least part of SW18) was now my cycling oyster.

Knowing that Vulpine had a wonderfully liberal attitude to employees getting on bikes at any opportunity, did I take absolute advantage of this and:

a) Take the rest of the day off and cycle three miles up the road from our office to have a jolly around Richmond Park?

b) Hop on the train from Earlsfield with her to Box Hill in an attempt to take on that climb?

c) Neither of the above.

Of course, it was c). The Grand Départ of my ride started at lunch-time in the corridor outside of our office, and ended yards later in a few laps around the car park. There was at least one thing I knew for sure before getting on a road bike for the very first time: having somewhere suitably quiet and flat to give it a go is a very good idea. That wide and smooth hallway on the second floor, along with the relative safety of a gated car park, was perfect. Spending sixty minutes riding gingerly around an industrial estate wasn't about trying to save social media face. I just needed to see what it felt like and what I felt like on Baadgyal without worrying about traffic buzzing around me or going over a pothole to come a cropper in the middle of Garratt Lane. To some, it may not have been the most riveting ride in the world or even the best way to find out what my road bike was capable of, but it was exactly what I needed to do. It gave me a chance to start familiarising myself with this beautiful but slightly alien machine – getting on this bike felt like another world. Even when I was sat as upright as I could physically get myself on Baadgyal with my hands either resting on the middle of the handlebars or holding on to the hoods (those rubbery things that the brake levers come out of at the top of the bars), this didn't much feel like being on my Dutch-style bikes. It was almost like I was lying down flat on the top tube of the frame. It was a bit weird and very disconcerting, especially when I was turning – or even attempting to turn my head to look around for the first time – and my centre of gravity felt like it was totally off its usual cycling radar. Being on her was going to take some getting used to. Although I was 100 per cent adamant about sticking to my guns about doing this my way (nice and slow), I knew a little help from my more experienced workmates wouldn't go amiss.

I probably couldn't have wished for a better situation to be in: five days a week I was working at a company that was all about cycling alongside friends who were all into different disciplines of cycling and everyone loved nothing more than to evangelise about the merits of ... cycling. This dream working scenario made the challenge of learning road cycling so much easier. A huge part of Vulpine's ethos was to promote and encourage cycling culture as much as possible amongst the staff, so at least one day a week we would all down tools and go for an extended morning or afternoon ride. You didn't *have* to own a bike or be into cycling to work there, but I could appreciate the thinking behind this. After all, the brand was all about cycling, so having staff who were encouraged to even just dip their toe into the activity meant you built a team of people with at least some understanding – or maybe even love – of cycling which could be poured back into the business. We'd switch our office brains off and get some fresh air in our lungs with a bicycle seat under our bums instead of a swivel office chair. These rides were totally different from the bike commute into Earlsfield, where the sole purpose was to get to a slightly uninspiring industrial trading estate and sit at a desk and stare at a computer screen for eight hours. Then you'd repeat that commute back home at the end of the day in the soul-destroying evening rush-hour madness.

Each week we would take it in turns to plot a route in or around Wandsworth (which of course would include a tea and cake stop) in which everyone could take part. It wouldn't be much of a ride if it excluded people from the team, so no matter what level of biking ability or what kind of bike you were on, you were always welcome. I'd normally do these work rides on my city bikes, but now it was time for Baadgyal to shine. This of course meant actually getting her back to the office. I'll let you into a little secret here – the first day of having a totally alien bike didn't feel like the right time to do my fourteen and a half miles' evening commute home via Westminster Bridge and Victoria Embankment entirely on my own. Instead, I worked late so I could take my bike on the train.

I went back to using either Frankie or Ratty to commute to work and go on the weekly jollies, leaving my road bike at home and popping out on her occasionally for rides around the block to get some practice in. That wasn't enough though – not to satisfy the burning desire I had to be out there on this glorious road bike and taste those sportier adventures that I had imagined going on. When my colleagues clocked that Baadgyal wasn't appearing on my commute, they kept encouraging me to give it a go. Truthfully, the best way for me to get comfortable with riding road was for me to *actually ride the bike*, and at least I would be able to do this with a group of people who wouldn't judge me on my riding. With every commute and office group ride I did on Baadgyal, the feeling of being on a road bike started to make more sense. Some of those lunchtime rides were a cycling awakening. That might sound a bit OTT, but climbing and descending Wimbledon Hill and actually knowing how to work the gears; learning how to use the drops – placing your hands on the lower and curved part of the handlebars which improves aerodynamics and increases speed when descending – with the support of my colleagues was an eye-opener to how astonishingly responsive a road bike is. Every little movement I was making – just like when I was trying to do those turns in the car park that day – was transferring straight to Baadgyal. More and more it felt like I was tuned into this bike and she was tuned into me: with each pedal, a bond was forming, like there was a physical link between my body, this bike and the road.

It took a good six months of cycling to work and doing more of the office jaunts on Baadgyal before I felt ready to take on a new challenge – something that I'd constantly hear other cyclists I knew talking about but was never quite sure that I had it in me to do. Without fail on a Monday morning the conversation in the kitchenette over the usual bean-grinding, espresso-making ritual would turn to some themes including, 'What rides did you get up to over the weekend then?' and 'What kind of distance did you cover?' I could still get involved in these conversations, even if my gentle #CoffeeCycleSaturday rides on Frankie around the city felt quite different to what some of my workmates were getting up to on their bikes. When I'd listen to them comparing notes on the beautiful places they'd cycled out to, how stunning the winding roads with their tough climbs and sweet descents were and how the beer at the pub stop at the end of the ride tasted like pure nectar, I'd feel the pull of a big ride. I could take or leave some of the GPS data crunching and Strava segment-smashing chat that came with it. But all of it always sounded like so much fun. And that was the key word: *fun*. Their weekend rides were never about competing against one another or who they were out riding with. It didn't turn into a pissing competition in the Monday morning catch-up chat, and my #CycleCoffeeSaturdays were just as valued.

Perhaps there was a *tiny* bit of FOMO in my mind when talk like this happened in the office. But now that I had Baadgyal there was nothing to stop me going for it. I was feeling more familiar with the ways of my road bike, and my handling skills and understanding of the gears were getting better. So I'd set myself a date for my first ride, and I knew exactly what it was going to be: a Sunday afternoon ride from Southsea to Bognor Regis and back, with Ian and our friend Jordan – a fellow bike lover who we became good friends with due to our regular visits to Southsea Coffee, where Jordan was a barista. I'd made a pretty public declaration about my intentions of doing it too, announcing it at the end of a segment on *The Cycle Show* with Matt Barbet that went out on national television the week of the ride. I guess there was no backing out once that was out in the ether. And although I felt pretty proud of myself in saying I'd be doing some road cycling out loud, it may also be that I'd said it as an insurance policy to make sure that I didn't back out.

Jordan had suggested the route and I'd been thrilled at the sound of it. Riding from seafront to seafront sounded wonderful. The whole route including the return was going to be about 82 kilometres (around 52 miles) and mostly flat, so I wasn't worrying too much about it – I just kept in mind that this wasn't a race and that we had a brilliant plan:

1) Meet at Southsea Coffee for 10 a.m. opening and grab some caffeine and breakfast.

2) Leave around 10:45–11 a.m. and set off towards Bognor Regis.

3) Get coffee somewhere along the route and just enjoy the ride.

4) Have a well-earned takeaway and fizzy booze when we were back in Southsea.

I was filled with optimism about the ride, which was a massive welcome change. The other massive change was what I was going to be wearing – full Lycra. Hanging on the back of Ian's bedroom door was a skintight jersey and matching bib shorts, all thanks to another of those beneficial quirks that came with working for a cycling clothing company. Vulpine wasn't in the Lycra business back in 2014, but they did become a title sponsor of a women's professional cycling team that year, which meant we got some official kit as a little bonus. It would have been bonkers not to show support for the awesome women's team we were backing and *not* go for a jersey and a pair of bib shorts. I couldn't deny the benefits of a bit of clingy Lycra any longer, especially for reducing painful rubbing and chaffing in places – you *defo* don't want that going on over more substantial distances. When you're spending more time on a road saddle, the chamois padding inside of those shorts (which, FYI, are designed to be worn without underwear as it's more hygienic for your sweaty nether regions) will make your cycling a hell of a lot more comfortable. There's one thing I never thought I'd see: me extolling the virtues of Lycra kit.

Sunday morning rolled around. I'd squeezed myself into my jersey and bib shorts (which I'd had to take off and put back on again as I'd already forgotten the golden rule about no knickers under the bibs) and stared at myself in the bathroom mirror. This was exciting. And also a little odd. I wasn't embarrassed about wearing Lycra but I was feeling embarrassed about the way my body looked in it. I knew it was going to be skintight. I knew it was beneficial for it to fit that way. It shouldn't have mattered but my mind was picking over things. Things like my belly being highlighted by the clingy material. And not being in the same peak physical condition as the women I actually knew who wore this very same kit in a professional capacity. Again, it shouldn't have mattered as I wasn't a professional cyclist, but I couldn't help but feel slightly self-conscious.

Standing outside Southsea Coffee with Ian and Jordan after our pre-ride breakfast, I caught a glimpse of us in the shop window: the two of them chatting about the route and switching their Garmins on, and me smiling to myself about the fact that I was actually about to do this – my first 'modern road ride'. Maybe it was the caffeine buzz kicking in, but I was feeling so energised. The weather was playing nicely, the guys were in a fantastic mood and even though we'd not set off, I was feeling comfortable about what was ahead of me ... a nice, gentle bike ride all the way to another seaside town.

Once I got my teeth stuck into the beautiful route that had been plotted out for us, I found my road legs and discovered a whole new level of cycling joy. It wasn't full of major climbs, but they were enough for me to feel the thunder rolling in my legs while I was doing them, and the exhilarating rush of the descents that followed. But the level of pain I started to feel in my shoulders and my lower back wasn't something that I was expecting to feel on that ride at all. Aches and pains in my back are nothing new to me, as I've lived with mild scoliosis (curvature of the spine) since I was a baby. It doesn't affect my everyday life, but the older I get, the more issues the S-bend in my back seems to cause me. Perhaps I should have realised there would be a difference between my body being on a sit-up-and-beg and contorting it into different positions on a road bike. By the time we arrived in Bognor, my left shoulder and lower back were starting to nag at me in a familiar way. My scoliosis had flared up. I'd had mild twinges of it when I was practising riding Baadgyal, but perhaps foolishly I didn't pay much attention to it, as those rides were short distance.

I popped a couple of painkillers, downed more coffee and assumed that it would eventually bugger off after resting for a while, but when we set off for the return cycle back to Southsea and started putting the long miles in again, the pain hit me with such force I could have screamed. Dropping further back from the guys with the agony of my back, shoulders and now my neck beginning to feel like bricks, I called time: I'd gotten to the natural end of this spectacular ride. I was a little gutted that I couldn't complete the return journey back from Bognor to Southsea, but this was one of those rare occasions where instead of pushing on, I listened to my body and what it was capable of coping with. I wish I had listened to the warning signs my body had been giving me in those early days of having Baadgyal. It wasn't that my body needed to get used to riding in a new position – I actually needed to get a bike fit.

A bike fitting carried out by a professional fitter perfects your posture on your bike, tailored to your body geometry. Other than your comfort levels being drastically improved, being fitted to your bike reduces the risk of injury or causing more distress to existing injuries or ailments.

I'd always associated bike fittings with elite riders and professionals. The furthest I'd ever gotten with a fit was making sure I bought the right size bike frame and that the saddle and bars were at a good height. When I had my fitting done in January 2016 (it took me a while before I sorted that out) – it changed everything for me and my back while riding.

I was lucky enough to have a one-on-one in 2016 with Tony Corke of Torke Cycling. It completely changed my attitude towards preparing for a ride, and I came away with a much better understanding and appreciation of what goes into a bike fit ... and why it's such a good idea to get one. I hadn't expected adjustments that looked like the smallest tweak could result in the biggest changes. The idea of throwing myself into bigger rides on Baadgyal without proper fitting is unthinkable to me now – especially with my scoliosis playing a factor on how my back behaves while riding. I felt a lot more confident about taking my road-riding adventures further, and knew I'd pay attention to any niggles that pop up when I'm on two wheels. I discovered how important it is to pay attention to your positioning from your head right down to toes. Doing this properly is imperative for your physical health if you cycle, so I totally recommend getting a bike fitting done, whatever level of cycling you are at.

However, back on that first ride, my back wasn't having any more of it. But neither Ian or Jordan made me feel bad about having to pull the plug – trying to cycle the twenty-odd miles back to Southsea through the crippling pains shooting through my crooked spine and spiking up into my shoulders would have been a rubbish way to end what had been a brilliant day. The painkillers weren't touching the sides, but I was stoked that I'd made it as far as Chichester on the return leg from Bognor – and was more than happy to hop on a train and relax for half an hour, get back to the flat and hop straight into a soothing bath.

Waiting at Chichester station for our train and while I still had adrenaline pumping around my veins that was probably keeping me upright, Ian suggested doing a little victory picture on social media to mark my first major road ride.

'I hope you're so proud of what you've just done, Jools – you were bloody amazing all the way,' he told me, and had me feeling like I'd just completed a stage of the Women's Tour of Britain.

I climbed up a few of the station steps, hoisted Baadgyal over my left shoulder, and through the throbbing pains in my arms, fist bumped the air with my right arm. And with anything you share on social media, there will always be comments ... and opinions.

As you may have guessed by now, of all of the words out there that get used in cycling to describe taking part in the activity, I have to say the one that gets on my tits the most is 'proper' – especially when I hear it being used in used in a certain context. I really don't mind receiving friendly hints and tips from people about how to get the best out of being on a bike – I'm all for it – but not when the cycling advice becomes condescending, or just a series of people commenting on a massive personal achievement saying you haven't done it properly. That just sucks.

After my first big ride on Baadgyal, I had a feeling that 'proper' would be lurking on the horizon with the second big ride I had coming. Two months after Bognor, I'd be back on the road again, but the circumstances of this would be very different. As much as I was excited about this next jolly on a bike, I was also steeling myself for someone to say something about how I'd do on it, especially because this would be a ride like no other.

The entire office was heading to Cheshire to take part in a rather special ride. We were going to be led out by an Olympic and World Championship-winning track cyclist, Sir Chris Hoy. As part of the publicity drive surrounding the collaboration between Sir Chris and Vulpine to create the HOY Vulpine range of road-cycling clothing, we were all going on a group ride with him. Not a bad office day out, right? Being surrounded by cyclists (and of course a well-known pro) who were all much more confident than me on a road bike, I was pretty happy to take my time on the ride and stayed steady at the back of the pack. I was still a novice to road cycling – I wasn't embarrassed by that and wasn't about to do something crazily outside of my comfort zone. I knew where my confidence was at on Baadgyal and being at the back of the pack was cool with me and for those who were kind enough to hang back with me too. The ride was going like a dream; we were whizzing through the gorgeous countryside, going off road and having a laugh.

As the ride progressed and I took on more climbs and descents, something started niggling away at the back of Baadgyal. I kept on hearing a clicking nose, like something was coming loose. I stopped, hopped off and had a look at the back. The chain was still in place, the rear wheel looked fine, as did the cassette and rear derailleur. So what the hell was that clicking?

'Probably something like a leaf or loose gravel had hooked into the spokes,' I told myself. We were out in the country after all, so that must have been it. Getting back on, and catching up with the others, I heard it again. Because I couldn't see a problem, I carried on riding, taking on the last climb on the route plotted out for us. The stunning descent at the other side of the climb was ahead of me and I was giving myself a mental fist bump for doing so well that day. I'd got into position on the drops and I changed my gears to delve into the downhill and with a clanging 'POP' my chain flew off.

'Oh shhhiiittt!' was perhaps the mildest expletive to come out of my mouth that very moment. In a split second, my heart was racing out of my chest. Panic mode took over as my legs were spinning around and I was convinced I was now stuck on the bike, descending headfirst down the hill and into an almighty crash. This had never happened to me before, so for it to occur while on my first major road-bike ride, being led by an Olympic gold-winning cyclist and not having a clue what to do was not ideal. I was still playing out the potential crash in my mind when I realised I wasn't actually glued to the saddle and was able to stop in time. I stood there, straddled over Baadgyal, feeling utterly dejected. A colleague stopped to help me out – to be honest I didn't notice he had parked up next to me as I was too distracted by the shock of what had happened.

'Didn't you spot the problem with the chain before?' he asked, immediately bending down to sort it.

'No', I mumbled, feeling like an idiot. But that wasn't true. I had known *something* wasn't right. I could feel it, but I didn't know what it was – perhaps because of that and not knowing the immediate answer to the problem, I had decided to ride on through it, hoping it would simply go away. In what felt like no time, he'd fixed it, sticking the chain back on in what felt like a matter of seconds, and giving Baadgyal a quick once-over too.

'You really should get the bike booked in for a service after this, Jools. This could have been pretty icky for you.'

Those words were ringing in my ears for a long time. I knew it could have been pretty icky for me if it had gone wrong, and I was so frustrated with the *fact I knew that* but hadn't done anything about it.

I needed to stop riding on luck (and relying on the good nature of other people helping me out) and learn more about bike maintenance. Getting comfortable with that side of things was essential for me to carry on with my bike life with no hiccups. But that meant finding somewhere I could get comfortable with maintenance and overcome my fears about it all.

If You Teach Them
(How to Fix It), They Will Come

I could fix a puncture and I could change my brake
pads and that was about it. I had no idea how the
bike worked – no clue how the gears worked ...
but I had them! I was like, oh – they do something,
y'know?

Jenni Gwiazdowski

I have a confession to make. I used to be absolutely rubbish at
bike maintenance. I'm much better at it now, and still learning
more about it as I go along. But once there was a point where
I couldn't tell you how to change a bottom bracket. Or what a
bottom bracket was.

Once upon a time I would never have made that admission

out loud. I'd be burying that kind of talk at the bottom of my Pashley basket, covering it with other dazzling cycling knowledge I had, all in the hope that no one would clock that I wasn't good at it. But why be so embarrassed about not knowing that stuff? No one is born with a bicycle maintenance manual hardwired into his or her brain, and everyone – even the most skilled mechanics out there – had to have started somewhere.

Jenni Gwiazdowski, founder and director of LBK (London Bike Kitchen), is another of my cycling sheroes who I had the chance to interview for this book. Jenni is an amazing example of someone who was into riding bikes but didn't know that much about bike DIY. She totally flipped that scenario on its head for the greater good. Not only did Jenni learn how to fix and build bikes, she then imparted that knowledge to others by creating LBK: a bicycle shop and open DIY workshop where you can learn to work on your own bike instead of giving it to someone else to fix. She's also a cycling author and has written a book, *How To Build A Bike: A Simple Guide to Making Your Own Ride*, with photos showing how messy and dirty it is to build a bike. Keeping it real with the grease that helps your bike gears turn? YES, JENNI.

While LBK has gone on to educate scores of bike lovers across East London and beyond since opening in March 2012, Jenni jokes that her initial thought behind creating the organisation was 'a little selfish'. Before LBK, Jenni worked in marketing at a small environmental charity, but had started to become disillusioned with her role. 'I enjoyed it but I didn't like the work environment. I was just getting into bikes at the time, and bought an old vintage frame that I fell in love with from a bike jumble sale to build up.' (Which is now the bicycle she rode in on for this interview – a beautiful circa 1960s black Claud Butler, with gold-trim details). Although bitten by the cycling bug hard enough to want to build her own bike, Jenni didn't actually know how to do it. The frame sat in her bedroom for two years, totally untouched as she didn't have the tools or know where to start with it. In January 2011, Jenni made a New Year's resolution to build up the Butler.

A familiar situation I could relate to when you are, as Jenni puts it, 'friends with lots of bikey people' is that you can keep asking around for help and get it. 'They will help you all the time! I had friends who were telling me stuff like, "You've gotta get the wheels sorted first" or "I'll help you get this part first," wanting to do it for me. That was really kind, but I was like – why isn't there just a class I could go to somewhere, and you could *teach it to me* so I could have that knowledge?' Knowledge is power, and what Jenni was saying is a bit like that old adage: '*Give* a person a fish and you'll feed them for a day; *teach* a person to fish and you'll feed them for a lifetime.'

Actually finding somewhere to go to – a safe space where you feel at ease and not embarrassed about asking questions on basic bike maintenance – is a problem many people encounter in cycling, and acts as a huge barrier to learning those essential skills. Jenni didn't know where she could go that would enable her like that. It was after a chat about this problem with her flatmate that she got the idea to start up a bike kitchen – creating a welcoming and empowering space for others like her to walk into. 'I was chatting with my then flatmate, who was also from California and had not long moved to the UK – she suggested bike kitchens like they have back in Cali. I didn't actually know what she was talking about so excitedly started researching them! Most bike kitchens are non-profit, volunteer-run projects in huge warehouse spaces, with vast tool libraries and second-hand parts you can access to work on your own bike. I was like – that's such a great idea, I'm going to create one in

London!' I could fix a puncture and I could change my brake pads, and that was about it! I think it actually helped being that naïve, because I was SO pumped by the idea. If I'd known how difficult it would be, I may not have done it!'

The first time I heard of LBK was via a newsletter I received in April 2012 from a brilliant (but now sadly defunct) cycling blog I used to follow, CycleLoveCC. In the newsletter was a picture of a woman standing outside the London Bike Kitchen shopfront, smiling and posing with a vintage blue bicycle. The blurb that accompanied the photo mentioned a brand-new bike kitchen that had opened in Hackney a month earlier. Even though it was so close to where I live and I'd been on the East London cycling scene for two years at this point, I'd never heard about Jenni Gwiazdowski (another woman of colour in the cycling industry and one who actually runs a workshop – what?!) or LBK when it launched that March. Nor did I understand what the word *kitchen* had to do with a bike shop. As Jenni explains, the name comes from the original Bicycle Kitchen, based in Los Angeles, California: 'They got that name because the space they set up shop in was originally an old soup kitchen!' They have since expanded and now have The Bike Oven and The Bikerowave, which are also based in LA. Before going ahead with her version, Jenni contacted the one in LA to ask if she could open up a bike kitchen in London: 'The LA team were like, "YEAH! No one owns the term – it's open to everyone and we all help each other out. We even get visits from other bike kitchens from around the world, which is really nice."'

Jenni's face lights up whenever she talks about founding LBK, what she set out to achieve with it, and why such an organisation is so badly needed. The majority of LBK's customers are people living in Hackney – an area of 'old East London', which is getting gentrified, resulting in a real mix of people coming into the workshop. As Jenni highlights, the teaching classes at LBK do not make enough money to create a sustainable business: their core financial source is 'young, white and male, and working in tech'. That demographic immediately bought into the idea of LBK and made up the shop's first customers, coming in to buy spare parts and take part in the classes. But one of Jenni's initial goals (aside from having a space for herself where she could continue to learn how to fix and build her bikes) was to start women and gender-variant nights.

Jenni explains: 'I wanted to do something really inclusive to all types of women: trans-fem, gender variant – *all women*. It was actually one of our first volunteers who is gender-variant who suggested our women and gender-variant group should be dubbed "the WAGs"!'

LBK needs to be financially sustainable to survive, but as a social business, this can be a real conflict. Rents in London – especially somewhere like Hackney with gentrification going on – can be high, both for housing and, as in Jenni's case, for premises too. Being able to pay staff a wage so that they can live and survive in the city is important too. Three staff members at LBK earn a wage, and Jenni herself openly discloses that she's only on £8,000 a year: 'It's enough to cover my rent and food ... luckily my social life revolves around bikes and all my friends are people who ride bikes and so really I'm paid back tenfold!' At its core, London Bike Kitchen is about education, empowerment and fun – that's always been their trifecta, but in order to keep LBK going, a compromise needed to be made which Jenni had to think long and hard about: offering repairs.

At one of their steering-group meetings, the notion of a repairs service was discussed. Even though LBK was all about teaching people skills to carry for life and helping marginalised groups, they couldn't keep on turning away business just because that business was people asking them to do repairs for them. As Jenni tells me, 'We focus on educating people but realised we couldn't continue doing that if we were turning away money. We had to just bite the bullet and open a second workshop [as their original one was too small] so we could start to fix people's bikes. The compromise was that the second workshop had to be used as a classroom on the weekend for our BYOB (Build Your Own Bike) classes.'

Jenni still loves what she does at LBK and being a part of the cycling industry – 'If I didn't enjoy it then I would have to leave' – but like me and many other women that I've met and spoken to, Jenni believes that changes still need to be made and there is plenty of space for growth within the industry. As highlighted in the 'Diversity Issue' of industry magazine *BikeBiz,* the cycle trade's worst-kept secret is its propensity to hire men in workshop mechanic positions. Even consumers acknowledge that in matters pertaining to their bikes, it is predominantly men who assist them. Jenni thinks that what she refers to as 'the cycling old guard' is hopefully changing and that she is contributing towards that change with the WAG DIY sessions, held at LBK. The idea behind these sessions is that they are a safe space where people can come in, and not feel they are being talked down to or condescended to: 'We'll see that it doesn't have to be a closed-off boys' club and not be welcoming other people into the fold – cycling and maintenance is for everyone.'

Also expressed in that issue of *BikeBiz* was the belief that the industry is not entirely responsible for its apparent gender imbalance, with front-facing engagement at equal fault. Bike shops – from major high-street brands to small independents – can be intimidating places to walk into as a woman. In 2015, a report conducted by the League of American Bicyclists on how to make bike retail more welcoming for women revealed that although women represent the new majority of adult bicycle owners, accounting for 51 per cent of ownership, 62 per cent of women who own a bike did not make a single visit to a bike shop the previous year, compared to 56 per cent of male bike owners.

Jenni has said in a previous interview on this subject that, 'it takes a certain kind of woman to walk into a workshop space and feel confident enough to just talk to the people in that space'. With the WAG DIY sessions, Jenni and her team have removed the hierarchy of having men disseminate the information, and have women doing it instead: 'It makes it more comfortable and easily approachable for, I would say, most women.'

The fear of walking into a bike repair shop and asking questions that many people would see as 'basic' or 'stuff that you should really know by now' was enough to keep me away from doing that for the first seven years of cycling as an adult. It wasn't until I signed up for one of LBK's Basic Maintenance Classes in 2017 that I could actually feel comfortable enough to openly admit my lack of knowledge and know that nobody was going to make fun of or patronise me. It was a space where I could ask whatever I wanted to – even if it was the same bike question, several times over. After all those years, I was finally able to seek out the tools to empower myself on a bike.

When telling Jenni stuff about how LBK makes me feel during our interview, she smiles and says, 'I feel like I've *done* my job when I get feedback like that from people,' but that certainly doesn't signify a 'my work here is done' attitude. Jenni aims to keep on empowering people through bike maintenance and educating every single person who walks through the doors of London Bike Kitchen. As she's said when it comes to the ethos of LBK:

'It's never going to be a case of LBK just fixing your bike – we

want to show you how to fix it yourself, because if you understand how your bike works, you are more likely to ride it. You
no longer see it as just a piece of metal. A bike can be a trans-
formative object in many ways.'

Talking Heads

Visibility is so important and I was ready to be seen again when my second *Newsnight* opportunity came up, this time to speak live in the studio about cycling culture in the UK.

It was a far cry from the relative safety of the pre-recorded section I had been in before and I hoped to talk about some of the issues that were at the forefront of my cycle mission by that point. The cycling hot topic which brought me back to *Newsnight* was the 2014 Tour de France. There was even more buzz in the UK surrounding the event, as the Grand Départ of the 101st edition of the race was happening in Yorkshire. An estimated 2.5 million people would line the route of the stages from Leeds to Sheffield. The combination of our strong Olympic performance and the Tour coming to the UK saw interest in cycling across the country surge once more.

I was appearing alongside Daniel Knowles, a reporter from

The Economist, who had written about the sociology behind the so-called cycling boom that was going on. It wasn't anything too heavy: we were two people who both enjoyed riding bikes after all, but I understood how discussions on *Newsnight* worked. We were going to be pitted against one another for a friendly debate on the subject.

I will always be freaked out about doing any public speaking, but I was also nervous for other reasons. Such as not feeling qualified to be there discussing cycling culture, especially if talk turned towards the Tour. It's an event I love to watch, but I wasn't an expert on professional cycling. I was nervous about my brain going totally blank and being thrown by the debate, or not getting the points across that I so desperately hoped I could. And, of course, I was more than aware of what for some might have been the elephant in the room: being the only black person there, talking about a predominately white-dominated sport. I'll admit didn't know much about Daniel before coming on the show, but if this was indeed a possible act of tokenism – and if I was on here as a black person but not able to talk about race or cultural difference – I was determined to not let that become the narrative, and to use this platform to the best of my abilities, if my nerves didn't do a number on me first.

The presenter, Laura Kuenssberg, posed a question: was there was an image problem with cycling in Britain and was it nothing but MAMILS on the streets? My friendly cycling opponent came out of his corner and took the floor first, describing the image of cycling in Britain as being very much an activity for forty-something, middle-class white men. I could agree with that – it seemed to be the status quo if you went by some of the media and marketing messages, and even organisations higher up the food chain were guilty of perpetuating that image too. I was rolling with this so far.

Then the divide started to appear. Daniel went on to drill down into who rides bikes, and how it's still only that particular type of man. He suggested that riding bikes only happens in Cambridge, where 'cycling culture really works' and Hackney, and that everywhere else you see nothing but aggressive MAMILS on their way into work. I knew that very little of this was true – he was merely perpetuating the image the media had built of what a cyclist should look like and what 'proper' cycling is. And I was sat right opposite Daniel as the complete opposite of that image!

I may not have been armed with hard data and stats to back up what I felt to be true, but I knew that my own lived experience, the people and groups I was meeting constantly in the world of bikes, totally went against what he was saying. Looking at how culturally diverse Britain is, it struck me as such a bizarre statement. He also suggested that it was near impossible to get hold of a decent second-hand bike. Schemes and projects exist to make sure it *is* possible to get hold of a bike that doesn't cost the earth – and they *don't* have to cost the earth to be a good bike.

Then it was my turn to speak. I talked about how I got Frankie through the cycle to work scheme, as I could never have afforded her otherwise. But what about others who don't have something like that as an option? Even I recognised that was a privilege I had. The existence of organisations like The Bike Project; The Bristol Bike Project (who provide an empowering service for underprivileged and marginalised groups of people within their community whose lives would benefit through having accessible and affordable transportation) and of course London Bike Kitchen are great examples of how varied cycling can be. But maybe this was a symptom of the blinkered view of cycling and how the activity is traditionally touted: you can end up missing the amazing mini-universes of cycling culture that exist.

However, we did manage to come to an agreement at the end of the debate, harking back to that previous *Newsnight* Netherlands feature: that the normalisation of riding bikes was missing and needed in the UK.

This appearance on *Newsnight* was very different to my first one just a year before. Although I was in the studio and doing it live in front of the nation, I felt more confident about it: partly because my confidence in public speaking about cycling had grown, and certainly because I knew I wanted to grab that platform and use it to talk about the things that got chopped from that segment back in 2013. This time round, I *had* to do it – I had to stick my head above the parapet and talk about the cultural differences that existed in cycling, which I knew about from my own lived experiences as a black woman and one now working in the industry!

Addressing those points and having this chance to talk about them on TV made me feel empowered and *listened to*. Even though I had no clue how people watching it were reacting and there was no live studio audience, I felt listened to because this time I could actually speak and no one could edit my words and silence the narrative. Having that platform (especially a very white-dominated one too) and this time being able to speak those truths felt incredible. It left me wanting the chance to do that more – not just on the BBC, but on any platform I could. I was going to grab every single opportunity with both hands, because of the promise I'd made to use my voice to amplify the voices of marginalised groups. Every time I get invited to take part in something like a panel discussion, or to go on the radio or on the TV, it frightens the living shit out of me. But maybe it would be even more frightening not to use the privilege of having such platforms to try and make some kind of positive noise.

I could never have imagined what a big part of my cycling journey the Tweed Run would become. I've made friends for life there, I've had work opportunities come from it, and I've covered the event every year on the blog. It's always special, but 2015 will hold an extra-special place in my heart.

The Tweed Run poster reveal is always something to look forward to. The artwork is invariably stunning as whichever illustrator is chosen always works closely with the team to capture the essence of the ride – 'A metropolitan bicycle ride with a bit of style'. Eliza Southwood had been chosen to design the 2015 poster. Already a huge fan of Eliza's work (I met her via seeing her work displayed at Look Mum No Hands! back in 2013), I was looking forward to seeing what she had created. A couple of months before the grand reveal, I got an email from Ted to let me know the poster had been completed, which was a nice surprise – everyone loves a sneak peek. However, I had to read his email twice to make sure I had the right end of the stick.

'Our 2015 poster girl may look a little familiar to you ... you're the inspiration for this year! Hope you don't mind!'

I got the biggest shock when I clicked on the attachment. The illustration was of a couple on a tandem bicycle: a white man on the front seat, a pipe in his mouth, focused on pedalling, and a black woman sat at the back, dressed in a houndstooth-patterned jacket and black skirt with a matching houndstooth pillbox hat, sipping a cup of tea while she cycled. I was utterly bowled over. Having to sit on the news for a while was the hardest thing when all I wanted to do was shout it from the rooftops. However, there was one thing I could do while waiting for the poster to be released: try to recreate the outfit that 'I' was wearing in the poster for the ride.

After donning a blazer and tailored shorts the year before, I'd already made up my mind that I was going to wear a dress for the 2015 run, as it would be so much cooler and to keep my cycle style for the event varied – I take my Tweed Run Wardrobe that seriously. It wasn't going to match the poster perfectly, but my compromise would be to wear a dress made from a houndstooth fabric as close to the illustration as possible. I was determined that this dress was going to be made in Britain in keeping with both my roots and those of tweed fabric, and by a stroke of luck, I knew exactly who to visit to make it happen.

I'd come across the brand 'Similan by Nisa' when Ian and I did one of our leisurely London rides to Old Spitalfields Market. Nisa's stall was a beautiful oasis of tweed: big-collared Harris Tweed coats and dress upon stunning dress, all handmade in her London studio. Looking through the rails, I'd made up my mind to buy something from Similan for the Tweed Run long before I knew anything about the poster. The thought of getting a custom piece of clothing had been far out of reach until very recently, and this felt like a huge indulgence. Going through all the Harris Tweed swatches with Nisa herself was a wonderful throwback to the days of Mamma V's career. After comparing swatch after swatch to the colours in the poster, we found the perfect houndstooth.

When the call came to say the dress was ready, there was a fair amount of excitement in the air. Unsurprisingly, given how much Nisa had put into making it, the dress was perfect. It was a belted A-line dress with two front pockets and a grand funnelled-neck. The quarter-length sleeves had pin tuck detailing all the way down the seams. The Harris Tweed houndstooth was in beautiful shades of brown, green, vibrant oranges and black. And the finishing touch would be a dark-red felt rose brooch – handmade by Nisa and given to me as a gift for the ride.

With the dress done, the next thing to sort out was the pillbox hat. Luckily, I didn't have to travel too far to find Bellapacella, a milliner recommended by Nisa and run by a woman called Jeanne, who also had a stall in Old Spitalfields Market. I won't lie – I've never really been a formal hat woman. I always loved the look of beautiful and ornate hats and fascinators, but never really thought they would suit me. Before that year, the only types of hat you'd find in my wardrobe were beanies and bobble hats, so getting a fancy one professionally made was a whole new experience. The Bellapacella stall was filled with a multitude of vintage-inspired hats ranging from 1920s-style cloches to cocktail and 1940s pillbox affairs. Jeanne was more than happy to create a bespoke hat for me and I had plenty of fun trying on the different styles, eventually entrusting to her the roll of tweed kindly donated by Nisa to match the dress. I returned in a couple of weeks to collect my piece of millinery magic. My pillbox hat was finished off with a pheasant feather, red netting and a diamanté cameo brooch. It was perfect.

When the poster was finally released, I put up a blog post of my preparation for the Tweed Run. It had an amazing response and fed my huge excitement for the day. I was like a kid before Christmas! The morning of the Run, we took a leisurely ride to Trafalgar Square (I didn't want to be a sweatbox in the outfit!), the starting point and where the usual official photocall was happening. I'll never tire of arriving to a sea of beautiful outfits and bicycles in all shapes and sizes, all gathered in one place and how it unfailingly gets an inquisitive and friendly response from onlookers. This time, I could feel I was one of the people that was getting stared at – people who followed VéloCityGirl clocked who I was, which resulted in posing for pictures before and after the official photocall. I was a bit of a spectacle, but there was such a joy in playing dress-up for the day. I made a point of finding Eliza and thanking her for the poster and everything it had meant to me.

During the ride, the poster came to life even beyond my outfit. As Ian and I pulled up to Red Lion Square for the Tea Stop, Mr Tweed Run himself, Ted, greeted us with a somewhat mischievous sparkle in his eye. We were instructed to park up our bikes and stay right where we were, and off he vanished. A few moments later Seb, one of the ride marshals, appeared and presented us with a rather modern touring-bike tandem! Neither us had ever been on a tandem before, so as you can imagine there was a bit of a wobble when it came to balancing and pedalling in sync. We managed a few revolutions before almost coming a total cropper. I had no idea how tricky it is to get used to tandem riding, and this was just going a few feet up a quiet side street, so I doff my pillbox hat to the couple that did Eroica Britannia on one!

It was unbelievable that once upon a time I had watched the Tweed Run via social media, hoping to one day be able to take part, and now I was the actual poster girl for the event. It had become a massive part of my cycling life – Ted and the hundreds of people who took part in it every year welcomed me into their community. That poster hangs on my bedroom wall as a reminder of how far I've come, and what chasing dreams can lead to.

The Open Road

I often think, 'Where would I be if it weren't for cycling?' I can't imagine what I would have done if I hadn't gotten into it. I would have to have found some other big thing ... but I can't imagine what on earth that 'big thing' would be.

Emily Chappell

In July 2017 I had the chance to interview one of the most kick-ass women on the endurance cycling scene, Emily Chappell: co-founder of The Adventure Syndicate, author of cycling memoir *What Goes Around: A London Cycle Courier's Story* and women's winner of 2016's Transcontinental Race – the entirely self-supported, 3800-kilometre race across Continental Europe. I'd met Emily a while before this interview (August 2015 to be exact, when I was in total awe of her after her keynote talk at London Bike Kitchen's WAG Festival), but I was still a bit nervous about having this conversation. Between all of her cycling projects, Emily is an incredibly busy woman, so grabbing sixty Skype minutes with her while she was back home in Wales resting was lucky, and like I said – she's one of *the most kick-ass women in cycling*, so it's natural to be nervous about picking the brains of one of your bike sheroes.

Emily has been cycling for over twelve years, and it was starting off as a cycle courier in London that got her into endurance riding. Cycling around the city delivering packages all day is a world away from riding non-stop around Europe, but it was doing this as a full-time job that built up the fortitude she took into her racing career: 'You get used to getting up and getting out on the bike no matter how tired, grumpy, ill, hungover or premenstrual you are.' During our Skype chat, Emily started echoing my thoughts on being surprised by what your mind and body are capable of on a bike, and I was taken aback. I know she couldn't have just woken up one day and suddenly be brilliant at long-distance cycling, but in my head someone like Emily just seemed like a biking badass – born with the gift of *doing it*.

'The first time I signed up for the Transcontinental, I realise in hindsight I felt like I was a total fraud,' she says, 'I always tend to think that I'm not good enough.' The curse of Imposter Syndrome in cycling – especially when it comes to going the distance – is something I know all too well, but Emily was one of the last people I would have expected to have it. Watching her in the summer of 2016 (by following her GPS dot on the live TCR tracking map online) become the first woman to cross the finish line in the fourth edition of the Transcontinental was incredible: Emily completed the race in 13 days, 10 hours and 28 minutes – just under two days ahead of the second-placed woman, Johanna Josten-Van Duinkerken, who did it in 15 days, 3 hours, 35 minutes.

A year before her huge achievement, I remember being incredibly inspired (along with all the other folks in the standing-room-only audience) at that WAG Festival, listening to Emily talk about her first attempt at the TCR in 2015. After eight days of non-stop riding, she had to pull out of the event due to chest pains which landed her in hospital. As Emily described that whole incident to me as 'unfinished business' in our chat, I could hear the determination in her voice as she said it: instead of putting her off from doing anything like that again, the whole experience spurred her on to trying again in 2016, and made her realise she was totally suited to endurance cycling: 'Actually I *was* completely capable of doing it, and should have been doing that kind of cycling for longer than I had been in my life!'

I could totally understand what Emily was saying and exactly where she was coming from. Although not as hardcore as taking on the TCR, after doing sportives such as the L'Eroica series, Ride London and things like cycling 104 kilometres around the harbours of Hampshire on my road bike for fun, I discovered that I had it in me to cycle longer and harder, pushing myself that little bit further each time, even though I'd keep on telling myself stuff like, 'You'll never complete this kind of event, Jools.' While telling Emily that, she immediately picked up on me doing myself down, despite the fact that I was doing more distance cycling than ever before: 'I see you as a classic example of quite a lot of the women I meet who tentatively dip their toes into a long-distance challenge and are more than capable of it,' she advised. 'You, along with a lot of those women I meet, have been capable of it for *years* – it's just a matter of building up at a pace you are comfortable with.'

There is also the curse of other people telling you that distance and endurance riding are the kinds of cycling you won't like and not the kinds of cycling a woman should be doing, especially alone. This is an attitude towards women's cycling that makes Emily quite frustrated (and quite rightly so): 'People saying, "I don't think you should do that – I don't think you'd like it" ... I'm more and more angry with that sort of attitude because, basically, those people are looking at women and judging our capabilities on the basis of the ride being hard, painful and challenging. It's saying we're not strong or intelligent enough to do deal with it, which is awful.' When it comes to the scary for Emily, she continues, 'I've done a lot of things that people thought would be difficult or scary that actually weren't and I've also done some things that *have* been difficult and scary ... yes, I was scared and it was hard ... but I did it.'

It's positive cycling disruptors like Emily who give me and other women and young girls out there the support and determination to give it (whatever that bike-related 'it' might be) a go. Through co-founding The Adventure Syndicate – a collective of extraordinary cyclists who happen to be women – Emily and her fellow 'Syndicateers' aim to challenge what others think women in cycling are capable of, by doing extraordinary things by bike to inspire, encourage and enable others, especially women and girls. In 2018 The Adventure Syndicate worked with five schools across Scotland in a one-year 'adventurous travel' project funded by the Sporting Equality Fund. Designed to inspire and enable pupils to feel capable of more, the project engaged with all pupils but especially teenage girls who would otherwise not choose to take part in physical activity. As I've talked about before, the focus on keeping and inspiring teenage girls to cycle is so important, as is breaking down the barriers that keep them off the saddle – which include things like feeling unsafe riding on the road and having no one to ride with. There is also the babying of women and young girls in cycling, something that Emily still comes across even after all these years of taking part in competitive races: 'There is a protective impulse people have towards women: people see women as very vulnerable in society, which I think actually is just infantilising women and young girls in cycling. Look at me – the number one question I get asked about endurance cycling is "Isn't it dangerous as a woman?" or some variant on that. Partly that's them assuming that the world is full of people who want to harm women and partly them thinking that as you're a woman, if a hard thing came along you might not be able to do it.' On this brilliant tangent, Emily asks an excellent question, 'Why the hell don't we encourage people to go and do things that are properly difficult? Most of us, when we do those things, have an experience that makes us a better person and *challenges us*. We're actually depriving ourselves of that sensation if we continue to tell each other it would be scary.'

This puts me in mind of the story of another female long-distance rider, Rebecca Lowe, a writer and reporter who in 2016 set off on an 11,250-kilometre year-long cycle from the UK to Iran. Rebecca was not a seasoned adventure cyclist – she had never used panniers on a bike before and hadn't ridden up a hill for six years prior to her trip. Writing for the BBC after completing her epic route, she said: 'I wanted to show that the bulk of the Middle East is far from the volatile hub of violence and fanaticism people believe. And that a woman could cycle through it safely. Not everyone had faith in my ability to do so, however. "We think you'll probably die," one friend told me before I left. A man in the pub said I was a "naive idiot who would end up decapitated in a ditch – at best" … yet I remained tentatively confident.' Rebecca completed her trip and did indeed return in one piece.

In all the years that I've been back on a bike, I feel like I'm still cementing my existence in the cycling world. Perhaps that sounds like a really deep thing to say when it comes to bikes, but that's something that I feel like I'm doing on my journey with cycling: the challenges and new experiences that I am giving myself on two wheels do make me feel like a better person. Even though I've had people say some really random and hurtful things about me (I'll never forget when someone said I should forget about road cycling because, 'Jools will never look natural on drop handlebars') it's always going to be up to me to decide if I want to try something new to find out if I'm going to enjoy it.

Women like Emily who trail-blaze and champion for a change of attitudes towards women's long-distance and endurance cycling are inspirational and keep the wheels of hope and encouragement spinning.

'I think, what would twenty-year-old Emily think if she could see me now? There are ambitions I had that kind of predated my ever getting on a bike but have come true via cycling ... like I always wanted to write a book – that was my childhood dream. I was going to be an academic but eventually I became a cycle courier and then it was like, "Goodbye, left brain, I'm just going to be a manual labourer now!" Then I started writing and *that's* when it all started to come true so it felt like I turned away from it but actually cycling led me *towards* it.'

Although one of her cycling ambitions as a child didn't happen exactly as envisioned (Emily wanted to become a professional cyclist, but realised she 'should have started ten years previously and everybody who was my age was retiring already'), she has been able to race at effectively world-class level:

'It's a very, *very* small field in endurance racing: it has been an amazing experience but I've learnt that being racy and competitive and winning stuff isn't the be all and end all that I thought it would be, so sometimes you know you're charmed and things come true and it's exactly what you always wanted and imagined. Sometimes you get where you never thought you would be and then you realise, *aaahhh* it's not actually what I expected of it, but I'm glad that I've had the chance to find that out – which again is something that cycling has given me.'

These words from Emily are a lesson that I carry forward with me on my cycling journey. When I got back on a bike in 2010 and started VCG, I didn't know the exact path those two things would take me down ... and to be honest with you, I never will. I can't predict the future – I can make plans, but there is no guarantee that they will go the way I'd envisioned them. That's happened plenty of times since I've been in the cycling industry (and some things and some people have burned me pretty badly) but you know what? That's okay as it's all part of the learning process and growing from those experiences.

Being on a bike has presented me with new opportunities and chances to discover myself ... and to see where my journey will go. And that's a feeling that I'm going to hold on to and keep cycling with for as long as I possibly can.

Beyond the Comfort Zone

Dark clouds are rolling in over my head, carrying the threat of more rain. I'm still soaked from the last horrendous downpour I got caught in about half an hour before; my leather cycling shoes are sodden, squelching whenever I move my toes, and my damp woollen cycling shorts and jersey are clinging heavily to my body. I've just climbed five hundred metres up a hillside on an old steel bike, over the muddy gravel roads of Tuscany ... all to take a seat on a lumpy old boulder. I ignore the screams of pain coming from my legs, along with the sheer drop to the right of me, as I gawp at the view: vast acres of the Dievole vineyard, surrounded by trees and rolling hills in every shade of green you could imagine.

This grey and thundery Sunday in October 2015 was beautiful. *Everything* in that moment, including how knackered but strangely energised I was feeling, was beautiful. I'd forgotten all about the fears I'd had over doing the Italian edition of

L'Eroica and riding across terrain that I'd never experienced on two wheels before. All I could think about was how amazing I felt for getting to this point on the sportive, and getting this far on my cycling journey. This was a whole new sensation, and I'm not talking about the lactic acid burning through my leg muscles … it was pushing myself further that I ever had on a bike, and the burning desire to complete the course around Tuscany and do even more rides like it. This was a far cry from my commutes around London, and a huge surprise to myself about what I thought I had in me when it came to life on two wheels.

This is what can happen when one journey that you have mapped out in your head can lead you to a totally different one in a heartbeat. It was in June 2015 that I returned to the Peak District to do Eroica Britannia. This time I had my wingman Ian with me for the adventure! He was desperate to do the event after listening to me bang on about how fantastic the 2014 festival was. He was even keener to do it, as parts of the cycle route were his old stomping ground as a child.

It was exciting just to be there together, but then an unexpected and amazing opportunity came up while we were there: Brooks England (one of the main sponsors of the Eroica events) invited us to experience L'Eroica in its birthplace later that year. There I was, mentally preparing myself to ride the Peaks again, while an agenda for my next Eroica adventure was being set in Italy. The answer was a resounding 'Yes!' Other than it being another amazing opportunity, I'd made a promise to continue challenging myself with more challenging rides – and from the stories I'd heard about the Tuscan countryside, this would certainly fit the bill.

Arriving in Pisa on the Friday and being driven to our accommodation in the town of Gaiole in Chianti, two things struck me immediately:

1) How beautiful it was.

2) Just how hilly the countryside was.

We were going higher and higher into the hills. With every bend in the road came a new breathtaking view of what was below us and road signs detailing the route of the ride. It was slowly dawning on me exactly how steep L'Eroica was going to be. Now, don't get me wrong – I LOVE a good descent, but going down these would be a whole new ball game. Going up? Well, I wasn't going to allow myself to think about that too much. As I gazed out the van windows, that tiny voice of doubt started to natter away in my mind ... but there was no way I was going to listen to it and miss out on riding that terrain. Other than the big day itself, one of the things I was hyped about experiencing at L'Eroica was the vintage bike market, along with the atmosphere of the village over the ride weekend. It's quite the sight to see: pretty much all of Gaiole comes out in celebration of the event. You're immediately welcomed in – look up and you'll see banners with messages of encouragement hanging from all the buildings. The small village lends itself almost entirely to a vintage bike market covering all bases for your ride – from old steeds and components to jerseys, banana helmets and shoes, it was all there and was magical to look through. Everyone was in the spirit and the romance of what was to come on Sunday.

Brooks had covered my bike hire so all I had to do was choose which of the bicycles in the shop would be mine for the day. We wandered into an Aladdin's cave – I had to stop myself from checking them *all* out and just focus on the group of bikes in my size. After cooing over frames, I gravitated towards what became my steed: an Andre Bertin road bike. It was technically a bit of an 'illegal' bike for the ride as the model was from around the 90s (so definitely not pre-1987) and the gears on it were indexed (when gears are indexed each click of the shifter will cause a single, simple shift up or down the gears, front or rear – for L'Eroica they should be non-indexed).

I joined the others in our group to get my bike tweaked and have a test ride around the village. I was happy with the fit and especially the fact that there were no cages on the pedals – I still wasn't ready for that – and the gearing was great. My one concern? The brand-new Brooks Swallow saddle the bike came with. It was an absolute beauty, but the thought of breaking in a new saddle on a 46-kilometre hilly ride worried me a little. After being assured that the saddle would be a dream, I didn't swap it out and hoped that they would be proved correct the next day.

The festivities continued into the evening with the 'Dinner of The Heroic' – an official meal laid on by L'Eroica the night before the event. In the best possible way it's an overwhelming experience: a huge white marquee hosts table upon table of participants, gathered to eat the traditional dishes of Gaiole and drink copious amounts of Chianti, which flows abundantly throughout the night. Sustenance is QUEEN! Stacks of bread, cured meats, bowls of ribollita, pasta dishes, grapes and biscotti served with Vin Santo ran as far as the eye could see. I totally loaded up on the courses. The dinner is intended to set the 'heroes' up for what they'll face the following day. Stuffing my face was 100 per cent the best plan. Going crazy on the Chianti? Not so much. Having had my fill, I took myself to bed to ensure a clear head for the big day.

The next morning I was a bundle of emotions: mainly excitement mixed with slight trepidation. Rain had been forecast and the early morning sky was brooding. Again that little voice started going off in my mind: 'You've never done climbs and descents like this before, Jools ... and in the rain?!' I listened to it for a moment, but it soon got hushed when we set off from the courtyard, cycling the long and snaking road down to the official start line. We gathered with the swathe of other riders setting off for the 75- and 46-kilometre courses. The sea of colourful woollen jerseys, vintage bikes and joyful conversations was drowning out any of my reservations. I immersed myself in the atmosphere and before I knew it we were shuffling along with the rest of the crowd towards the start line. It suddenly felt very real when I noticed everyone around me was pulling their brevet cards out of their jersey pockets or saddlebags, ready to get their first stamp.

All L'Eroica rides have predetermined checkpoints, known as 'controls'. Each rider carries an official brevet card that has to be stamped at each control to prove completion of the course. Our first one was the start line, which meant after that it was time to head off into the Tuscan hills to get to the next one.

For the next few hours it was nothing but stunning open roads, pedalling, fresh air ... and rain. The dark clouds gave up the obvious secret they had been keeping: that the day would be incredibly wet. God knows what had been going through my mind but I didn't have a single piece of waterproof clothing on me. No packable jacket in my pocket, no water-resistant cap stowed away in my musette, not even a bin liner to stick over myself (as I saw others doing, which was genius) – it was just the beautiful, retro, woollen jersey, padded shorts and a cap that stood between me and the downpour. Usually, a small shower dampening my day would be liable to produce a small tantrum, and this was a full-on weather assault. But this time something inside of me came to life in the rain. I have no explanation for it, but I absolutely loved it. Being told by lots of seasoned riders of L'Eroica that this was the worst weather they had ever seen at the event only spurred me on. A mix of the atmosphere, strangers shouting 'Allez, Allez!' as I cycled along, bumping into friends on the ride who were also battling up climbs and down descents, and the Strade Bianchi essentially becoming mud tracks made it all the better. Through wobbles, drenching and tiring cycling, the one thing that was constant was smiles and laughter. Every corner turned revealed a new adventure – be it a brilliant food station, a breathtaking view, more familiar faces, or wild grapes providing extra sustenance, there was constantly something new to relish and enjoy.

The rain eventually stopped, but there was still plenty of terrain to cycle through, made even more treacherous thanks to the downpour. After many more kilometres of mud, the desire to push on never faded and eventually the end of a truly heroic adventure was in sight. Arriving back in Gaiole, I was once again immersed in a sea of riders. We were all messy, damp and tired but revelling in the feeling as we crossed the finish line. Celebratory hugs and drinks and dirty bikes were the order of the afternoon in the centre of the village, and with that, one of the best adventures I'd ever had on two wheels was done. We all felt like heroes.

On a chilly February evening in 2016, I stood outside the Design Museum and took a deep breath before entering the building. Partly to calm down after hopping on a Boris bike and pedalling in the frantic rush-hour traffic to get there on time, and partly to steady my nerves for what lay ahead of me later that night: chairing a panel discussion which was completely outside my comfort zone.

In November 2015, the Design Museum had launched the

last large exhibition they'd be holding at their Shad Thames site before relocating to a new home in Kensington. It was the 'Cycle Revolution' exhibition: celebrating the diversity of contemporary cycling in Britain from everyday commuting to Olympic-level competition. The show would also focus on cycling design and innovations and where they could take the riders of the future.

I'd met with the show's curator Donna Loveday in the summer of 2015 as part of the Vulpine team. One of the company's Original Rain Jackets had been selected to go on display as part of the 'cycling design and innovation' section, and I was there to discuss the logistics of getting the jacket (and any back-ups required) to them for the show. An unexpected surprise was Donna telling me at the end of our meeting that she was a follower of VéloCityGirl and the Design Museum wanted me to be involved in a panel discussion they'd be putting on as part of the exhibition later down the line.

They wanted me to chair a panel in a February talk titled, 'Never Mind the Bikes – Do We Need a Cycle Revolution?' Each speaker on the panel would need to answer the question (yes or no) and explain their reasoning with a short presentation, and then have a discussion about it all with their fellow panellists.

I immediately said yes to chairing it: I've got to take those opportunities as they come along, right? It's not every day you're asked to speak at the Design Museum, and this was a platform that I never imagined myself being on.

The panellists that I would be chairing and speaking alongside were a world away from the kind talks that I'd been part of before. On the panel were: Will Butler Adams (MD of Brompton), Donnachadh McCarthy FRSA (co-founder of cycling campaign group Stop Killing Cyclists), Jon Marshall (co-founder and director of MAP, working with a start-up on the design of an intuitive cycle navigation device) and Vincent Stops (Labour councillor for Hackney Central Ward and a cabinet member for environment, transport and planning).

And there was me – the cycling blogger, part-time TV presenter and by now a familiar face in the cycling scene. I was pleased to have been invited to be part of this by the Design Museum as I would have plenty to say on the subject and wanted that platform to do it on. But at the same time, I was feeling the pressure of being the only woman and the only PoC on a panel made up of middle-aged white men. There are times when being that sole voice weighs heavy on your shoulders ... along with the fear of being pigeon-holed into the same role over and over again. Still, I was praying that night when I walked into the building that I wasn't there as an act of tokenism.

Each of us came to the discussion with our differing cycling backgrounds. Scheduled to speak last meant I was able to watch the presentations and gauge the reactions of the audience. My fellow panellists were all calling for a similar kind of cycling revolution, and their talks were filled with statistics related to design, business and city-cycling infrastructure. I came at it from a completely different perspective. I stood up at the plinth, clicker in hand to load up my presentation. Staring out at the audience, I was trying to read their faces, even though the spotlight was on the stage.

I started clicking through my slides: pictures from my childhood of me on that tricycle. My beloved hand-me-down Raleigh Burner from my sister. The day I got Frankie from On Your Bike. The amazing people I had met on my cycling journey. *This* is what I was going to talk to them about. I could feel the moisture vanishing from my mouth and my throat turning to sawdust as I started to speak. I talked about what cycling meant to me as a woman and specifically a black woman. I talked about widening participation for all women in cycling, and the importance of keeping such an important conversation going, the impact cycling has had on my own mental health and the ways it has opened my eyes to so much more of life. My argument to the question posed by the panel's title was that a cycling revolution was *already* happening, but there was a need to recognise the intersectionality of it and for brands, voices and organisations to recognise that and the social change around cycling and to engage in the dialogue that surrounded it.

I said I wished there were more women from a range of different backgrounds and other marginalised groups up on this stage to talk. I wished there was more inclusion. I knew I wasn't representative of all people of colour, women or marginalised groups in cycling, but I was doing my best to encourage those that I did know to start cycling. I'd been doing that via the platform of my blog, other panel discussions that I had been part of that were specifically reaching out to these groups. I talked about the reasons people from these under-represented backgrounds had that stopped them from getting into cycling: financial restraints, the preconception that cycling is an activity for the elite only, lack of self-confidence – all of which were very real factors.

I can't speak for everyone, and nor would I ever dare to. I was just a voice that wanted to talk and encourage others to talk and have such platforms to do so too. We all need to be listened to, we all need to be represented – and we will all be heard in the revolution. So we needed to keep talking, and keep the wheels of the revolution moving.

The end of the talk certainly wasn't the end of the discussion – I ended up having conversations with members of the audience who wanted to chat, and ask questions about my cycling background. Those conversations were fascinating, and many people were wanting to chat to me about the organisations I'd mentioned (such as London Bike Kitchen and The Bike Project) and the journey I'd been on – because, as one of them put it, 'I'd never really thought about cycling from those other perspectives that you talked about, as I guess I never really had to.'

Different Strokes

On Monday 7 March 2016, my 05:30 a.m. alarm went off as usual. I'd get up at that slightly insane hour of the morning to give myself enough time to get ready and make the commute from East to South West London. On paper, the commute via train takes 62 minutes. In real life with delays on the Jubilee Line and the unpredictability of things going wrong at Waterloo with South West Trains, it could take up to two hours. I could hear my phone beeping on the bedside table, urging me to get up. That woozy, just-five-more-minutes haze covered me, and I could feel myself trying to reach for the alarm.

That was the first indication something wasn't okay – *trying* to reach for the alarm. Perhaps it was that sleep-fog hanging over my head, but while lying on my left-hand side, I couldn't pull my right arm up to hit the phone. I was just lying there, struggling to move. The sound of the alarm became incessant and as it fully roused me from my sleepy state, I soon realised that something was very wrong indeed. Not only was my arm still asleep, my right leg wasn't having any of it either. Nothing was working properly and the right side of my face and mouth was completely numb too. I've never had a tonne of bricks collapse on me before, but this suffocating and claustrophobic sensation I was experiencing was the only thing I could liken it to.

Panic and fear drowned me as I tried to talk, shout or even moan but the only sound I could make was a series of slurred noises. No matter how desperately hard I tried to speak or use all the energy I could muster, my body simply wasn't responding to my commands. The numbness eventually passed and the right side of my body slowly decided to wake up. This terrifying sensation may have only lasted for a matter of minutes, but it felt like an eternity. Finally sat up in bed, my mind was in two places: I couldn't really process what the hell had just happened, but I also convinced myself that I was fine. 'Perhaps it was just a weird form of sleep paralysis,' I said to myself. I had a busy day of work ahead and stuff to get on with and there was no way it could be anything sinister.

As I travelled into work that morning, I felt absolutely awful. Bouts of wooziness came in waves, and I had a feeling it was probably more than just the usual crush of being in a packed London Tube carriage in rush hour. I couldn't handle getting on my bike to cycle over to South West London feeling so bad, but the train didn't help either. I made it into the office, continued to ignore my instincts and decided I just needed to get on with my day and whatever this was would pass. Coffee: that should fix it.

Come early afternoon and copious cups of coffee later (probably not one of my best ideas), I still wasn't doing very well. If anything I was worse. Tiredness was hanging over me like a cloud, and a severe headache had me feeling like I'd been punched in the head. I knew I had to talk to my doctor. It's funny how something as simple as phoning the surgery was giving me cold sweats. I nipped out the office to give them a quick call – all I needed to do was casually explain what had happened to me, get told it was nothing to worry about and maybe take a few painkillers and get some rest, right? Of course, my 'casual' chat with the receptionist to explain what had happened wasn't that casual at all.

'I'm going to get the doctor to call you straight back for a consultation when he's free, but did you call or go to the hospital after it happened?'

'No ... I snapped out of it after a few minutes so I thought I was fine.'

'Okay ... like I said, I'll get him to call you right back.'

I was barely back in the office when I saw 'Doctor' flashing on my phone display and for a split second I didn't want to take the call. I didn't want to talk about it for fear of finding out something really was wrong. As I explained step-by-step what had happened to me, I felt frightened and failing.

'Are you still at home, Jools?' the doctor asked, sounding calm but quite concerned.

'No, I'm at work, in South West London.'

A brief pause from the doctor hung in the air.

'By the sound of what you've told me, you may have had a TIA, which is a mini-stroke, and you need to be assessed. St George's Hospital is the closest A&E to where you are, I'd suggest you go straight there.'

I don't really remember the rest of the conversation. I excused myself from work and dutifully made my way to A&E, just like he told me to.

It sounds like madness, but I didn't call anyone until I'd arrived at the hospital and got myself booked in. Alongside not wanting to cause worry, I also still couldn't admit to something serious being wrong. In the grand scheme of things, I felt fine: I mean, I was still feeling knackered, but I was awake, alert and talking – which is a far cry from what I thought a stroke was supposed to be like. This was nothing like I saw in *Holby City*, so on balance I was probably fine. Telling that to my family however, as I revealed what had happened earlier that day, didn't negate their panic at all. Mamma V went to pieces, and Ian downed tools and escaped from work as fast as he could to get back to London. Until he could be there, I called Iszi – one of my closest friends who used to work with me at Vulpine. She didn't live that far from St George's, and before I knew it she was by my side, doing an amazing job of keeping me calm and making me smile. Granted, it may not seem like a laughing matter, but defusing the fear and finding the humour in such a surreal situation was something I didn't realise I so desperately needed to keep me sane. There was no chance this was going to be a quick stint in A&E – I'd played myself thinking that would be the case! Ian took over from Iszi on the late shift waiting for me, while I received the full works from the Stroke Unit.

I'd never been subjected to so many tests in my life: bloods were taken, ECGs were run and a few scans were chucked in for good measure – all to see what the hell had gone on inside that brain of mine for a few minutes. My average Monday had taken a turn for the bizarre that I was never expecting and my future was looking as muddy as my road bike after a gruelling session in a rainstorm.

The hours spent in the hospital unit dragged. God knows how Ian must have felt sitting in the waiting room, but I was slowly losing my mind. I was like a sitting duck in a not-so-flattering gown, waiting for the next round of tests, any kind of news or just an update telling me I was free to go home. As the damage was being assessed, none of what was going on was making much sense. I needed to do something – anything – to cling on to my sense of normality. In that moment social media was a real saviour. I have my ups and downs with it, but being able to tell a world of friends what was going on and hear back from them within an instant kept me grounded and stopped me from panicking.

It was a long night. At 12:30 a.m. I was still sitting there, dressed in that far-from-fabulous blue gown, wondering what my fate would be. It was like waiting for a date that you kind of hoped would stand you up, so you could just walk away from it. But this date did no such thing, the bastard. The doctor who was assessing me finally walked back into my cubicle to talk to me. She had the news I was absolutely dreading: I had suffered a TIA. Her delivery of the news wasn't harsh – the entire team who had been looking after me was wonderful, and they knew the events of the last twenty-four hours had knocked me sideways, but she might as well have just thrown a bucket of cold water over my head.

I was numbed by the news – like a cruel joke had been played on me. But there it was: thirty-three years old and with nothing worse than a few asthma attacks in my medical history, yet I had suffered a mini-stroke. The hospital weren't able to give me a super-detailed insight as to what definitely caused it, but the word 'stress' was being said quite a lot. 'That's enough information, thanks,' I thought, deluding myself yet again that this would be it. This TIA had already become TMI for my befuddled brain to take in. I'd been awake for nearly twenty-four hours, and it was making me restless, anxious and agitated. I just wanted Ian to take me home and not have to give this any more thought.

Conversations about what happened next were on the hospital's agenda, however, and there was no escaping from them. I knew that it was serious, and looking back now it sounds like I was being utterly nonchalant about the whole thing. Imagine

The definition of a slow puncture is, according to etyres. co.uk, 'when a tyre gradually loses pressure over a period of time due to any one of a number of causes, including an object embedded in the tread such as a nail or damage caused by pot-holes'. That feels an apt metaphor for what had happened to me. You don't immediately notice a slow puncture, but underneath it all, something is going slightly wrong and it's caused by a bit of damage that happened earlier somewhere on your travels. Being at home on bed-rest and away from the busy hustle of it all gave me plenty of time to think. Trying to figure out exactly what my pothole was or the object that had embedded in me felt like an almost impossible task, but I had to look back and sift through it all to find out.

I was dumbfounded by what the bad things could be – awe-some stuff had already happened to me in 2016, just three months into the year. Weeks before this TIA nonsense occurred, I'd been on top of the world as I started tackling one of my big-gest anxieties: doing more public speaking. I love talking about cycling – from presenting on TV to being on panels, it's one of the things I thrive on because cycling is such a huge part of who I am. Unfortunately, getting up in front of a crowd is also some-thing that has me shaking like a leaf and paralyses me with fear. Yet I'd managed to chair a talk and give a presentation at the Design Museum for their Cycle Revolution exhibition. I pulled it together mentally to host London Bike Kitchen's WAGfest evening to a packed Look Mum No Hands!. This was all 'the good shit', there was nothing wrong. And there was the prob-lem: I'd convinced myself that everything was perfect.

While I was busy papering over the cracks, I'd stopped paying attention to anything that was wrong, or any warning signs that it wasn't hunky-dory after all. Owning up to some home truths meant the road to recovery was going to be even harder than I thought. I was far from enjoying my 'month in the wilderness', which was peppered with visits to the Outpatients Stroke Clinic. I'd never bounced between so many hospital departments in my life, and even that was mentally exhausting. From the Neurology Unit, to the Vascular Lab, Phlebotomy to Neuroradiology – all bases were being covered, and all credit to them, the team I was under was doing an amazing job. I was being looked after, yet I was as internally ungrateful as it was knackering. All over again I was in a fragile state, worried sick about what they would find. A common theme started to develop on each visit – the conversations that happened before the tests.

'You're only thirty-three? That's quite young, isn't it . . . '

or

'What could have got someone like you in here?'

That was the general nature of the small talk I'd have to listen to. My answer would be a shrug of the shoulders or making some witty quip about having a brain fart. Truth is, I probably knew what the answer was and didn't want to admit it. When the rounds of tests were done, and I saw a consultant at the very end, what I suspected to be a cause of the catastrophe was confirmed. Stress. I'd quite simply pushed too hard and stressed myself out.

I'd got myself into this mess by powering on through situations that made me unhappy, instead of stepping back and trying to address them. Why on earth had I done this, and allowed this to happen to myself? It was almost like I had broken one of my own golden rules of cycling – I had stopped going at my own pace and was desperately trying to keep up with everyone else around me. I *had* felt that something was about to go very wrong underneath my feet . . . and yet I kept pedalling on – speeding up to keep up and heading straight into total burn-out. It was time to start slowing down and look after myself properly.

Freewheeling

I knew something had to give. The fact it took my brain almost *giving up* on me to have that conversation with myself was another example of me not going at my own pace. I was trying to hastily paper over the cracks instead of fixing them and making out that everything was okay. It wasn't. That wasn't me – that wasn't how I dealt with things. I had to do something about it.

The month I was away from the office gave me space to think about exactly what I wanted out of life. Considering how scrambled my brain was, it was insane that those four weeks post-mini-stroke produced some of the clearest thinking I had done in a long time. The term 'life is too short' suddenly had real meaning to me – which is a scary thing to process. But it gave me the push to finally make one of the biggest decisions that had been hanging over my head for a while. It was one of the hardest, but it was the right one, if I was going to attempt to move forward and be completely open to new opportunities without burning myself out. After four years with Vulpine, I decided to go freelance. On 4 April 2016 I handed in my notice.

While I was signed off, I was still in regular contact with my line manager (sickness absence regulations and all that). Every time I spoke with her on the phone, I could feel the words 'Kate, I really need to talk to you about something' trying to come out of my mouth, but they just kept on getting stuck in my throat. I was terrified of putting the wheels in motion for leaving. This was totally different to me saying goodbye to my UEL days. First there was the practical side of it: when I quit admissions, I was walking away from one job straight into another. Yes, the position with Vulpine could have fallen through at any moment (one of the risks of joining a start-up, especially as the very first employee, was that nothing was certain), but I had a safety net ready to catch me – there was no such guarantee with going freelance.

Secondly, there was the emotional side of leaving Vulpine. When I landed that role, all through the power of VéloCityGirl and my love of cycling, I was convinced it was my dream job. I was working for a brand-new clothing company which held the promise of making changes that would turn the industry on its head with inclusivity and diversity at the core of its ethos. My whole world, friends and family and of course my online cycling community believed it was my dream job too, and why wouldn't they? From the moment I could shout my new job news from the rooftops, through to every single wonderful experience I had in my role, that's all people who knew me would hear me talking about. I wondered what they would they think if I were to walk away from it all ... probably that the mini-stroke really had frazzled my mind.

Running parallel to life at Vulpine was VéloCityGirl, morphing into this ... *thing*. The blog had taken on a new life and was giving *me* a new life. It was all so much bigger than I could have ever imagined. The panel talks, the platforms, the marginalised groups I was able to reach out to and connect with ... all of this made me feel so alive in cycling! I wanted to be able to continue to use my voice and use my platforms to amplify the voices of others. That was where my head and heart were at – I was feeling so restricted in my job and the hold it seemed to have on my freedom in the industry that I needed to break away from it.

I knew that if I wanted to do more – both professionally and personally – I had to take a major leap into the unknown.

The resignation conversion with my line manager happened over the phone. As I was still signed off, it wasn't possible for me to do it in the office. It felt so alien to do it that way – like this was the ultimate sign of how detached I had become from the company that I was once so in love with. When I told her my news, the first thing she said to me was, 'I knew it, Jools.' She'd picked up on my unhappiness at Vulpine months before, but didn't say anything to me about it just in case she had got it wrong and it was something totally different that was playing on my mind.

I didn't realise it had become so obvious, and it terrified me how disillusioned I was starting to feel with the cycling industry. There were elements of those old sparks going off in my head again too. I wasn't happy working in the industry any more. I had grown tired of the promise of change when everything around me seemed to be following the old crowd. I needed to take myself out of that situation, to rediscover my love for cycling again, as losing sight of the open road and forgetting the joy of freewheeling wasn't an avenue I wanted to go down again.

My first step back into the world of cycling post-mini-stroke wasn't actually a bike ride. As advised by the doctors in A&E that night in March 2016 (and further drummed into me at every stroke outpatients appointment I attended for those investigations), rest and recuperation was key to recovery and *no cycling* was to happen in those four weeks. But I wasn't told that travelling to go and look at bikes wasn't allowed ... and that's exactly what I did that April.

While resting at home (and seriously mulling over my life choices) that March, an email from Phil and Tessa Taylor, founders of Bespoked UK, that prestigious handmade bicycle show in Bristol where I fell in love with my Colourbolt bike, appeared in my mailbox. They were inviting me to be a judge at the show in April for two of the categories: the 'Outstanding Design' award and, get this – 'The Lady Vélo Choice' award for Women's Bicycles! I had to re-read their email several times to make sure my brain was processing this information correctly. Not being a frame builder myself, it was an absolute honour to be invited to judge at a show as authoritative as Bespoked UK – but to have my own named category to give an award out under? *That* was totally mind-blowing! Sat on my sofa feeling disillusioned and questioning my place in the world of cycling, this email from Phil and Tessa could not have arrived at a better moment.

It was incredible to be returning to Bespoked UK not as 'Jools who works for Vulpine', but as *Lady Vélo* – a member of the show's 2016 judging panel. As I walked through the grand archway entrance of Brunel's Old Station and stepped into the main exhibition hall filled with beautiful bike upon beautiful bike, I took a deep breath. The gravity of what was happening really hit me. Founders and frame builders who I knew and who were seriously respected in the industry like Caren Hartley (of Hartley Cycles) and Jay Pond-Jones (of Colourbolt) were somewhere in that hall, and I was there to judge their bikes.

I couldn't let Imposter Syndrome steal my thunder on this one. No way was I going to listen to that niggling little voice telling me that I should have stayed in my lane. I was there under my own steam! My love and appreciation for beautiful bicycles and my opinions on them, as expressed on VéloCityGirl for the last six years, were respected and deemed judging-worthy enough by the founders of the most revered bike show in the UK.

Of course, there was another thing about being at Bespoked in that capacity that was such a big deal for me: I was a *woman* in a predominately male-dominated sector of the cycling indus-try doing this! All those feelings and fears I had about being stifled, not being able to progress further and constantly bang-ing my head on glass ceilings – they hadn't all suddenly been magicked away by attending Bespoked, but my requested and desired presence in *that space* went some way to remind me that changes in the industry can happen.

Judging at Bespoked between those two categories was quite the experience – with 108 exhibitors, there was a lot to see, take in and talk about. I'm certainly not complaining: the chance to get to chat with the frame builders and designers and get the stories behind their builds was brilliant.

Catching up with friends I'd not seen since the TIA (or thought I'd not really see again because I wasn't working full time at Vulpine any more) and finally meeting some people who had been on my radar for ages was another thing that made a big day of walking around, making notes and talking loads even more enjoyable. And of course getting my camera out and rekindling my love of taking pictures of bike frames at different angles to upload on my social media channels was a lot of fun too. I had missed doing stuff like that – old-skool VCG blogging.

I couldn't get over how being part of Bespoked UK made me feel. I say it a lot – perhaps because I set myself a lot of challenges – but I felt like I was about to take on one of *the* biggest challenges of my life by going freelance, in an effort to recapture the cycling happiness I had at the very start of VéloCityGirl. Sink or swim. Fail or fly. It didn't matter … what did matter was going out there to grab my happiness, or at least find out if I could reach it. I had been so inspired by some of the other amazing women that I knew (including some of the female frame builders I met at Bespoked and around that time) who had made the leap to do their own thing, chase their dreams and make strides towards achieving them, that I so desperately wanted to do the same.

This was the start of something brand-new, on my terms. It was time for a new adventure.

The New Skool

There's lots of moments where I'm like, 'No, I can't do this anymore – it's not right.' But then I just ride my bike – a bike that I've made – and it makes me so happy ... and that's why I started building and riding bikes. I just sense-check that and then get back at it when my head is less cloudy.

Adeline O'Moreau.

Thinking back to those initial months of freelance life with VéloCityGirl, it's probably easier to count the times where I felt *100 per cent legit* about what I was doing than all those instances where I didn't. I've lost count of how many times the doubts crept in. Those moments where I thought I'd made a huge mistake: leaving a 'powerful' position I held within the cycling industry to try to make a difference by going it alone, on my own terms. Perhaps I wasn't good enough to do this, and maybe the positive things my friends and other people were saying were nonsense.

I'd be lying if I said that didn't happen any more. My mind still plays those games with me, and I have to work *really hard* to fight those thoughts, to be able to look at what I'm doing and think to myself, 'Yeah – actually walking away from Vulpine wasn't a moment of complete madness after all.' Even though I had a bit of a plan, little did I know exactly where it would end up taking me ... but sometimes it's great to just freewheel and ride the path that life decides to take you on.

Someone else I know in cycling who went down a similar 'unknown' path is bike racer and frame builder Adeline O'Moreau. The first time I met her in real life (Adeline is another person in cycling I first got to know through the power of the Internet) was April 2016, when I was a judge at Bespoked UK. Adeline was working at Google as a creative designer, and was racing with the London collective The 5th Floor (a cycling team who also have a group of riders based in NYC). That same month Adeline had also completed a frame-building course at The Bicycle Academy in Somerset and built her own bike. Fast-forward a year and Adeline had launched her own frame-building company, Mercredi, and was now making bikes for other people. Her work was that good she was nominated for two awards at Bespoked 2017, winning The Columbus Choice Award and runner-up for The Chris King Choice Award. Not bad going for someone who had spent very little time in a workshop, and had never brazed a single piece of steel bike tubing in her life.

The Belgian-born, London-based designer turned her hand to frame building after becoming increasingly frustrated with off-the-shelf bikes. Adeline races Cyclocross (sometimes called Cross or CX – a gritty style of bike race that takes place over terrain including pavement, grass, wooded trails and steep hills, and has obstacles that require riders to dismount quickly, navigate around the obstructions while carrying their bikes and remount them again), but she could never find a CX bike that worked for her. The bikes that she bought didn't fit properly, nor did they suit her riding style. Tired of never having one to race on that was perfect, Adeline decided to fix the problem by signing up for a frame-building course to make her own. As she puts it, she wanted a bike that 'fits perfectly, has all of the clearance and none of the compromises smaller off-the-shelf frames always seem to have'.

I still remember how strong the pride was that radiated off Adeline while we sat together that April in Workshop Coffee (one of my favourite coffee shops in Fitzrovia, and one of the sponsors of The 5th Floor cycling team) as she told me about completing the course at The Bicycle Academy. At the end of it, she had a perfect bespoke CX bike that she had designed, fitted to her own specifications and built from scratch – all in the space of just ten days. Sat with Adeline in Look Mum No Hands! fifteen months later for this interview, she was smiling from ear to ear, with even more pride and enthusiasm radiating from her – which was understandable, considering the whirlwind of events that had happened since our last meet.

'There wasn't a plan to launch my own company!' she tells me with an energetic bounce. 'I just wanted to build a highly functional bicycle that would be perfect for my kind of performance ... every decision we [Adeline and the team at The Bicycle Academy] made was informed by how the bike was going to perform.' After Adeline had created her 'perfect race machine', she noticed that, other than it improving her riding, her CX bike also gave her something else – power. This wasn't power related to just the physical side of racing. As Adeline explains, it was also a boost to her mental strength: 'It allows me to go so far out of the comfort zone I had before. That's a really good reminder and always makes me think to myself *I made that bike* and *that bike* gives me the power to do those things.'

It's clear that frame building for Adeline is more than just making something she can stand back from, look at and think, 'What a beautiful machine' – it was the empowerment that came with that first frame which made it so much more. And that became a feeling she wanted to give to others. Although there was never a goal to start her own company, events began to conspire in her life which would make that happen. As well as those feelings of satisfaction Adeline experienced while in the workshop using her hands and tools to create her CX bike, she was also becoming disillusioned with working in the advertising industry. Eventually, she quit her job in that field, thinking, 'There had to be more to life than late nights in the office working on pitches.' As fate would have it, life took Adeline back to The Bicycle Academy when an unfortunate event happened to a friend of hers. 'My teammate Clare got her crossbike stolen and I was like, "Shit! She's such a good rider and now she doesn't have a bike – I wish I could make one for her!" And then – like life does sometimes – I'm in the office and Andrew from The Bicycle Academy calls me and he leaves me a message like, "Oh, hey Adeline, it's Andrew, I've got some good news for you – give me a call me back," and I'm like, "Well, OK – what's this about?!"'

The good news Andrew had for Adeline would prove to be life-changing. That year at Bespoked, Shand Cycles (an independent British bicycle manufacturer based in Scotland) had won the Columbus Spirit Award, and the prize was a set of Columbus steel tubing of their choice. Although a brand-new set of top-quality tubes is *always* welcome at a bike manufacturer, Shand – already a thriving business – decided to pay it forward and donate the prize to another up-and-coming business or builder, understanding the impact a new set of expensive tubing would have on someone who is just starting out. As Adeline explains, 'Shand Cyles got in touch with Andrew and said, "Who can we help out with this set of tubes? Who is going to benefit the most from receiving it?" and then Andrew thought of me because I had had such a good time making my bike *and* I had told him that I wanted to make more but I didn't really have the know-how to go about it.' Not only did Andrew offer Adeline the tube set, he also offered her space at The Bicycle Academy to build herself another bike. 'Andrew asked me if I had an idea of what I'd like to do and my answer was pretty immediate and was something like, "Uh, yes ... I'd like to make a bike for my teammate Clare because hers got stolen!"'

The timing of this offer was perfect – Adeline couldn't wait to get brazing again and Clare had recently left her job so didn't have cash to spare to buy a new crossbike – but then another thought crossed Adeline's mind. 'I wanted to try and make this crossbike a bit differently to mine ... I decided I'd like to try and make a batch of them and make Clare's one alongside two other bikes.' Adeline found two other people on the CX scene who were in the market for a new bike and were more than keen on her making their machines. She designed them in BikeCAD (specialist bicycle design software used by custom frame builders and fit specialists), bought more tubing to make those two bikes, and headed back to Somerset to build once again in the BA workshop.

Adeline wanted to give accessibility to a sector of the cycling market that she felt was under-catered for: shorter people (like herself) or very tall folks who fell outside the statistical norm. It turned out making those three bikes in a batch was a eureka moment for Adeline regarding this problem – and one that led to the birth of Mercredi Bikes. 'I discovered if I make three bikes that are kind of similar in their features – although the geometry is completely different because they're made around three bodies that are completely different with different abilities – it's just repeating the same action three times instead of just doing it one at a time ... and it makes it much faster and much more straightforward. And if it's faster it's cheaper ... and if it's cheaper then more people can have it.'

Accessibility to that market regarding cost and the experience of getting a hand-built bike was important to Adeline too. Understandably, having *anything* made bespoke can be an expensive business – but it can also be an intimidating process, which in turn can make it feel like a very exclusive members' club. I often think about how much I'd *love* to commission a totally bespoke bike (both aesthetically and physically – especially because of my height, and the shoulder/arm reach issues I have with the scoliosis in my spine) but dreaming about it is as far as it gets. At present, I can't afford it, and (despite working in the cycling industry, knowing a thing or two about bikes and having once judged at Bespoked UK) I feel like a novice who wouldn't know how to describe what I want to a frame builder. This is a thought echoed by Adeline, who gets just how unnerving it can be. 'I think accessibility doesn't just come down to the price you have to pay to get the object – I think there is an element of custom bikes that can be a bit daunting for someone who's not gone though that process before. When those bikes become quite complicated and have a selection of components on them that the customer isn't familiar with – which is totally OK – it can feel like in order to go to a frame builder and say, "I'd quite like you to make me a bike please," you'd need to have that gigantic bike knowledge already. Feeling like you don't know enough to go to a frame builder, even for a chat, makes it less accessible and that's a problem that shouldn't exist.'

Although I'm not a Cross racer (though never say never), it's hard not to get swept up in the enthusiasm Adeline has for what she is doing, and feel inspired by her to ride your bike as hard and as far as possible. You immediately get the vibe from her that she's on a mission to make cycling more accessible – from the method she uses to build her bikes, right down to being able to speak to her in laywoman's terms about what you'd like. Adeline keeps the whole process as pure and simple as possible, and understands the importance of making a connection with whoever she is building a bike for. That personal touch is a massive aspect of what Mercredi is about for her: 'The first step when someone comes to me and would like me to make a bike for them is always that we meet each other and talk about what they want to *do* with the bike. At that stage I am absolutely not interested in what kind of bottom bracket you want to have, or what cable routing you think would be the right one – forget the components! What I want to know is what you hope to do with that bike: just go to a place in your mind where you can see yourself riding it ... what are you doing? Are you going on adventures, are you racing, are you going on a long ride ... will this bike make you feel confident going downhill again? That's the starting point of any build and I think it's then my job to help the person to understand, if they don't know already, what they want to do with their machine.'

Adeline works in a slightly different way to other frame builders; she makes all of her bikes in batches of three or four. This allows her to be as effective as possible, while keeping the quality of the builds up and the price of them down. Simplifying the design of her CX bikes (at present, Adeline is completely focused on frames for cyclocross racing) means that she can focus on how well the bike rides for its racer – and at the end of the day, as Adeline points out, the joy of actually riding a bike that works for you is one of the most crucial things. 'If the industry designed around every rider's body, we could bring that made-to-measure bicycle to riders who would not usually want to get one because it's too expensive or because it's perceived as this object to cherish and look at rather than jump on and ride *really* hard. So I just tried to prove to myself *that* building process makes sense and it could work ... and it did!'

When it comes to the aesthetics of a Mercredi bike, there's a real fun and creative element in Adeline's designs. One of my favourite examples of this is the metallic-green Sausage Dog Camo CX racing bike she made, which was the winner of the Columbus Choice Award at Bespoked 2017. This is exactly what you think it is – a bike frame covered with dachshunds ... eighty-seven of them to be precise. There was a humorous story behind the design that the rider and Adeline wanted to convey: the sausage dog symbolised the power and determination of the rider and their bike – 'innocent-looking but absolutely unstoppable'. The inspiration may have come from the customer but being able to bring that emotional connection between the human and the machine alive through design is something Adeline does incredibly well. 'I'm a designer by trade and I want to sweat on the details and I want to make something super-crisp and pretty, but also I know from my design career that in order to make a good design you have to state yourself a really clear mission.' As she's explained before, her initial thoughts on a build will always be geared towards the fit and performance of the bike for the rider and what they'll get out of it, but there has to be that emotional connection to the bike too – after all, it becomes a part of the person and their whole story, so the two go together. 'You don't want to make something that's pretty that's not got a mission – I want to make something that works. And then my design process needs to be refined around that one mission which is *make a bike that rides as best as it can* and *make sure that the rider will ride it as hard as they can*. And then every decision that I have to make, I have to think about that again: "Is this going to make the bike ride better? Is this going to make the rider want to ride her or his bike more?"'

Since launching Mercredi Bikes, Adeline has gained a lot of positive attention and plaudits in the cycling world. Between admiration for her unique design process and winning awards for both her custom builds and racing (Adeline was crowned women's Single Speed CX European Champion in 2018), there is something else that has drawn quite a lot of attention to her: being a female frame builder in a male-dominated industry. Being a woman in that domain doesn't faze Adeline, as she goes on to explain: 'I just happen to be a woman who is a frame builder. I have a job and it's to make good bikes, and the fact that I'm a woman is, I think, irrelevant to the equation. Obviously having lived twenty-seven years as a woman has given me different sensibilities because of the experiences I've encountered. Your output in the world is always tempered by your story and what's happened to you in life and some of the stuff that's happened in my life has to do with the fact that I'm a girl, but the fact that I'm a female doesn't change much – it doesn't make me make weaker or stronger bikes. I don't think I've been *lucky* not to encounter any battles – I just think the industry is smart enough to not care.'

Having worked in the tech industry surrounded by tech bros for years before moving into cycling, Adeline is familiar with that kind of male-dominated work scene. 'I've come from an industry where I've often been the only girl in my team and where I've sometimes been in job interviews and people have said they want to hire me because I'm a woman and they need to put a woman on their team ... and I'm like, "NO – I want you to hire me because I'm going to do a really good job because I'm a really great designer!"' Adeline applies this school of thought to Mercredi Bikes: 'I think people who want me to make bikes for them don't give a shit if I'm a girl or a boy. They want to ride their bike really, really hard and they think about their bike in a way that *they* identify to it ... and that has nothing to do with my gender.'

There are undoubtedly quite a few young women and girls who see Adeline as a trailblazer in her field. This was a subject that I had to broach with Adeline, as it's still (sadly) considered unusual for a woman to be in that sector of the cycling industry, so surely there will be others out there who will be looking up to her as a role model. This is something that Adeline does feel 'emotionally attached' to – growing up in Belgium, she never felt any barriers stopping her from doing anything that she wanted because she was a girl: 'I grew up with two brothers and my parents made me wear the clothes that my older brother had grown out of so I was never really defined by my gender. Even as a small child, I was just a kid and I think that allowed me to grow up without thinking there were jobs for girls and jobs for boys and that there were hobbies for girls and hobbies for boys ... I enjoyed running around in the forest and daring my brother to eat a slug as much as I enjoyed trying new, inventive but not-so-great haircuts!' Talking about it more, Adeline says she feels really lucky in that sense, as she knows a lot of people who didn't get a chance to define themselves as they were growing up. 'It was their education or society or the city they live in [that defined them] so I'm really conscious of how lucky I am.'

This luck or privilege that Adeline had growing up is something that she recognises, and she understands that it's pretty special to be someone in the industry that other people can identify with: 'I'm a woman frame builder and if I'm inspiring lots of women to cut metal and set things on fire, then I would be extremely proud and extremely happy about that. I still want to inspire all kinds of people though – like *anyone* who thinks they can't use a drill, can't get busy with a blow torch or they can't quit their job and start a business of their own ... if people can identify themselves when they see me do something and they get inspired to do it then that's wonderful too.'

There have been a few moments when it struck Adeline that some folks didn't expect her to be doing what she does in frame building and running her own cycling business because she's a woman. She gave an example of being on a stand with one of the CX bikes that she'd made: 'The person talking to me is like, "What is this bike – who makes it?" and I'm like, "Well, that's me," and they say, "Oh, so you paint them?" and I say, "No, I make them with metal and fire and my own hands." And they're like, "Wow, but that's such a manly activity!" and I just tell them, "Well, no, actually ... it's not!"'

As Adeline continues to build Mercredi Bikes, she also continues to positively disrupt the industry and get people out riding. The name Adeline gave to her company is pretty fitting as well: Mercredi is Wednesday in French, and on Wednesday afternoons in Belgium schools close so that the kids can go off and have all kinds of fun. And that's exactly what Adeline hopes people who ride Mercredi bikes will do – have all the fun, going anywhere you want, with no rules stopping you.

Empowerment, encouragement and energy are at the core of her designs – and those are feelings she's determined to pass on to anyone who swings their leg over the top tube of one of her CX bikes: 'That's why I made the bikes – to give that power to somebody else and that's why I want to keep on making bikes. Having a bike that works with you allows you to go to all those places, those physical places and those places inside yourself, that you can't really reach otherwise. And so, it's good to ride to remind myself of that when I'm like, "Oh no, this is all bullshit I'll never be able to make it work" – it can be really hard but it's definitely all worth it, because if my bikes make other people feel good, that makes me feel so good too.'

Going Up a Gear

May 2016 – two months after having the mini-stroke, more cycling opportunities for VCG started rolling in thick and fast. In another episode of 'Exciting Cycling Emails that Lady Vélo Receives', Brooks England got in touch inviting Ian and me to take part in the inaugural Eroica Limburg event that July. My blogging relationship with Brooks was going from strength to strength: they enjoyed my fresh take on doing the Italian L'Eroica so much, they asked me to cover the newest European addition to the sportive series, which was taking place in Valkenburg, Holland.

When Brooks contacted me, I was still under the care of St George's about that pesky mini-stroke business, so the first thing I did (well, the second thing, after screaming for joy) was consult with the medical team who were looking after me. I'd stayed off the saddle for those initial four weeks like they told me to ... and I hadn't actually cycled since the mini-stroke happened. As I wasn't feeling like the living dead any more, I had a hunch that it would be all right, but knowing how serious the whole thing had been, I needed to make sure doing something as intense as an Eroica ride would be allowed. The timing of Brooks inviting me to Limburg couldn't have been better, as the TIA Stroke Clinic had updates for me on all the investigations they'd done. The initial blood tests I had when it happened had come back clear. The carotid artery ultrasound (a scan that looks at your carotid arteries, which run up either side of your neck) the outpatient clinic carried out was fine: there wasn't a blood clot, fatty materials or air bubbles blocking an artery to my brain again. The MRI scan I had returned no abnormalities. Everything was okay. Even though I got this good news, I still had a chat with my GP to be double sure. Both gave me a medical thumbs-up to go ahead and do the ride. But there was still worry surrounding me taking on what would be my biggest and hardest bike ride since having that mini-stroke just four months before.

I assumed that after that period of no riding and going stir-crazy about it had passed, I'd have hopped on Frankie or my Colourbolt quicker than the speed of light. But I didn't. While I was recovering, if I had to go out, I'd use public transport or walk to my destination. I got stuck in that groove well after the four weeks had passed and I wasn't even mad about it. If I wanted to take a walk, that was okay. If I wanted to take a long bus ride and zone out on my journey, that was okay too. I was remembering to go at my own pace again and do what worked for me, which is something I'd been guilty of forgetting for way too long.

That invitation – the chance to do something so challenging after such a difficult time – was appealing though. I guess because it was something brand-new in cycling to get my teeth stuck into and a chance to show myself what I was capable of if I put my mind to it, I wanted to do this! No disrespect to Frankie, who will always be my first bike love, and perhaps it sounds potentially self-destructive after what my body had been through – but I needed something that wasn't a gentle commute in London to remind myself that I was alive.

Ian was 100 per cent up for doing Eroica Limburg – of course the roadie in him was! Just like me, he'd never been there before, and was up for taking on a new adventure with me ... but he was also worried about me doing something as extreme as the ride that we were reading about on the Eroica website. As with each Eroica sportive, the ethos of the Sunday ride was the same: to celebrate the beauty of old-skool road cycling and for it to be damned hard in places. Described as 'the beauty of fatigue and the thrill of the conquest', Limburg was putting itself out there as a ride to be reckoned with. We were looking at doing 65 kilometres (40.3 miles), which is the short route (the longer routes are 125 kilometres and 200 kilometres). I'd done thirty miles on Eroica Britannia, so ten more didn't seem like that much of a stretch for me. Ian's anxiety about me doing the ride was assuaged by the all clear that I'd got from the docs, and how hyped I was about getting out there and doing something like Limburg – he was a rider, so he really got it! Before I could go back to Brooks England and give them a definite 'yes please', I just had to convince Mamma Vélo that it was going to be fine ...

'I've had the all clear from the hospital *and* the GP – honestly, I'll be okay, Mum.'

I remember stressing this point to Mamma over a cup of tea in the kitchen. Sat on the opposite side of the kitchen table, she took a sip from her cuppa, while giving me one of *those looks* over the top of her glasses. I was straight back to being that kid on the tricycle riding a bit too fast through the passageway. Mum squinted and set her tea aside.

'And Ian is going to be with you *all* the way on this ride, right?'

'Yes Mum – *all the way*,' I answered. Even though I'd been cycling for six years and had thankfully never come a cropper on my bike, Mum always takes more comfort in me cycling if she knows that Ian is riding with me. I knew it was a combination of Mum's thinking on this: safety in numbers and someone she knows and trusts watching over me because she couldn't ... Bless her.

Mamma V picked up her tea again to take another sip and gave me another of her looks. This time I was that kid getting her tricycle out from under the stairs to go on a big ride around the grid.

'Well, make sure you're both careful. And get some nice pictures of the ride.'

Just like Britannia and Gaolie, Eroica Limburg was a weekend-long affair. We flew out to Valkenburg on the Friday and had a relaxed afternoon with the rest of the Brooks team. There was more riding going on that weekend than I'd let on to Mamma V, as I knew that she would just worry herself sick. On the Saturday, Brooks had planned a 'modern road ride': instead of riding on pre-1987 road bikes, Brooks supplied each of us with a modern-day road bike and road-cycling kit for us to take in the sights of the city.

Going out for a ride on the Saturday before the race was an ace opportunity to see the city and get a feel of what the big event would have in store. The beauty of the scenery was breathtaking – blue skies (before the burst of rain caught us towards the end), vast fields, a few climbs and descents (with the odd herd of cows and coffee stops along the way) and seeming reasonably flat, it was a joy to cycle through on my borrowed Bianchi. Part of the ride warm-up incorporated some of the Amstel Gold Race route (the very same Spring Classic that Amy and I ended up watching on our first visit to LMNH) and was led by ex-pro-cyclist Marc Lotz. Now I'm not gonna lie: I couldn't keep up with him for dust, but it was still nice to ride alongside him and pretend to be of that standard for a few moments. Taking a leisurely pace that morning was my plan, knowing that Sunday would be a long day on the saddle. I saw hints of what was to come on the Eroica route – official sign-posts were appearing along the roadside, some leading towards gnarly-looking gravel roads and pools of mud. It was certainly worth keeping that in mind as I cycled back to Valkenburg, to enjoy the rest of the relaxed vibes.

Ride day arrived, and as our wave of Brooks B1866 clothing-clad cyclists made its way to the start line, those gravel roads and rough terrain I'd spotted the day before played on my mind. The sky looked like it wasn't going to hold up for ever, and at some point I suspected that plenty of mud and rocky roads would be on the agenda. I knocked back a couple of espres-sos, gathered for the group photos and lost myself in laughter, catching up with friends and hanging around with some of the cycling legends who were riding the course that day.

The start of the route took us through Lourdes Grotto accompanied by a light show and videos of The Muppets singing 'Mah Nà Mah Nà' projected on to the cave walls. This was already shaping up to be unlike any Eroica route I'd been on before. Starting the route off with laugher was a tonic, as a few minutes later this Lady was not laughing. On the other side of the grotto was the Cauberg. This was a climb that took me and my legs by surprise. I gave it a go, but my legs were screaming, and this was only the first climb of the route. Unlike Marianne Vos, I didn't smash Cauberg in one thrilling go. There was plenty of panting, a whole lot of push-ing and some serious walking to get to the top. Beyond that climb, which I thought was already the end of my legs, came the stunning countryside and fields I'd had a taster of the day before. Rolling fields of green, with bursts of wheat, corn and poppies, lined the route. With great beauty comes great pain. This ride taught me that more than most. Those gravel roads and mud baths that I had clocked on Saturday were waiting for me. It was almost unrelenting: with every twist in the course came a new climb and descent. I swear there were points where the gravel was morphing into boulders and sink-holes under the skinny wheels of my bike. I've no idea how I managed to stay upright and not get floored.

By the time I reached the first and only food stop on this course, the thirty-two kilometres it had taken to get there had started to feel like a cruel joke. There was no let-up as I struggled to cycle on: I was getting increasingly irritable, feeling dizzy and at the point where I couldn't cycle in a straight line. Being mindful of my recent TIA and remembering that I had to listen to my body, I got off the bike and walked for my own (and everyone else's) safety. For the first time in six years of cycling I had 'bonked'. After being told that's what was happening to me (or rather having it drilled into my head as I wasn't quite 'all there'), I got seated and knocked back more food than I thought possible. Despite having breakfast and taking on fluids along the way, it hadn't been enough sustenance for my body to deal with how brutal that first leg of the route had been. An incredible hunger hit me like a wall, and I carb-loaded and downed glass after glass of orange juice like never before. There was no rush, so I allowed myself time to recover and get my energy levels back up before back on the bike I went.

Although there still wasn't much let-up on the roads, the rest, refreshment and food (plus extra portions stashed away in my jersey pockets) I'd taken on board gave me a boost and allowed me to ride the remaining twenty-eight kilometres. When I looped back to Valkenburg at the end of a very long day, that finish line looked like heaven. For every moment when I felt like I was about to lose my shit because of the amount of tyre-ending gravel, steep climbs and bike-swallowing mud, I remembered the beautiful descents I let myself loose on, and the camaraderie of the ride.

Me and my aching body had made it through all the gnarly stuff. It was something to be celebrated and be proud of, and even if it was 'just the 60-kilometre' course, no one can take away the absolutely glorious feeling of riding something so brutal, bonking and coming out the other side smiling.

Four months prior to this, the thought of riding a course like Limburg would have been impossible. I had doctors (as wonderful as they are – always bless the NHS) prodding and poking at me, telling me that I needed to stop riding for a while. I listened. I continued to listen to them and also to my body and mind, which eventually became happy to let cycling take a back seat while I sorted myself out. But I also had to listen to my body when the desire to do something totally out of the normal for me on a bike came up. How could I not? I pushed myself to a limit (and still managed to listen to myself when I did end up bonking) but I made it to the end ... with a medal around my neck to prove it. Coming this far so soon after everything that had happened meant everything to me and reminded me that I was indeed very much alive and kicking, and that nothing could hold me down.

It had been a while since I'd attended or worked at a large-scale cycling trade show. I'd grown wary of them during my time working on that side of the industry for many reasons, including how uninclusive and formulaic they had become. There needed to be a *really* big pull for me to want to go back to one again. It had to be something that would make a difference from the usual narrative that I would pick up from those kinds of show (that cycling is an activity for the more affluent end of society and that it's predominantly aimed at men), which was always so ... soulless. In August 2016, one such pull came along. I got a call from a client I used to work with in my old job, telling me about an idea they had put together with the UK's biggest cycling trade shows. Instead of being put off at the mention of the words 'cycling trade show', my interest was piqued.

Back in my sales and operation days, I used to work with VeloVixen – an online store which specialises in selling female-specific cycling gear. VeloVixen were one of the stores that carried Vulpine's women's range, so after speaking with them on a weekly basis (stock requests, sales figures – that kind of thing), I had built up a great professional and personal friendship with Phil and Liz Bingham, the husband-and-wife team behind the small family-run business. Since launching in 2012, VeloVixen have been keen supporters of women's cycling, and are known in the industry as the 'home of women's cycling kit'. They're consistently recognised every year in industry awards and have won some major accolades including 'Best Women Specific Retailer' and 'Best Online Store'.

Almost a month after doing my Limburg adventure and still feeling like I could take on the world, I got a call from Phil. We'd not spoken much since I'd left my old day job so it was a wonderful surprise to hear from him. What was even more wonderful was the reason he had given me a ring.

It was that time of year again in the industry calendar – cycling trade show season – and Phil and Liz would be bringing their hand-picked selection of women's gear to Birmingham in

September for The Cycle Show. That's not *The Cycle Show* I was a presenter on – this Cycle Show is a three-day event held at Birmingham's National Exhibition Centre (NEC). It's the biggest cycling trade show in the UK, showcasing over three hundred exhibitors and five hundred brands, and is a chance for the general bike-loving public and industry insiders to see products that are coming to the market for the first time.

There is no question that The Cycle Show is an incredibly well-organised event by a very excellent team. When it came to the logistical side of things, the operations manager in me was always impressed with The Cycle Show ... and would break out in a cold sweat thinking about how much planning goes into putting on an event like that! However, the female cycling-blogger/bike rider in me wasn't that blown away by the vibe of the show. There were plenty of exhibitors and brands that I enjoyed checking out, but what was on offer beyond that wasn't representative of how diverse cycling culture is.

I'd always been baffled by this – The Cycle Show is the biggest one of its kind in the UK, and the cycling scene/cycling culture here is much broader than usual tropes that were being peddled. The range of cycling personalities that were being invited to give talks on the main stage of the exhibition always seemed to fall into the same demographic too: male elite, professional cyclists. Where were the women? Where were the PoC? Where were the grass-roots cycling groups and campaigns? The project that Phil told me about bringing to life with The Cycle Show was going to attempt to remedy that problem.

VeloVixen were upping their contribution to women's cycling with the VeloVixen Women's Cycling Hub. A year in the making, Phil and Liz had created a huge space at The Cycle Show solely devoted to women's cycling. The Women's Cycling Hub would be offering a mix of female-specific clothing brands to try and buy, and a speaking area solely devoted to women in cycling, ranging from elite to grass-roots. They were quite literally giving a platform to women from different backgrounds to tell their stories. When Phil gave me a taster of some of the range of the confirmed speakers for their stage, I was more than impressed. It included:

Jo Rowsell-Shand – who had recently returned from Rio 2016 after winning Olympic gold in the team pursuit

Manon Carpenter – former mountain-bike world champion

Emily Chappell – ultra-distance cyclist and recent winner of the TransCon race

Adele Mitchell – cycling blogger and journalist

Sarah Perry – organiser of Tour de Force (amateur cyclists riding the length of the Tour de France)

This was already sounding like quite the refreshing mix. It's always fantastic to see well-known names on the main stage at shows of this scale, but when you're bringing together Olympic gold medallists with lesser-known female cycling advocates, endurance riders, mountain-bike legends and grass-roots cycling, you're on to a damned good thing. All of these women have different voices and different stories to tell.

I had assumed that Phil had called to fill me in on what VeloVixen was doing at The Cycle Show, because he knew this was something I and readers of VéloCityGirl would be interested in. But when he asked me if I would be one of the speakers at the event – as well as being the host for the Cycling Hub, I was blown away. The answer was most certainly yes to being there in September!

Remembering not to let my nerves eat me alive, I got on with the task in hand – which was to remain totally professional in handling the stage and Q&A sessions I was running, while also getting totally immersed in the fantastic cycling stories being told via the panels and talks. In this situation, being awestruck over all the amazing women I was speaking to is more than allowed, right? How could I not when you have the likes of Shu Pillinger and Emily Chappell talking about racing across continents with no holds barred on how challenging it is? Then sitting down with Jo Rowsell Shand and Dani King – another extraordinary Olympic gold medallist whose reputation precedes her – for one-on-one Q&A sessions talking Olympic gold, the hard work and the sacrifices that go into being in that world and what the future holds for them? I even felt inspired to dip my toes into the world of mountain biking one day, thanks to sitting down with Manon Carpenter.

Honest and frank talks about carving a career in cycling as a woman were on the agenda too. As a woman who had recently gone freelance in that world, hearing these voices was really important and inspiring for me. Listening to women in the industry who had 'made it' like Liz Colebrook (bike-frame builder and owner of Beaumont Bicycle) and Joyce Bereton (founder of female-specific cycling clothing company As Bold As) was incredible. They discussed in frank terms the difficulties and joys of their paths, and how to make changes for other women wanting to go down that road.

One of the fastest growing customer sections in cycling is female road bikers, which begged a very obvious question: 'Why isn't there more for women at these shows ... or more women *on* the line-ups?' In creating the Women's Cycling Hub, VeloVixen started to carve out the path for change and are continuing to do so: after its successful debut at the 2016 Cycle

Show, the Women's Cycling Hub became a regular feature of the event.

Seeing a cycling industry mainstay like The Cycle Show have the Women's Cycling Hub as part of the event is encouraging and should be celebrated. But while applauding them for their progressiveness and turn towards inclusivity, that doesn't mean the problems women and marginalised groups in the industry face have been solved – changes *still* need to be made. More companies, brands and events further up the top of the chain (who in my opinion still hold the most power) need to start implementing these kinds of change too: have more panels like the Women's Cycling Hub at your trade shows and look beyond the obvious headliners; engage with the wider cycling demographic that really *does* exist; employ more WoC/PoC and other marginalised groups at your companies; expand your marketing tactics beyond the demographic of affluent white men!

Variation and intersectionality are key to getting multiple messages across. I had grown tired of what these large-scale shows were usually like – keeping to the well-ridden path of names and faces. Those names and faces are brilliant, but the industry was crying out for some diversity. Knowing VeloVixen had worked hard to break that barrier and do something different was impressive, and warmed my stone-cold trade show heart.

Working with one of the nicest teams in the cycling industry who are moving towards real change was incredibly refreshing. It was pretty pleasing to have been a part of this with VeloVixen *and* The Cycle Show leading the way in showing other large-scale events how it should be done. Inclusivity should be something *everyone* in the industry is striving for, and not just something that's just displayed as a knee-jerk reaction, or because it's trendy to focus on it for a while. This *has* to be constant; this has to be a movement. We all have voices and stories that should be listened to, and the world of cycling would be enriched so much more with wider representation. It's time to really open up the stage and the floor to every voice that should be heard.

Although I hadn't gone clipless straight away with Baadgyal back in 2013, that didn't mean the idea of doing it wasn't crossing my mind on a regular basis. Curiosity about doing it popped up every time I went out for a ride on Baadgyal and saw other roadies with their shoes attached to their pedals, powering to their destinations. I'd get a case of the 'what ifs':

'What if it's not as scary as I think it is?'

'What if it does give me a bit more power on my ride?'

'What if I don't suck at it and I'm actually quite good?'

It took three years of owning Baadgyal and owning my confidence on her to feel ready to take on the challenge. Clipless cycling would only happen when I was ready – not because I was feeling pressured into it, and I'm so pleased that I listened to myself on that. First I had that bike fitting in early January 2016, which included having my cleats and pedals set up precisely to my measurements. Knowing that they were ready to be used whenever I was ready to give it a whirl was so reassuring. Next, it was all about practising using the cleats and pedals without the fear of breaking something – including myself!

I had to keep that positive momentum that I'd got from the fitting that month with Tony going, and a gem of advice from friends who rode clipless stuck with me – 'practice makes perfect', so for the rest of that month, clipping on and off the bike on a regular basis in a safe space was so necessary. Doing it in familiar surroundings that were close to home and I was comfortable in was key. Now when I say close to home, I really mean that: I'd prop Baadgyal up against the kitchen counter (I didn't have a Turbo Trainer, so this was the next best thing – I also still need to get myself one after all this time!), step on the pedals and get 'that clicking thing' going on. I practised twisting my feel and clipping in and out until it started to feel more natural. Remembering the euphoria of getting the hang of it during my bike fitting and doing it in the kitchen was putting my mind at ease, but this wasn't quite the same as rolling the bike out of the house, hopping on it and actually riding. So that's what I did ... in one of the children's parks close to my house! It wasn't the scale of Canning Town Recreation Ground, which was once my playground on the Burner, but the tiny little pathways in the kiddies' park were enough for me to get started on.

After a month of practising between my kitchen and the kids' park, I was feeling ready to go much further and do the real thing. I wanted the experience to be fun and with someone who could put up with me having inevitable 'moments' on the bike ... and laugh with me should I tumble and fall. Ian has always been my wingman on new cycling adventures, but I really wanted to do this with another woman. Having that shared experience of what it's like going clipless for the first time and what it felt like out on the open road as a woman was important to me – it would be an inspiration! I knew exactly who I wanted to do this with: luckily enough I can call the amazing Adele Mitchell a friend and she was more than happy to take me for Sunday cycle in roadie mecca ... Box Hill in Surrey.

We'd set a date – 7 February (which coincidentally was exactly a month after I'd had my bike fitting). Adele put my mind at ease about the whole thing in the lead-up to our Sunday spin: she knew how excited but nervous I was about finally riding clipless in the 'real world' and I knew that she wasn't going to make us do anything crazy. I kept on telling myself, 'It's a bike ride, Jools – just with a slightly different twist.' Sunday arrived and the weather gods were on my side: the skies were blue, the air crisp and there wasn't a rain cloud in sight. Adele texted me a picture of the Surrey Hills looking glorious earlier that morning to encourage me, and I couldn't wait to get cycling with her.

I needed to get to Dorking, where Adele lived, but there was no way I was riding all the way there from Canning Town! I cycled over to Waterloo to get the train from there in my Lycra kit, but not in my cleats: I stuck those in a little musette bag on my back and wore a pair of Converse trainers for the journey. You can actually cycle in flat shoes on clip-in pedals – it's a little tricky as there isn't as much surface area for the soles of your shoes, but it's doable when you get the balance right. It was great to get into Dorking and see Adele waiting for me outside the station but it also dawned on me that this is where going clipless would really begin. I changed into my cycling shoes, clipped in with my left foot and pushed off with my right. Click – both of my feet were locked on. We had a little practice ride around the empty station car park ... so far so good. With encouragement from Adele and gaining more confidence in that moment, we set off towards Box Hill along the cycle path.

As we rode along the path, I kept on twisting and unclipping each foot, one at a time to make sure I still had the hang of it. There were a few hiccups doing that though: as some of the 'snap-clicks' turned into my toe fumbling to flip the pedal over and the cleat slipping off it with each attempt – ARGH! Frustration started to rise just a little and then came the doubts in my mind: 'This isn't me ... I'm never going to get the hang of this ... this system doesn't work for me and I'll be stuck on Box Hill for ever!'

And then eventually it clicked.

BOTH my feet remained attached to the pedals and I was still moving. I felt pretty good: the nerves were starting to settle down, but thinking ahead, I was fully aware of what would naturally come next: stopping. We'd talked about this beforehand and I'd kept in mind what Adele was saying about taking a foot out with enough time to anticipate coming to a halt. She pointed out a crossing ahead we'd be coming to on the route, which became my marker for the first attempt at stopping. That fumbling right foot of mine suddenly became my natural unclipping side and with a good twist of my heel and enough time, I got that foot out, balanced again on the pedal and made it to the crossing without falling. The rhythm of the ride was coming together – we were climbing, I was clipless and Adele was doing an amazing job reminding me of this and keeping me going.

The ascent of Box Hill, something I never imagined myself doing, was now under the wheels of my road bike. There I was, pedalling amongst other Sunday morning Surrey hill climbers, saying hello and all heading for the top. I'd done hill climbs before, but as we got higher and I kept on pushing, I started to realise something felt very different – I had more control over what I was doing on the pedals with my feet being locked into place.

'Just one more corner, Jools, and you're there – and remember to start unclipping!' shouted Adele as she rode ahead of me. There it was: as I rounded that last corner, the top of Box Hill appeared. I went from feeling pretty good to near on fantastic. Mind you, that feeling was probably further aided by the sheer amount of cake that was also on offer at the top.

Suitably sugared, caffeinated and buoyed up by bumping into some familiar faces at the café, an hour later it was time to roll on, and what goes up must come down: it was time to take on the descent. Now, I love a good bit of downhill riding, and doing it this way was something else. Previously, and when at speed like at L'Eroica, it had felt like I had to 'push' myself into the pedals to remain steady and on the bike. Doing it clipless? That feeling went and it felt like I had so much more control of the bike, and myself. I loved the feeling a hell of a lot more than I expected. As the route came to an end and Dorking station was back in sight, it all seemed way too good to be true: I'd managed to climb up and down Box Hill, was unclipping my right foot in time to stop and having a blast.

Of course it had to happen. We'd joked that I'd avoided the obvious, so my euphoria enabled the completion of my rite of passage: a slo-mo clipless fall. I'd slowed down for the final crossing, yards from the station, but my right foot just wasn't coming away from the pedal. I was coming to a halt yet as if in slow motion my entire being fell to the right ... and BOOM, she was down. I'm glad to report I was laughing as I was going and Adele had my back and my arms as she got off her bike and hoiked me out of the road, still attached to my bike.

It may have ended with a drop, but it couldn't take away from what was a brilliant day of riding and yet another cycling learning curve for me. Going clipless was probably one of my biggest fears about getting into road cycling. It took one day for me to be converted. I was itching to keep on riding clipless and build my confidence ... one clip at a time.

Nine months after my first clipless cycle, Team VCG (me and Ian) was invited to cover the launch of the collaboration between cycling holiday company Love Velo and British Cycling. In November 2016, Love Velo had been announced as British Cycling's official travel partner and was holding a special day at the National Cycling Centre in Manchester to mark the news. To celebrate joining forces, Love Velo offered a group of everyday riders a session on the NCC's Velodrome and indoor BMX track. The rather special twist to this experience? You'd get coaching throughout your sessions from Rio 2016 medal-winning Olympians and Paralympians.

Neither Ian nor I had been on a velodrome track before and it had been a very long time since either of us could claim to have been on a BMX either. There was plenty of excitement building as we got on the train to Manchester, though some trepidation as to whether we'd get back in one piece. I'd spoken to a few friends who'd done track cycling plenty of times, and after I'd told them I'd ridden fixed gear before, they all had the same advice: build up your speed and you'll be fine. That was all well and good, but the combination of being fixed, clipped and without brakes on a steep track was giving me pause for thought.

Entering the empty Velodrome at 8 a.m. on a Monday morning was breathtaking. The vastness of the track and the seats looking over it really hits you, and the knowledge of champions who have cycled on the track hangs in the air. Knowing that I'd be donning my kit and having a go on it was both thrilling and daunting. Being greeted by Callum Skinner (a member of Team GB who won silver in the individual sprint at the 2016 Olympics and a member of the British team that won gold in the team sprint) and Megan Giglia (a British Paralympic gold-medal track cyclist who competes in C3 classification events) was incredible. They were so down to earth and excited for us, putting everyone there at ease.

Clipped in and holding on to the railing, coaching began with a rundown of the track and re-familiarising myself with being on a fixed-gear bike again. Starting to ride around the apron – the flat area between the infield and the track – the feeling of relaxing on the bike kicked in. It'd been a while since I'd done fixed (I'd had the pleasure of being loaned a Clubman – a fixed-gear bike – by Pashley for a review and ended up with it for eighteen months, which was a lot of fun!) and although I'd not forgotten how, this was brand-new territory.

Feeling more confident after a few gentle laps, it was time to progress on to the blue of the cote d'azur, which is the start of the Velodrome. Those light-blue painted boards signal the edge of the track. This area is marked off by foams in time-trial events like the individual pursuit, which stops riders taking a shorter route around the track and gaining an advantage. As I was going around, I had Megan giving me feedback on how I was doing. After a certain amount of laps and picking up speed, she encouraged me to graduate up to the black and eventually the red line of the track. It was quite surreal having her talking to me as I was riding and telling me that I was improving with each lap. With each revolution, I was taking on more and more speed, faster than I had ever been on a bike before. I loved it. My legs had gotten into a wonderful cadence and before I knew it, I'd gone beyond the blue line and was riding high up on the banks of the track. Coming down in every sense of the phrase was awesome: being on a high like that from cycling – especially a form of cycling that I never thought I would do – was amazing. I got a chance to chat briefly with Megan after listening to her tell us all about her journey into cycling for Team GB, and the fact it all started with her having a stroke really struck a chord with me.

My mini-stroke was still on my mind – it'll never leave me, nor will the fear of it being the thing that could have stopped me from cycling. But that mini-stroke also made me stronger and opened my eyes to life-changing decisions that I needed to make.

After some much-needed carbs and tea, more inspirational talks and cradling some medals, it was time to don new gear and head over to the BMX track. I did mention it's been a while since I was on a BMX, right? I'm talking a while ago like 'my first bike' while ago. When I got the Raleigh BMX Burner my brother restored for me, I loved riding it, but seeing the indoor track and meeting Quillan Isidore (a former under-16 world champion and multiple-time national champion) fast made me realise what I had done before was nothing on the scale of what a BMX can execute. I've wanted to get back on one for a long time, but just never got round to it. I'm going to be honest with you: I was not as good at BMX as I was on the track. Even when I had a one-on-one session with Quillan – on his personal bike may I add, which was lovely of him – I wasn't quite getting into the stride of it as fast as a certain bloke I know.

Ian took to the BMX track like a duck to water and it was a joy watching him tearing it up! Although I didn't quite get the hang of it, and it was possibly best for the health and safety of others that I ended up watching from the sidelines for the rest of the session, that's not put me off wanting to try it again.

The biggest joy of the day was that there wasn't any pressure on you being good enough to ride either of the tracks. It brought back the absolute joy of just going out on a bike and trying something new. Being a total novice that day wasn't an issue, even when you end up making an embarrassing social media faux-pas ... like photobombing Olympic gold medallist Callum Skinner, which is exactly what I did. Perhaps I should have noticed Callum posing for the photographer in the inner ring of the Velodrome as I was going around it. Instead of speeding up to get out of the way, I panicked and slowed down. When Love Velo released their official launch pictures and one with me looking mortified on the track behind Callum was included in the press pack, it took pride of place on the VéloCityGirl write-up of the day.

There will be moments in life that totally throw you. Something that will come along out of nowhere and push you to your limits – testing your resolve and seeing what you're made of. I'd experienced plenty of those on my cycling journey, but I had no idea that taking part in RideLondon would be one of those moments.

This was *really* going to be something else.

RideLondon is an annual weekend festival of cycling held in London. It was developed by the then Mayor of London Boris Johnson, London and Partners, and Transport for London (TfL). RideLondon was designed as an annual legacy from the London 2012 Olympic Games and first held in 2013. The format consists of a series of cycling events on closed roads around London and Surrey for amateur cyclists, families and children and professional riders, culminating in the London–Surrey Classic, a one-day international road race held on the Sunday. The big event for novices is the closed-roads amateur sportive ride (either the 100-mile 'full' version, or the 46-mile version).

I always had a burning desire to do RideLondon (even back in the days when I wasn't 100 per cent ready for a sportive like that) and would follow the same routine every year the ballot opened: I'd apply for entry online, wait for months in anticipation of getting a place and then get that dreaded

Commiserations magazine in the post. Getting a place on the event really is a lottery: around 25,000 cyclists take part in RideLondon, and in 2018, 80,000 people applied via the public ballot for places.

'That's cool,' I'd tell myself every time I didn't make it; 'maybe I'm not supposed to do it this year,' and leave it at that. No big deal. This time my chance had finally come to take part. Instead of watching RideLondon set off from my proverbial back garden, I'd be on that start line in Stratford with thousands of other cyclists on Sunday morning, ready to ride all of those glorious miles ahead. London Marathon Events (the company which organises RideLondon) offered me a three-day gig working at the cycling exhibition show they were doing at the ExCel centre. I'd be one of the guest speakers on the main stage: spending Thursday through to the Saturday before RideLondon talking to thousands of participants coming to collect their registration packs (and see the exhibition) about the 'rules of the road' and good riding etiquette for a sportive. I was now qualified enough to do something like this, which felt pretty amazing. As well as working at the event, one of the perks of this freelance gig was places for me and Ian on either the 46- or 100-mile route. Although my confidence on doing long-distance rides was strong, as a first-timer I opted for the 46-mile route.

The timing of being offered a place to do RideLondon that year was perfect. Physically I was ready – I was riding more, and doing more jaunts on both Baadgyal and my other commuter bikes had built up my strength. I now had quite a few sportives under my cycling belt, and my confidence on a road bike felt like it was hitting its peak. When I say peak, I don't mean I had come to the end of the road on a bike and doing RideLondon meant I had achieved everything that I ever wanted to do on two wheels! This opportunity was another incredible route for me to explore on my cycling journey, and I was beyond hyped to be doing it. But even in the midst of awesome events like RideLondon, fear can still strike.

I had reached an incredible point in my life: I could look at a long-distance ride and tell myself, 'I have it in me to do this,' but my own niggling self-doubts and panic could still get the better of me. This wasn't just about the worry of crashes with other participants or annoying mechanical issues along the way. Here's where I need to admit to something: despite being so excited about the event, I'd been in a weird head space about my relationship with cycling for a while, and on the morning of RideLondon all those thoughts started to rear their ugly heads. My worries – kept at bay by all that excitement – returned the moment I woke up. Ian picked up on something not being quite right with me – he'd been doing a stellar job trying to boost my mood all morning. 'Not today, mate,' I was telling myself, this wasn't allowed to happen after having been on such a glorious high. I was hoping it was the mix of bleary-eyed tiredness and pre-ride anxiety making me feel a bit rubbish, but I knew I couldn't dismiss it as that. It was too late. Suddenly, all I could think about was all that stuff that hadn't clouded my mind for a few days. All that clarity I had was rapidly fading and my mind became foggy with random thoughts. I knew it wasn't a race or a competition, but I had of course pitted myself against my own worst enemy: Me.

Suddenly I was thinking I had something to prove to the rest of London, like doing the event was some kind of weird rite of passage that I needed to take as a 'London Roadie'. I'd done a few long rides a few weeks before the event, but diving into social media that morning, checking the hashtags and comparing myself to others, it felt like I hadn't done enough. No, I wasn't out there with any cycling clubs doing early morning laps of Regents Park or climbing Box Hill every Sunday until ride day ... but I had to keep in mind that comparison is the thief of joy! I was doing it at my own pace, and that was totally okay. I took a deep breath and re-focused on what the day for me was all about, and what the bigger and better picture was in my cycling life. It's human nature to compare yourself to others, and that's something I know I'll always end up doing, and I made peace with that as much as I possibly could.

I couldn't allow the day to turn sour before I'd even left the house, so I needed to focus on the good stuff to push the self-doubt away. I looked over at my kit hanging on my bedroom wall before pulling it all on. A little spark of joy reignited again. My road cycling wardrobe had recently grown thanks to new additions from a shopping spree I'd gone on. A bobet blue jersey and hot-pink coral bib shorts were waiting to be worn along with my brand-new, gleaming white Giro Espada road shoes. The kit all looked damned good, and it would make me feel damned good too. There was an element of power dressing for the day – I see it as a way of armouring myself for a ride.

Feeling a lot more serene, Ian and I set off at 7 a.m., cycling to the other side of Newham. It was blissfully quiet at that time of the morning, but that started to change as soon as we joined the Greenway. You see plenty of people on bikes where I live, but this was something else. Bunches of cyclists seemed to be appearing at every cross-point along the route, all heading towards Stratford. Everyone was looking at each other's rider number and giving a knowing nod and smile. Despite the fact that some of them would have been on the road a LOT earlier than me and Ian, their happiness for the day ahead was glowing under their yawns. My mood started to push upwards, and as we pulled into Queen Elizabeth Park, the air was thick with positive energy.

Our very lovely set-up for the day meant that we could hang around in the Velodrome and grab an extra breakfast before setting off. It also meant there was an opportunity to do some serious people-watching. I could look through those high windows that towered over the park and clock almost everyone who was streaming into the grounds. Seeing thousands of Lycra-clad bodies congregating got some of those earlier thoughts whirring around my mind again. You can't help but notice what the demographic of this event is like: predominantly male, middle-aged and white. Even on those years when I wasn't taking part and had watched from the sidelines I noticed it. But actually being there and shuffling along to the start line? I felt it more acutely than ever. Even though cycling is pretty much 90 per cent of my life and what I 'do', I'd be a liar if I said I didn't feel a little bit out of place. I've found my corners of it along the way but each new event brings a new hurdle to overcome. That was one of my biggest fears – feeling alone and like this wasn't a space for me or women like me to be in. I wasn't going to turn around and go back home though. One of the things I was encouraging people to do while talking at the ExCel was to share their #ReasonToRide, and I got to thinking about the message I'd put out on social media the night before:

> The thrill, freedom and personal challenge . . . and for every little black girl and woman I didn't see at the start of my journey? My 46 miles are for you.

That was my reason to ride, and that was the mental push that got me over the start line. The countdown ended, the flag was waved, and the moment I clipped back in and started my ride, I started to feel good. I cycled through the closed roads of my hometown, I rode alongside people that might have been 101 times better than me, but I didn't give that a second thought while I was out there. I had 46 glorious miles laced with laughter, friendly faces, struggling a bit on Wimbledon Hill, getting a tiny bit wet in the rain, and crossing the finish line with a massive smile on my face. I'd done it. I'd actually done it, and that dark dog of doubt was banished to its kennel for the 3hrs:27mins:36secs I did the course in.

Even though it was wonderful not to let them get the better of me on that day, I know that, looking at the bigger picture, my cycling fears and doubts will never fully go away. I'll never be in control of when they decide to manifest – that's something that's way beyond my power and of course that makes me anxious. But I started to accept that. There is no 'perfect happy ending' when it comes to my cycling journey – yet I can now put my hand on my heart and say that I'm okay with that. Every push on the pedals and rotation of the wheels beneath me leads me to a new adventure, and with that come potential forks in the road.

I just need to continue to make peace with the bumps in the road ... and keep on riding forwards.

Maintenance

'Seven years of no punctures? Did you actually make
a deal with the devil?'

'You know what? That could well be true ...'

@swiftlaura and me on my Instagram, 2017

One of the biggest lessons I've learned on my cycling journey is
that in order to keep on going, you have to know how to maintain your machine. Riding a bike isn't just about those glorious
days filled with sunshine, and breezing through the city looking as stylish as possible. It's also about those less glamorous
moments, like getting your hands dirty and really understanding how the nitty-gritty of it all works. That's so important.
Having that know-how of what to do when something goes
wrong is essential for life both on and off the bike.

And believe me, it's definitely a case of 'when' and not 'if' something on your bike goes wrong, as it's inevitable something will ... no matter how lucky you think you are or how many deals you've made with the maintenance devil.

In the first few months of being back on a bike, I imagined and talked (mainly to myself) about all the amazing mechanical things that I wanted to learn, and set myself goals of getting that knowledge nailed. Yet somehow those months morphed into years and not once did my hands reach for a wrench – instead they went no further than grabbing on to my handlebars. I was never getting my fingernails dirty with the glory of oiling my own chain. It's not like I didn't have the time to either. I had a full-time job and I was caring for Mamma V, but there was always time available to get learning. There were so many free evenings, days off work and weekends that would have been perfect for getting stuck into it. I could have fired up the laptop and searched for local classes online, scanned through YouTube and watched videos on how to take my bikes to pieces on the living room floor. I mean, what's the absolute worst that could have happened? Maybe fucking up a few components, getting a bit frustrated and starting all over again. That probably would have been one of the *best* things that could have happened. The worst thing for me was exactly what I ended up doing: almost nothing at all.

I was constantly finding excuses and falling back on others (including Ian) helping me out. I'd always be watching others getting stuck in and getting ready to roll with what looked like utter confidence, doing their vital checks before each ride, tool bags packed and no essentials forgotten. I'd have mine too and fumble my way through using it if needed. Tyres fully pumped and debris-free? I could do that, but would spend the ride praying it would be a puncture-free zone. Chains lubed and not broken or loose? Something else I could do as well, but fingers crossed it doesn't snap or come off while we're out and about.

Gears adjusted and in perfect working order? I could just about get away with going on the single speed or hope for the best – and a bit of help – if I was on my road bike. My reluctance to own up about not knowing this stuff was making me feel like an outsider. I'd been cycling for so long, but still believed I knew next to nothing about it.

I was completely intimidated by all of the knowledgeable people I was surrounded by. In my head, being a part of 'that scene' and still feeling like a newcomer was as awkward as hell ... but all I could do was just roll with it. Friends weren't going to judge or laugh at me – real friends wouldn't, and deep down inside I knew that, but the main thoughts which swirled around my head when it came to facing up to maintenance were: 'When is someone going to find me out?'; 'How long will it be before this explodes in my face?'; 'When will I be exposed as being an utter fraud?' The kind of paranoia you get as a kid in school, asked a simple question in front of the whole class and really not having a clue what the answer is.

Of course, there was also a bit of 'Vanity Vélo' in this. I felt like I'd unintentionally painted this idyllic cycling/life picture that I was about to destroy.

Try again. Fail again. Fail better. This wasn't happening, and I knew that hands-on experience was one of the best ways to learn about anything practical. I'm a creative person and getting stuck into a new project usually excites me. I guess it was a bit like a tiny lie. But you know when the lie starts to get bigger, takes on a life of its own and then gradually gets completely out of control and feels unstoppable? THAT. My 'tiny lie' started when Frankie came into my life. I was freshly back into cycling and learning absolutely everything all over again ... except for the 'maintaining and fixing your own shit' side. It's not that I didn't want to – it just wasn't the first thing that I dived into. Maybe that was a symptom of never having been exposed to that side of cycling as a young girl ... I don't know, but it seemed utterly bonkers. I had the bike of my dreams and was relying on it daily to get me from A to B safely yet learning how to maintain it wasn't at the top of my 'cycling things to do' list.

'I'll get on top of it soon.'

'I'm still getting used to being back on a bike as it is, so I'm doing this piece by piece.'

'I have plenty of time to learn about that stuff anyway.'

I'd tell myself things like this over and over again, while my 'tiny lie' continued to snowball. Owning just one bike had quickly become a thing of the past, and of course with that came more mechanical elements for me to get my head around. My journey into cycling had notched up to whirlwind speeds and before I knew it, I was fully immersed in the industry. I was completely surrounded by folks who all 100 per cent knew their stuff. And there was I – coasting along on sheer luck, borrowed time and empty promises I was making to myself. In one sense it was the perfect situation to be in – having what felt like 101 people around me who I could ask my 101 questions *and* could help me out when I was a bit stuck. It didn't feel like that though. One of the many brilliant things I realised about the cycling community is that there is always someone on hand to help; somebody who has that top-notch level of information stored away in their brain about bikes is only ever a gear change away. Of course I was always grateful for this when I encountered it, because it was nice thing to do for a fellow rider.

'Don't worry, Jools – we'll pack it down into the box and build your bike back up for the shoot.'

'We'll give it the once-over and make sure it's all running okay.'

'Just leave it with us and we'll get it sorted out for you.'

Whoever it was, they would always exude such confidence in their vast knowledge that I'd always be like, 'Yeah ... this is fine actually. I know I can leave my bike with you and every-thing will be cool.' So I fell into the habit of always relying on someone else to do it. I thought to myself, perhaps I shouldn't be worrying so much about crappy stuff happening to my bike or feel guilty about not sorting it out myself because that friendly help was being offered to me. Again I'd tell myself over and over that I would get on it eventually because deep down inside, I knew I had to. Either I would find a way for it to happen ... or I would continue to find an excuse. There's a term that gets bandied about a lot in cycling (and probably in other sports activities too) – 'all the gear and no idea'. It's one that makes me flinch a little for a couple of reasons.

Yes, in the beginning you'll buy 'all' the kit you think you need (and inevitably a bit more than that) and you'll need to figure out how to use it properly.

No one was born an expert and we've all been 'newbies' at something at some point.

I can hold my hand up and say I've been both of these and I totally embodied them when it came to all matters concerning bike maintenance. I had almost all the gear you could think of. I'd buy it because I knew that I should have this stuff with me, for the 'just in case'. But would I really have a clue what to do with it if one of those moments happened? Not really, but the chain of thought was 'Just make sure you have it anyway, Jools.' There were extremely generous companies and brands sending me tool kits to use, to help me on my cycling journey, and of course friends and family members buying me super-thoughtful bike-related gifts with every birthday and Christmas that swung round. Always making sure that I was never caught short ... always making sure that Jools was well equipped when 'she's out there on that thing' as Mamma Vélo would say. I was thankful for all of it. I appreciated every single mini-pump, tyre-lever set and multi-tool that came my way ... yet I honestly had no idea what to do with them. Well, I knew what they were for, but having rough ideas based on seeing others using them vs stone cold 'I'm fully versed on what I'm doing here!' levels of knowledge? Let's just say the latter certainly wasn't the case.

This is where my unfortunate alter-ego 'Vanity Vélo' would totally take over. All I could think about was how much of an utter arse I'd reveal myself to be by letting three simple words tumble out of my mouth: 'I don't know.' I hadn't schooled myself on the very basics of what made my cycling tick, yet there I was, on my bike or writing about being on my bike, going on TV to talk about it and evangelising about how fantastic it all is to anyone who'd listen. So admitting that I couldn't look after my own bikes beyond giving the frames a loving wash and polish in my back garden was laughable.

The more I knew I could count on help from wonderfully kind fellow cyclists, the more reliant I became on it. Eventually, that reliance turned into a crutch and one that I didn't seem to be in a hurry to kick from underneath myself. I'd bedded down into a false comfort zone, and I say 'false' because for me it wasn't actually that comfortable at all. Although I was desperate to learn, the motivation to do it was missing. And the run of good cycling luck that I was living on wasn't shaking me out of my maintenance complacency either. Something had to give. It didn't seem to matter where I went or what I put my bikes through, good fortune always seemed to be on my side. Like the summer of 2011 when I went cycling with Ian and some of our friends in the New Forest on Frankie. Taking a town bike like a Pashley Princess across mountain-biking terrain doesn't sound like the smartest move, but I have to cut myself some slack here: she was the only bike I owned back then and the route we took wasn't that harsh. Still, everyone was convinced that it was going to end in disaster. But it didn't. Not a single mechanical problem cropped up on the ride. However, the biggest lesson I learned was realising what a disaster it was not to have worn some form of padded underwear on a bumpy ride like that.

I'd gone seven whole years without a puncture. Just imagine, in all that time, I'd cycled so much and in so many different places, like the broken-glass-peppered streets of London, over the rough and jagged terrain of the Tuscan Hills and in the muddy and thorny valleys of Limburg ... and yet never picked up a single flat in any of those situations. No one including me could believe that was even possible. Surely this streak would eventually run out, and after such a long period of Lady Luck being my best mate, there was part of me that was actually willing her to unfriend me. It sounds completely insane to put a jinx on such a good thing! My problem was, nothing was giving me a hard enough nudge towards picking up any tools, so my thinking was this: if something a bit shitty happened while out on my bike – not shitty enough to land me in hospital, of course – it would surely act as a catalyst for me to roll up my sleeves and get stuck in. Maybe finding myself up shit creek without a paddle – or on the roadside with a problem, a multi-tool and no bloody clue – could be just the thing to get my DIY confidence going. Jumping in at the deep end probably isn't the most logical way of approaching the issue, but I was running away from confronting my own fears and needed something to give me that jolt. As it turns out, that jolt was actually just around the corner – my super-lucky relationship with cycling maintenance was about to encounter a seven-year itch.

Whenever the UK is blessed with beautiful weather during the summer months, I try to get out on my bikes as much as possible. 2017 was one of those glorious summers and I'd managed to get lots of rides in. Quite a few of them involved Baadgyal, and since that bike fitting back in 2016, rides with her always filled me with joy. We were seeing plenty of action together and I felt like the more rides we did, the more familiar and confident I became riding clipless. When that summer swung round, I'd been riding with my feet attached to the pedals for a year, so with each adventure together, my confidence would grow a lot more. Testament to how much my clipless confidence had grown was deciding to do the Thames Bridges Challenge in October of that year, Thames Bridges is an annual charity bike ride organised by the Stroke Association and has been going since 1997. As this was a cause incredibly close to my heart (and Ian's – he would be doing it with me too) and an opportunity to see some of London's most beautiful landmarks on my road bike, I was totally up for doing this! We registered for the 35-mile route, which would hopefully be a lovely way to spend a Sunday cycling through the city. Starting in Chiswick, looping through Central London and taking in some of London's iconic bridges then back to Chiswick at the end, it was a ride I could really get my teeth stuck into.

The week of the Thames Bridges Challenge and while on a short morning ride around the block (training for a big ride doesn't have to be huge chunks of riding), my cycling spidey senses started tingling about tiny little niggles with Baadgyal. Overall, everything seemed fine, and because I couldn't put my finger on exactly what felt wrong, I brushed my maintenance concerns aside. After all, I got round the RideLondon course with no issues that July and when Ian checked the bike over for me before that ride, all was well. Surely all was still okay and I was just being overly paranoid. Deciding not to trust my instincts (reader – always trust your instincts when it comes to the care of your bike), I just focused on how excited I was about Sunday. Baadgyal would still need a little check to make sure she was ride-ready though. A once-over before a major ride is always a good idea.

Of course, I wasn't the one who'd be doing any of that thorough checking. And to be totally frank with you, it was rarely ever me doing that for any of my bikes. It was now three days to go before the Challenge. I decided not to head out for a morning ride and instead have a rest day at home. Don't get me wrong – getting some training in is a good idea and always a lot of fun but giving yourself a break to recharge your batteries is just as necessary too. That and just lounging in bed with a cuppa while listening to the radio is utter bliss. The sound of 6 Music's *Breakfast Show* and my slow tea-slurping was interrupted by noises I recognised all too well coming from downstairs. The back door being unlocked and opened. Then the clanging of stuff being moved out of the downstairs cupboard, followed by a rapid chorus of 'click, click, click, click, click', the distinct sound of rear wheels and their loud hubs in motion. Hmmm. I came out of my room and took a seat on the steps. Peeping through the gaps in the bannister, I could see the all-too-familiar pre-big-ride scenario unfolding before me. Ian had wheeled both of our bikes out of the house and set them up alongside the standard collection of accessories in the garden:

One can of lubricant spray.
A sponge and dry rag.
A bucket of water.
A bottle of bike cleaning fluid.
Various cleaning brushes in different shapes and sizes.
One multi-tool.
A track pump.

Knowing that I needed to just chill, he was kind enough to go ahead and give Baadgyal that pre-ride spruce-up. This was a routine which over the years had become what you could call 'the usual' – not me being too lazy or knackered to look after my own bike, but Ian being the one prepping for any big ride. He would always check over my bike before his, and chat with me about he was doing. He wasn't patronising me and he certainly wasn't being a dick about it – he's my best mate in all things cycling, and his intentions were nothing but good. But I'd always be standing there while he was tinkering away, internally kicking myself for just watching and never having the confidence in myself to try.

'He's a good lad, eh?' I thought to myself. 'But I can't keep on letting this happen.'

A wave of positive determination came over me, which made an amazing change. By the time I hauled myself off the stairs and joined Ian in the garden, he had already finished cleaning my bike. Crouched on the floor, he was inspecting Baadgyal's wheels. Nothing too unusual there, except for the slightly puzzled look on his face.

'Everything all right?' I asked.

'Hmmm,' was Ian's response as he started gently squeezing a few of the wheel spokes. After that my bike was upended off the path and turned on her back with her wheels in the air. He started checking the spokes again, this time plucking each group of spokes like a harp as he spun the wheels around. Okay – so he's being thorough, which is good, but the look on his face was telling me this was far from fine.

'Did your bike feel a bit weird or different to you on the last ride you did?'

Ah. So something *was* wrong.

'Nope, nothing strange to me,' I said. Although on that last ride I did around the block something was a bit off ... but yet I said nothing to him.

Ian did a final round of strumming the spokes and another spin of the wheels.

'They're both buckled, Jools ... and a few of the spokes in them are a bit loose too.'

Oh. Well, that was a surprise that I wasn't expecting. There was I just moments earlier feeling hyped-up and ready to leap in. Even if my knowledge in this situation wasn't going beyond making sure my tyres were filled with air, and my bike was still physically in one piece by just glancing over the frame, I was so up for chucking my two pennies' worth in. And now this. Having no idea that was going on with my wheels (especially after all the rides I'd been putting in that summer), I went straight back to feeling like I wouldn't really know what I was supposed to be looking for.

'Is it really bad? I mean, are my wheels about to collapse on themselves? Should I have felt something before?'

Questions like that were flying out of my mouth towards Ian at a hundred miles an hour. I wasn't asking them out of learned curiosity, it was out of sheer panic. This magnificent road bike of mine that I was finally bonding with was unwell. I'd noticed something was up but ignored it out of feeling clueless. I felt like a cycling fraud all over again. Although it didn't seem like it at the time, this wasn't actually the end of the world for my wheels. Logically, the more you use something, the more wear and tear you'll put it through, and over time that happens to your bike wheels. This leads to the once-tensioned spokes loosening. With a lack of tension holding them in place, the wheels will buckle. And end up slithering from side to side as they go round. Imagine them moving like a snake and you'll get the idea. To get them back to how they should be I needed to true my wheels: that's tightening the spokes so that the rims straighten up again, bringing the wheels back to their 'true' roundness. I wish I could have calmly explained it to myself like that when it happened. Instead I was convinced I'd failed yet again and finally ridden one of my bikes to utter ruin.

'I'd give tightening them up a go for you, but we don't have a spoke key,' said Ian. Out of all the tools we had between us, one of those keys, a nifty little tool that clamps on to your spokes so you can turn them with ease, wasn't amongst them.

'I've done a little tighten on them as they're only finger loose, but it's probably best to get it to a shop to be trued and looked over properly.'

Ian was totally right. While he was more than cool about not DIY-ing this one, I was feeling red-faced about not spotting my wobbly wheels and once again being out of my maintenance depth. There was absolutely nothing wrong with getting a professional to fix it and supporting your local bike shop is always a bonus too. I called my LBS, explaining to them what was wrong with Baadgyal – thanks to being told by Ian – and seeing if there was any chance of her being looked at ASAP due to the upcoming ride. Of course they could do that. I shouldn't have even doubted they'd be more than happy to help me out.

'If you can get it to us before the end of the day, Jools, we can slot the repair in and have your bike ready by Saturday morning.'

Ready the day before the ride was perfect, and thank goodness Baadgyal would be checked over with enough time beforehand. There'd be no physical issue getting her to the shop either as Baadgyal was still roadworthy: the spokes weren't totally ruined and the rims were not on the brink of collapse. My confidence, however, was. I didn't feel 'brave' enough to take her there myself. Once again my fear of looking like a fool got in the way. Ian, being the absolute gem that he is, cycled her over to the shop for me, dropping her off for the repairs. Turns out it was a good job that we didn't attempt to DIY it at home as the bike shop called me later that afternoon with an unexpected update. They'd given Baadgyal a complete check-up and found a few other issues that neither of us had picked up on. Her gears and brakes were a little out of whack so needed adjusting. As did the headset – the bearings system that attaches the fork of the bike to the frame and allows the fork and front wheel to turn – which had also become a little loose and was giving a bit too much play. When a headset is working the way that it should, you don't even really notice it, so perhaps I could cut myself some slack over not clocking that. But it had come loose so the steering would have been suffering. That's loose spokes, wobbly wheels and dodgy steering. Again, it wasn't an 'end of the world' situation as the bike shop told me it could all be easily sorted, but that suddenly felt like quite the list of ailments Baadgyal was suffering with.

I couldn't help but question myself. When on earth did all these things happen, and why didn't I trust in my feelings that something was up? I was surprised that Baadgyal hadn't fallen apart under me, from her buckled wheels up. But I couldn't dwell on this. My beautiful road bike had been serviced and was back in rude health. I went and collected her on Saturday morning and it felt awesome riding her back home in top condition.

Even though all those issues Baadgyal had were fixed the day before the ride and everything was in perfect working order, the following morning I got a stark reminder about how sometimes in life things are just way beyond your control.

I woke up on the day of the ride feeling horrendous. What started off as a few annoying sniffles on Saturday night had morphed into a full-blown cold on Sunday morning – and looking out the window didn't help matters either; it was grey and wet outside.

'This was not the plan,' I grumbled to Ian, next to me in bed. A huge part of me really wanted to stay there and hide under the duvet. It's one thing riding through the beautiful rain at L'Eroica in Tuscany – a soggy October morning in London on a road bike with a head cold is quite a different matter. Ian peered out the window, frowning when he saw the rain.

'Ah,' he sighed, but I knew something optimistic would follow. He always tries to see the best in a bad situation. 'This weather could pass and you'll probably feel better after breakfast. It's still early enough for the day to change.'

And early it was. We had to be at the start line for 10.30 a.m., and with that start line being in Chiswick, the latest we could leave home to get there on time (via a train from Waterloo) was 7 a.m. As tempting as a sick-day in bed was, I had a ride to do and there was a chance that being out on my bike could make me feel much better. After a decent breakfast, layering up in weather-appropriate cycling kit and still feeling groggy, we managed to roll out of the house at 7 a.m. as originally planned. The heavy rain had calmed into a light drizzle, so there was some hope of the day not being a total damp squib. I'd started to feel positive about it all again when, less than 5 minutes into our journey, Ian signalled that he needed to stop. He'd got a puncture in his front wheel.

We had a track pump at home, which would be much quicker than using one of our mini-pumps to sort the puncture, so we turned back so Ian could fix it. We were so close to the house, it would have been madness not to. The events of the morning seemed like a series of bad omens: waking up with a random cold, the appalling weather and then Ian's almost instant mechanical issue. The day felt cursed and the warmth of the house was tempting me to stay put. But before I could even utter the words 'Let's just sack the whole thing off' Ian's tyre was sorted, and we were back on the road again.

My head was still feeling like fuzz, but there is actually something quite lovely about riding in the City of London on a Sunday morning. We made it to Fenchurch Street, part of our route to Waterloo station. That area on a weekend is a different story to a weekday – at the ungodly hour we were cycling, the commercial skyscrapers looked like glass giants sleeping in the

clouds. While looking up and admiring the grandeur of buildings like 20 Fenchurch Street (the 'Walkie Talkie' building),
Baadgyal – who had been riding like a dream – suddenly felt
very different underneath me.

Squidge, squidge, squidge.

'The roads feel pretty rough in this rain,' I thought to myself
as I kept on pedalling.

Squidge, squidge, squidge, again.

This time followed by Ian, who was cycling not too far
behind me calling out my name.

'Hang on, Jools, we need to pull over!'

Unclipping, I slowly came to a stop by the side of the road
with Ian, and we both got on to the pavement.

'You've got a puncture, Jools,' Ian said, pointing at my bike.
'Your front tyre is almost completely flat.'

You've got to be kidding me. I got my very first puncture
and I didn't even realise. Other than thinking my bike felt a bit
'squidgy' in the rain, I had no clue this had happened, or even
at what point on the journey!

I stood there in the drizzle, holding on to Baadgyal by her
handlebars, staring at the deflated and sad-looking tyre – which
was exactly how I felt. Familiar waves of annoyance and embarrassment washed over me. I was annoyed because the day had
turned into a nightmare and embarrassed because I got my very
first puncture without knowing it and didn't know how to fix it.
I leant Baadgyal against the wall of the building we were stood
in front of, and carefully clip-clopped to the back of my bike –
walking in cleats is tricky enough – doing it on a wet pavement
makes it even more perilous. I unzipped my saddlebag and
pulled out the necessary puncture repair kit from it – a spare
inner tube, a couple of tyre levers and a mini-pump. At least I
knew what was needed. Without saying a word, I handed them
over to Ian.

'Are you sure?' Ian said to me, offering me a lifeline. I shrugged my shoulders and stepped back again. He released the front wheel from the bike and got on with fixing my puncture.

I felt utterly defeated – this 'I have no clue about maintenance' shit was happening to me all over again. My bike had been sorted twenty-four hours before, but perhaps I should have got stuck in then. Ian would have happily guided me on how to do it, but my frustration got the better of me, and already running late for the ride meant I just wanted to get it sorted out as quickly as possible. As he was hunched over the detached wheel, prying the rubber off with a tyre lever, I took a picture of Ian and posted it to my Instagram. Explaining to my followers what was going on (and moaning about how cursed the day was), this picture was going to serve as a milestone on Fenchurch Street: the first time Lady Vélo got a puncture after seven years of riding ... and the last time anyone would ever fix it for her. It was time to finally get my hands dirty.

It may have taken much longer than expected, but I was finally on the road to bike maintenance. Those mishaps with my road bike certainly stirred something inside of me to put my learning wheels in motion: in those moments I didn't have a clue about what was wrong with her, and someone else had to step in and fix the issues. I had to keep telling myself that was totally okay: I wasn't a failure because it wasn't me sorting out my bike, and nor was it an admission of defeat. It was fantastic to get Baadgyal serviced and given back to me in top condition before the Thames Bridges ride, and awesome that Ian fixed that puncture for me. But when I started thinking about my other bikes and what it'd be like to spot problems myself, that actually felt quite good. And then having the ability to recognise and perhaps even prevent them from happening? Well ... that felt like it could be incredibly empowering.

I needed to be in a comfortable environment where it was okay to learn. Back in 2010 when I had that initial spark of wanting to learn more, the types of cycling classes I was finding out there didn't feel like they were aimed at someone like me. At one end of the scale were the way too advanced, like City and Guilds Cycle Mechanic Courses. They offered existing mechanics professional vocational qualifications, taught at industry-standard levels. Errr ... a bit much for me. Then at the other end there were the major cycling retail chains that put on their own group sessions. At first glance I thought these could be the right fit, but when I saw all the technical things they covered I was overwhelmed. One included being taught how to change an inner tube 'in double-quick' time. I'd never even changed one full stop, so that ruled me out – especially when the group was likely to be filled with people ten steps ahead of me on that kind of stuff.

Once again I found myself feeling like the Goldilocks of cycling – this time desperately trying to find the maintenance course that was just right. The mild frustration of not finding exactly what I was hoping for was enough to make me stop looking. I hadn't found anywhere suitable, so I went back to cycling on sheer luck and surrounding myself with people who could help me. That would have to do. It was baffling though – there was a real lack of options available for the skill level I was comfortable coming in at, and on top of that, the cost of some of those classes was a barrier to entry. *Others must have noticed this*, I thought to myself. Surely I couldn't be the only person on the planet who was (albeit internally) screaming out for an alternative to what was on offer. Turns out I wasn't ... and of course there was a workshop practically on my doorstep in East London which would become the perfect fit ...

It all changed when Jenni Gwiazdowski from London Bike Kitchen slid into my inbox. She'd seen my 'puncture on

Fenchurch Street' post on Instagram and sent me a message telling me about LBK's Intro to Maintenance Course. Jenni was incredibly tactful about it: she'd figured that I might have been embarrassed about not being able to fix my own mechanical issues (which I totally was) but also didn't want to offend by suggesting a beginner's class to someone who had cycled for seven years! She hit the nail on the head though – and as I learned, this was a feeling she had been familiar with once upon a time.

The Intro course sounded fantastic. It covered basics, like learning the names of common bike parts and what they do along with discovering the essential tools for maintenance and how to use them properly. It didn't stop there – the course, which would be taught over two days of three-hour classes, was totally hands on too. It focused on practical leaning: you'd be working on a bike (either your own or one LBK provided), doing stuff like fixing punctures and replacing tyres, and taking off and replacing a bike chain. The idea of messing around with my own bike didn't freak me out … in fact it was the total opposite! Even though I was pretty much sold on doing the course, what sealed the deal for me was the class numbers. LBK cap their classes at four students maximum. Being in a workshop with three other people on the same bike level as me was more than I could have hoped and wished for. This course sounded like The One.

I'd missed the October intake so signed up for the next round, which were evening classes in November. I decided that Ratty – my single-speed Colourbolt – would be the bike I'd use for the classes. The Intro course wasn't going to be covering gears (they had a separate Gear Indexing class for that) so it made sense to come in with my most basic bike to get started.

I arrived at LBK for my first class on a chilly Wednesday evening. It was a bitterly cold ride that night, but I forgot about the cold when I wheeled my bike into the workshop. The wonderful welcome I got from Nelson and Ellie – the LBK staff who would be teaching the course – was enough to warm my soul. I knew them both already from being friends via the cycling scene, so I knew I would be in friendly hands. Even though I was totally gassed-up about the course, I had wondered if feelings of being the 'new girl' at school would creep in – that fear of the unknown and entering much later into a cycling world that had already bonded with the knowledge that they had. There was none of that at all. I had nothing to worry about, which was absolute beginner's bliss.

The class was even smaller than I expected. It was just me and one other person who'd booked on to the course! I introduced myself to my new classmate – a young woman called Mary, who was also a keen cyclist but not that clued up or confident about maintenance, just like me.

'I always go to my dad, who helps me out with any bike problems,' Mary said to me as we both put on our heavy-duty workshop aprons, stained with grease and smelling of bike lube spray. They smelled like maintenance success. 'He's really into bikes, so knows exactly what to do.'

I lifted Ratty and hung her up on my bike repair stand for the course, clamping her in place by the seat tube. 'Time for a change, I'm guessing?' I asked back with a smile. 'It's the same with me and my boyfriend always helping me out ... well, him along with all my cycling friends who know their shit because I don't!'

'Totally time for a change!' Mary said, laughing with me. 'Jools, I think we're gonna be the ones to DIY the shit out of our bikes from now on!'

'Oh yes, Mary!' I said in confident agreement with her. 'YES, we are!'

And with that we rolled up our sleeves, collected our tools and got busy getting our hands dirty and our heads filled with cycling knowledge.

It's never too late to learn and London Bike Kitchen helped

me realise that. To some it might sound like madness: cycling on pure luck for all those years and never doing a class like that until I actually got a puncture. An unfortunate but inevitable incident was the catalyst for me to go learn – I knew my luck would run out at some point. But there were so many factors holding me back: low confidence, utter embarrassment about not 'knowing everything' about that side of cycling and feeling like I didn't have a safe and comfortable space to learn in or admit to my lack of knowledge. I shouldn't have been so hard on myself for not doing it sooner as bike maintenance can be a very intimidating scene. I've spoken to so many women who felt the same way: that the maintenance classes they had come across were not spaces for them. Stories of women who had signed up for courses but got so intimidated by the vibe that they never returned, or being in classes and wanting to ask questions but being so afraid to for fear of looking like an idiot. I can relate to that so clearly and totally understand where they are coming from.

I wasn't the only woman out there who harboured those cycling insecurities, and if you find yourself feeling similar fears, I want you to know that you are not alone, and that there is space out there for you where you can feel at ease. I still feel blessed to have somewhere like London Bike Kitchen, and I hope that this gives you a boost to find a workshop or organisations like that which could work for you too.

Gaining that practical knowledge boosted my confidence: being able to observe what Nelson and Ellie were doing, but also working with the real thing – my own bike – was invaluable and empowering. I felt motivated and enjoyed it so much.

Maintenance is about arming yourself with the tools and support to keep on going … knowledge is power! Finding the space to gain that knowledge and confidence is invaluable. When you really understand how your bike works and what to do when something on it goes wrong, you're more likely to ride it harder and further (both physically and mentally) than you'd ever imagined. If you take one thing from this, I'd love it to be to continue your journey; you'll be surprised at where it could take you.

The Road Ahead

Whenever any doubts about what I'm doing with my life creep in, I like to revisit my blog post about getting Frankie and bringing her home from the bike shop. I open my laptop, load up VéloCityGirl and click on the archive section for 2010. Even though that day in March will always be crystal clear in my memory, it's always good to remind myself of that moment and how far I've come.

I look at the picture that goes with the post. I'm dressed in the 'bike-collection day outfit' that I had planned out a few weeks before: a pair of black patent-leather winkle-pickers, skinny black jeans, and a grey and pink flannel check shirt. You can't see the shirt because of the purple-felt, double-breasted dress coat I had on. On the lapel of the coat was a vintage brooch in the shape of a bicycle, encrusted with diamantes. I was parked up on Cable Street, posing on my brand-new Pashley Princess, with a massive smile on my face. I had no idea what lay ahead of me. All I could see was my immediate future, which was the bicycle I had wanted for so long and the rest of the Cycle Superhighway that would guide me back to Canning Town, leading to the commutes to work that I'd be doing in a few weeks' time on that bike. I couldn't see where getting that Pashley would really end up taking me. The entire journey that bike put into motion – all the highs and even the lows have been incredible. They've shaped me and continue to do so.

It's been nine years since I decided to get back on the saddle, and my definition of what cycling is, is still being broadened and enriched. It all gets me thinking about the eighteen-year-old me who left it all behind. But my love for cycling never really died. Yes, it waned and fizzled out, but it was more like a dormant volcano. It was still there, bubbling under the surface, waiting to erupt again. It took ten years, but I ended up back on a saddle again. I've come to terms with the reasoning behind my long hiatus, but I now can't begin to imagine what my life would be like without cycling. The cycling crew I used to hang around with all the time still exists: perhaps not with the same people or in the same places, but certainly in a new guise. They're those inspirational women who I've interviewed in this book, my partner Ian, who is one of my biggest supporters, the wonderful people that I've worked with over the years, and of course the online cycling community who welcomed me into their peloton when I launched VéloCityGirl.

I've pursued ambitions that I didn't even realise I'd have when it came to cycling, and working within the cycling industry, which was one of them, was an eye-opening experience. When something that's your dream turns into a very different reality – one far from what you'd expected – it can be a shock to the system. Instead of letting that knock me back, I decided to do something about it. Making positive changes and disrupting the status quo could have been a risky move – but it was one that

I was willing to take to try and shake up the narrative. I'm not looking back any more. I'm only looking forward.

The world of cycling is such a rich and diverse one when you look beyond the same stereotypes that are constantly pushed out there ... my hope is that I'm doing something to bring change to the future of that, one revolution at a time. And if I can encourage others to feel like they can get on a bike, see that it's a space for them and enjoy the journey? Well, that's also bringing about change and that would be incredible. It's okay for that journey to go a little or a lot off track. It's yours and no one can take that away from you. It's okay to ask questions and question situations that just don't seem right. Nothing changes if we don't take action. It's okay to go your own way, wherever that path may take you, and enjoy it.

I started this book telling you that cycling is more than just a bicycle, and I hope that *Back in the Frame* has shown you that it is. But this is just the tip of the iceberg. I hope that you carry that thought with you on your journey and that your journey takes you to amazing places.

The Perfect Ride Q&A
Rachel Cullen & Jools Walker

Jools Walker, aka Lady Velo, is a blogger, TV presenter and public speaker. *Back in the Frame*, her debut book, is a brilliant memoir of bikes, blogs and riding through depression. Here, Rachel and Jools discuss the practicalities, as well as the essence, of the perfect ride...

Let's start practical! When you think about The Perfect Ride, what is the weather doing?

Rachel: The sun is shining, obvs! But there is also a slight breeze. If we're talking temperatures, then we're looking at 16/17 degrees; and a blue sky – I don't mind if there's some fluffy cloud dotted about here and there.

Jools: It would definitely be filled with sunshine! I've always been pretty frank about being a bit of a fair-weather rider (although cycling in the rain can be fun at times), but I'd much rather a bright, clear day, with a nice breeze to keep me cool.

What is your preferred bike? What other equipment must you have with you?

Rachel: I love my Giant Deft Advanced 2. It's a beautiful road bike, and although it's carbon, it's not the lightest on the market but it's robust and weighty enough to feel secure. Some road bikes feel too light and flimsy for my liking! It's also got some built-in suspension which really helps with the rolling hills around here and minimise vibrations. I absolutely love it. In terms of other equipment – I always carry a tubeless repair kit, my iPhone (for emergencies and selfies!) a drink and some food, plus a shell top / jacket in case the weather turns or gets cold on the top of the hills.

Jools: That's a really tough one to answer! Over the years my obsession with cycling has led to owning more than one bike (which was never the plan...) so it depends on the kind of ride I'd be going out on. At the moment, my Brompton is my preferred bike. It's nifty enough to ride around the city, and fold down and stow away if I need to hop on the tube! I'd have a small bike pump and a spare inner tube with my phone, to search for coffee shops and other interesting places to stop at, and me!

Are you alone or with someone else? If so, who?

Rachel: I love riding alone.
Jools: I'd be with my partner, Ian. He's been my best cycling

buddy since I got back into bikes in 2010. He loves cycling and it's always a joy for us to spend time together on our bikes.

Where in the world are you?

Rachel: I'm out riding on the Yorkshire hills where I live. The views are spectacular; there are so many options for different rides. I prefer small country lanes – usually snaking up a hillside and then a fast downhill on the other side. I live in the countryside for a reason, and I wouldn't want to be anywhere else. If I was to choose a place further afield, I'd have to say through the paddy fields in Vietnam as a complete contrast to the terrain back home – flat as a pancake, but equally beautiful and incredibly tranquil.

Jools: It's probably going to sound soooo predictable, but we'd be in London! Even though it's home and where I'm from, since getting back on a bike I'm discovering something new about it on every ride. There is something really joyous about being a tourist in your own city, and discovering hidden gems.

What route are you taking and how long are you cycling for?

Rachel: I have a selection of local rides I'm very familiar with. These range from 10-30 miles in distance. Although I've done events longer distances than this, this is my preferred range for my own rides (and taking into account the hills around here – they're hard enough!)

Jools: On days like those, we rarely have a set route, but we would certainly be cycling for the whole day... or as far as our legs can take us!

Are you following a set circuit, going from A to B, or just cycling where your feet take you?

Rachel: I always ride with a planned route in mind – I always have a route in my head/mapped out, even if I vary it on the way. It feels much safer that way and helps me to gauge my pace/fuel and work out how long I'll be! I couldn't just set off riding without any idea of where or how far I was going. My head doesn't work like that.

Jools: We'd be cycling where our feet would take us. That's the fun of knowing your city, but deciding to go off the beaten track (or roads, I suppose) and seeing where that turn or side street that'd you usually not take leads you to.

What is the terrain like?

Rachel: Hilly!! End of. Just that.

Jools: Reasonably flat, but I don't mind the odd climb here and there to test my legs and make sure I've still got some strength in them!

What are you snacking on? Do you stop for a picnic?

Rachel: I always carry a couple of emergency gels and a protein bar. And some electrolyte juice. Rarely more than this – you can always call at a coffee stop on the way, or design the route to include one! It doesn't make much sense to ride carrying more than is absolutely necessary, and sandwiches always get squashed in my rucksack!

Jools: Random, but I always have Jelly Babies with me when I go for a day out on the bike. I think it comes from my running days where I'd have Jelly Babies stowed away in my pocket (or bum bag that I sometimes run with) as they were perfect bursts of fuel for me! We would defo stop somewhere for food... probably at a nice café, coffee shop or pub for lunch. This is again the joy of having a bike you can fold up and stow away!

What are you emotionally feeling as you ride along?

Rachel: Happy! Filled with joy and freedom (if the weather is as described above, and I'm feeling good.) Rides like these are just the best. Looking out onto panoramic views of the countryside and seeing endless green fields makes me feel peaceful and grateful to be there. Plus, after the hard effort of a long climb, it's brilliant to have a fast downhill section which can be exhilarating as the breeze hits your face and makes you feel alive. It's worth the effort.
Jools: Feeling free. That's an emotion I always feel when I get on a bike. The freedom to go anywhere I want to, and the freedom to be able to do it means everything to me.

Does the perfect, comfortable seat even exist?

Rachel: Not perfect – sadly. I've struggled with this issue and have settled with a female-specific Specialized Mimic seat designed with us in mind! I've tried several seats and do suffer over long distances with frontal pressure. This is the best one I've tried, but sadly it's still not perfect and I wouldn't describe it as 'comfortable'. More tolerable which for me is as good as it gets!
Jools: I know that my most comfortable saddle is the Brooks B66s that's on my Pashley Princess – it's had ten years of 'breaking in' and it is now moulded perfectly to the shape of my bum! In all seriousness though, you need to find a saddle that's the

right size for your body, and make sure that the set-up of your bike is correct for your body too. Factors like the width of a saddle and how it feels on your sit bones is so important. I totally recommend taking the measurements of your sit bones to work out the sizing of the saddle and the type of saddle you need. There are quite a few types of saddle out there (narrow, wide, comfort, gel, just to name a few). Any good bike shop will be able to help you out with this instore or with guides online, so defo check those out.

What one thing can you not ride without?

Rachel: My bike! Joke – sorry. I don't like riding without sunglasses, even if they're clear lens ones because otherwise there's too much dust and spray being thrown back into my eyes. So glasses for me.

Jools: I'm gonna have to say my phone… it's so useful for looking up new places to check out while I'm out… and also if I get *very* lost, I know I can at least GPS my way out of it!

After a long ride, what do you do to feel more human and less person-who-is-now-an-extension-of-a-bike?

Rachel: Eat something and then get straight in the bath with a cup of tea and some biscuits! It's always a winner after a long ride, when my muscles are achy and I feel sweaty and grubby. I love a post-ride long bath. It's like a ritual for me.

Jools: Stretches when I get home, and a looooong shower always gets me back together! If it's been an especially long ride (like when I've done a sporting event) nothing beats getting a takeaway delivered and having a huge meal too!

Acknowledgements

I have to start by thanking my agent, Jo Bell, as without her *Back in the Frame* would never have become a reality. Thank you, Jo, for sticking with me through this, and for your guidance every step of the way. Your faith in me as a writer means more than you could ever imagine.

To the team at Little, Brown but especially my editor Rhiannon Smith – thank you for believing in my story, giving me a chance and helping me shape every single draft into an actual book. You pulled so much out of me every time I hit a wall or was convinced that I was mentally spent. Thanks for your encouragement, for carefully nurturing my words and making this all happen.

To the women (who I'm also lucky enough to call my friends) that I interviewed for this book: Adele Mitchell, Jacqui Ma, Ayesha McGowan, Emily Chappell, Jenni Gwiazdowski and Adeline O'Moreau – a huge thank you for sharing your personal experiences with me and every single person who will read *Back in the Frame*. All of you are a huge inspiration to me and I'm damn sure your words and wisdom will inspire others out there too. I'm forever grateful.

Thank you to my family for all your love and support on this journey, and for letting me delve into some of our family history in a book that's supposed to be all about bikes! To my sister, Michele and my brother, Anthony – thank you for being two of the biggest inspirations on my cycling journey, imparting your taste in clothing and music to me and, between the two of you, getting me on that Raleigh Burner and on the road that's led me here.

To my dad, Leo – even though you're thousands of miles away in Jamaica, I could feel your love and support for me while writing this book through every FaceTime and WhatsApp chat we had. Thank you for encouraging me to chase my dreams.

To Mamma Vélo – I can't thank you enough for being so honest and allowing me to share parts of your life with the world in the way that you have. Thank you for always having my back and believing in me in everything that I do. You're the strongest person I know, my best friend and my inspiration.

I also have to thank every single person in my cycling and social media family – and I call you family as for the last nine years of doing VéloCityGirl, that's what you've all become. Thank you to all of you who encouraged me, believed in me and supported me . . . not just in the writing of this book. You all make up a huge part of who I am and what I do. I'm forever grateful for you being in my life.

And finally, most special thanks and absolutely huge amounts of love go to my soul mate and ultimate cycling buddy, Ian James. You're always by my side (not even living in separate cities could stop that) and I couldn't have done this without you. I've also lost count of the cups of tea and amazing dishes you made that kept me going long into those big writing nights. Going out with a chef has its perks. Thank you for your incredible patience, support and most of all, your love.

Resources

VéloCityGirl
velocitygirl.co.uk
Twitter: @ladyvelo
Instagram: @ladyvelo

Emily Chappell
thatemilychappell.com
Twitter: @emilychappell
Instagram: @emilyofchappell

Jenni Gwiazdowski/London Bike Kitchen
lbk.org.uk
Twitter: @money_melon/@LDNBikeKitchen
Instagram: @ldnbikekitchen

Jacqui Ma/Good Ordering
www.goodordering.com
Twitter: @Goodordering
Instagram: @goodordering

Ayesha McGowan
aquickbrownfox.com
Twitter: @ayesuppose
Instagram: @ayesuppose

Adele Mitchell
adelemitchell.com
Twitter: @adelemitchell
Instagram: @adele_writer

Adeline O'Moreau/Mercredi Bikes
mercredi.co.uk
Twitter: @Ecunard
Instagram: @m_rcredi

Eliza Southwood – Illustrator
ElizaSouthwood.com
Twitter: @ElizaSouthwood
Instagram: @ElizaSouthwood

The 5th Floor
the5thfloor.cc
Twitter: @The5thFloor
Instagram: @the5thfloor

Adventure Syndicate
theadventuresyndicate.com
Twitter: @adventuresynd
Instagram: @adventuresynd

Aprire
aprire.cc
Twitter: @aprirebicycles
Instagram: @aprirebicycles

As Bold As
asboldas.com
Twitter: @asboldasbold
Instagram: @asboldas

Beaumont Bicycle
Beaumontbicycle.com
Instagram: @beaumontbicycle

Bespoked UK
bespoked.cc
Twitter: @BespokedUK
Instagram: @bespokeduk

Bikeability
bikeability.org.uk

Bikekitchen
bikekitchen.ca
Twitter: @bikekitchenUBC
Instagram: @bikekitchenUBC

Bikeminded
bikeminded.org
Twitter: @BikemindedRBKC
Instagram: @bikeminded

Bikerowave
bikerowave.org
Twitter: @BikeRoWave

BikeSnob NYC
bikesnobnyc.blogspot.com
Twitter: @bikesnobnyc

The Bike Project
thebikeproject.co.uk
Instagram: @the_bikeproject

The Bristol Bike Project
thebristolbikeproject.org
Twitter: @bristolbikeproj

Brooks England
brooksengland.com
Twitter: @brooksengland
Instagram: @brooksengland

The Bicycle Academy
thebicycleacademy.org
Twitter: @BicycleAcademy
Instagram: @thebicycleacademy

British Cycling
britishcycling.org.uk

Canyon Bicycles
canyon.com
Twitter: @canyon_bikes
Instagram: @canyon

Colourbolt
colourbolt.com
Twitter: @colourbolt
Instagram: @colourbolt_

Copenhagen Cycle Chic
copenhagencyclechic.com
Twitter: @_Cycle_Chic
Instagram: @cycle.chic.republic

CycleScheme
cyclescheme.co.uk
Twitter: @cycleschemeltd
Instagram: @cyclescheme

The Cycle Show (ITV)
Twitter: @thecycleshowtv

The Cycle Show (NEC)
cycleshow.co.uk
Twitter: @cycleshow
Instagram: @cycleshow

Electra Bikes
electrabike.com
Twitter: @Electra_Bicycle
Instagram: @electra_bicycle

Eroica Britannia
eroicabritannia.co.uk
Twitter: @eroicabritannia
Instagram: @eroicabritannia

L'Eroica (International Series)
eroica.cc
Instagram: @eroica.cc

Fat Tire Tours
fattiretours.com
Twitter: @heyFatTireTours
Instagram: @FatTireTours

Hartley Cycles
HartleyCycles.com
Twitter: @HartleyCycles
Instagram: @HartleyCycles

LFGSS (London Fixed Gear and Single Speed)
lfgss.com

London Cyclist
londoncyclist.co.uk
Twitter: @londoncyclist
Instagram: @ londoncyclistblog

Look Mum No Hands!
www.lookmumnohands.com
Twitter: @1ookmumnohands
Instagram: @1ookmumnohands

National Cycling Centre
nationalcyclingcentre.com

Pashley Cycles
pashley.co.uk
Twitter: @pashleycycles
Instagram: @pashleycycles

Ride London
prudentialridelondon.co.uk
Twitter: @ridelondon
Instagram: @ridelondon

Shand Cycles
shandcycles.com
Twitter: @shandcycles
Instagram: @shandcycles

SPIN Cycling Festival
spinldn.com
Twitter: @SpinCyclingFest
Instagram: @spincyclingfestival

Tatty Devine
tattydevine.com
Twitter: @tattydevine
Instagram: @tattydevine

Torke Cycling
torkecycling.com
Twitter: @torkecycling
Instagram: @torkecycling

TotalWomensCycling
totalwomenscycling.com
Twitter: @TtlWomenCycling
Instagram: @ttlwomenscycling

Tweed Run
tweedrun.com
Twitter: @tweedrun
Instagram: @tweedrun

Velominati
velominati.com
Twitter: @Velominati
Instagram: @the_velominati

VeloVixen
velovixen.com
Twitter: @velovixenuk
Instagram: @velovixenuk

Vulpine
vulpine.cc
Twitter: @vulpinecc
Instagram: @vulpinecc

Health Support in the UK

NHS Stroke
www.nhs.uk/conditions/stroke

NHS Depression
www.nhs.uk/conditions/clinical-depression

Stroke Association
www.stroke.org.uk

Notes

p7: *2017 analysis carried out by Transport For London (TfL)'*
Analysis of Cycling Potential 2016, Policy Analysis Report,
March 2017, TFL

p10: *Newham is still ranked as one of the most deprived
areas in the UK*
The 2015 English Indices of Deprivation published by gov.co.uk
shows Newham went from being the 2nd most deprived local
authority in England to the 25th

p60: *Affordability is a significant barrier to entry, especially
amongst ethnic minority groups*
'What are the barriers to cycling amongst ethnic minority
groups and people from deprived backgrounds?' Policy Analysis
Research Summary, November 2011
http://content.tfl.gov.uk/barriers-to-cycling-for-ethnic-mnorities-
and-deprived-groups-summary.pdf (page 3)

p89: *Emily Chappell has written an excellent article on 'flap
mash' if you want more of this content*
https://www.casquette.co.uk/know-how/2017/4/22/saddle-lore

p170: *As documented in a study by Trust for London and the New Policy Institute, Kensington & Chelsea has the greatest income inequality of any London Borough*
https://www.trustforlondon.org.uk/data/boroughs/kensington-and-chelsea-poverty-and-inequality-indicators/

p170: *according to a recent report by local Labour MP Emma Dent Coad, in the World's End council estate, residents have an average income of £15,000 a year, while owners of nearby homes on the other side of the King's Road have average earnings of £100,000*
https://www.theguardian.com/inequality/2017/nov/13/grenfell-tower-mp-highlights-huge-social-divisions-in-london

p192: *Mayor of London, Boris Johnson, at a press conference for the inaugural RideLondon–Surrey Classic. He gave a soundbite about his plans to get London to not be a 'great fleet of people with their heads down, wearing Lycra, who feel that they've got to get from A to B as fast as they can'*
Boris Johnson, BBC *Newsnight* 07/08/13

p202: *without equity, patterns of discrimination are difficult to see*
'Here's Why We Should Care More About Equity, Not Equality'
Muslimgirl.com/46703/heres-care-equity-equality

p244: *As highlighted in the 'Diversity Issue' of industry magazine BikeBiz, the cycle trade's worse-kept secret is its propensity to hire men in workshop mechanic positions*
The Diversity Issue, *Bike Biz*, July 2018, issue 138, page 5

p244-245: *In 2015, a report conducted by the League of American Bicyclists on how to make bike retail welcoming for women revealed that although women represent the new majority of adult bike owners, accounting for 51 per cent of ownership, 62 per cent of women who own a bike did not make a single visit to a bike shop the previous year, compared to 56 per cent of male bicycle owners*
'Bike Shops for Everyone – Strategies for making bike retail more welcoming to women'
bikeleague.org/sites/default/files/Bike_Shops_For_Everyone.pdf

p247: *An estimated 2.5 million people would line the route of the stages from Leeds to Sheffield*
BBC News: 'Tour de France 2014: The "grandest" of Grand Departs' https://www.bbc.co.uk/sport/cycling/28188083

p259: *Rebecca Lowe, a writer and reporter who in 2016 set off on an 11,250-kilometre year-long cycle from the UK to Iran. Rebecca was not a seasoned adventure cyclist – she had never used panniers on a bike before and hadn't ridden up a hill for six years prior to her trip. Writing for the BBC after completing her epic route . . .*
'Is it foolish for a woman to cycle alone across the Middle East?' https://www.bbc.co.uk/news/magazine-39351162